Alps & Sanctuaries

of Piedmont & the Canton Ticino

E. Gogin

Sicut vos estis nos fuimus,
Et sicut nos sumus vos eritis.

Alps & Sanctuaries

of Piedmont & the Canton Ticino

Samuel Butler

Sta Maria della Neve

ALAN SUTTON
1986

ALAN SUTTON PUBLISHING
BRUNSWICK ROAD · GLOUCESTER

First Published 1881

Copyright © in this edition 1986 Alan Sutton Publishing Limited

British Library Cataloguing in Publication Data

Butler, Samuel, 1835–1902
[Alps and sanctuaries of Piedmont and the Canton Ticino].
Alps and sanctuaries.
1. Italy—Description and travel—1861–1900
I. [Alps and sanctuaries of Piedmont and the
Canton Ticino]   II. Title
914.5′049   DG427

ISBN 0-86299-283-4

Printed in Great Britain
by The Guernsey Press Company Limited,
Guernsey, Channel Islands.

Author's Preface to First Edition

I SHOULD perhaps apologise for publishing a work which professes to deal with the sanctuaries of Piedmont, and saying so little about the most important of them all—the Sacro Monte of Varallo. My excuse must be, that I found it impossible to deal with Varallo without making my book too long. Varallo requires a work to itself; I must, therefore, hope to return to it on another occasion.

For the convenience of avoiding explanations, I have treated the events of several summers as though they belonged to only one. This can be of no importance to the reader, but as the work is chronologically inexact, I had better perhaps say so.

The illustrations by Mr. H. F. Jones are on pages 95, 211, 225, 238, 254, 260. The frontispiece and the illustrations on the title-page and on pages 261, 262 are by Mr. Charles Gogin. There are two drawings on pages 136, 137 by an Italian gentleman whose name I have unfortunately lost, and whose permission to insert them I have, therefore, been unable to obtain, and one on page 138 by Signor Gaetano Meo. The rest are mine, except that all the figures in my drawings are in every case by Mr. Charles Gogin, unless when they are merely copied from frescoes or other sources. The two larger views of Oropa are chiefly taken from photographs. The rest are all of them from studies taken upon the spot.

I must acknowledge the great obligations I am under to Mr. H. F. Jones as regards the letterpress no less than the illustrations; I might almost say that the book is nearly as much his as mine, while it is only through the care which he and another friend have exercised in the revision of my pages that I am able to let them appear with some approach to confidence.

November, 1881.

Table of Contents

List of Illustrations

15

Alps and Sanctuaries

Chapter I

Introduction

MOST men will readily admit that the two poets who have the greatest hold over Englishmen are Handel and Shakespeare—for it is as a poet, a sympathiser with and renderer of all estates and conditions whether of men or things, rather than as a mere musician, that Handel reigns supreme. There have been many who have known as much English as Shakespeare, and so, doubtless, there have been no fewer who have known as much music as Handel: perhaps Bach, probably Haydn, certainly Mozart; as likely as not, many a known and unknown musician now living; but the poet is not known by knowledge alone—not by *gnosis* only—but also, and in greater part, by the *agape* which makes him wish to steal men's hearts, and prompts him so to apply his knowledge that he shall succeed. There has been no one to touch Handel as an observer of all that was observable, a lover of all that was loveable, a hater of all that was hateable, and, therefore, as a poet. Shakespeare loved not wisely but too well. Handel loved as well as Shakespeare, but more wisely. He is as much above Shakespeare as Shakespeare is above all others, except Handel himself ; he is no less lofty, impassioned, tender, and full alike of fire and love of play ; he is no less universal in the range of his sympathies, no less a master of expression and illustration than Shakespeare, and at the same time he is of robuster, stronger fibre, more easy, less introspective. Englishmen are of so mixed a race, so inventive, and so given to migration, that for many generations to come they are bound to be at times puzzled, and therefore introspective ; if they get their freedom at all they get it as Shakespeare "with a great sum," whereas Handel was "free born." Shakespeare sometimes errs and grievously, he is as one of his own best men " moulded out of faults," who " for the most become much more the better, for being a little bad ; " Handel, if he puts forth his strength at all, is unerring : he gains the maximum of effect with the minimum of effort. As Mozart said of him, " he beats us all in effect, when he chooses he strikes like a thunderbolt." Shakespeare's strength is perfected in weakness ; Handel is the serenity and unself-consciousness of health itself. " There," said Beethoven on his deathbed, pointing to the works of Handel, " there—is truth." These, however, are details, the main point that will be admitted is that the average Englishman is more attracted by Handel and Shakespeare than by any other two men who have been long enough dead for us to have formed a fairly permanent verdict concerning them. We not only believe them to have been the best men familiarly known here in England, but we see foreign nations join us for the most part in assigning to them the highest place as renderers of emotion.

It is always a pleasure to me to reflect that the countries dearest to these two master spirits are those which are also dearest to myself, I mean England and Italy.

Both of them lived mainly here in London, but both of them turned mainly to Italy when realising their dreams. Handel's music is the embodiment of all the best Italian music of his time and before him, assimilated and reproduced with the enlargements and additions suggested by his own genius. He studied in Italy; his subjects for many years were almost exclusively from Italian sources; the very language of his thoughts was Italian, and to the end of his life he would have composed nothing but Italian operas, if the English public would have supported him. His spirit flew to Italy, but his home was London. So also Shakespeare turned to Italy more than to any other country for his subjects. Roughly, he wrote nineteen Italian, or what to him were virtually Italian plays, to twelve English, one Scotch, one Danish, three French, and two early British.

But who does not turn to Italy who has the chance of doing so? What, indeed, do we not owe to that most lovely and loveable country? Take up a Bank of England note and the Italian language will be found still lingering upon it. It is signed "for Bank of England and Comp*." (*Compagnia*), not "Comp*." Our laws are Roman in their origin. Our music, as we have seen, and our painting comes from Italy. Our very religion till a few hundred years ago found its headquarters, not in London nor in Canterbury, but in Rome. What, in fact, is there which has not filtered through Italy, even though it arose elsewhere? On the other hand, there are infinite attractions in London. I have seen many foreign cities, but I know none so commodious, or, let me add, so beautiful. I know of nothing in any foreign city equal to the view down Fleet Street, walking along the north side from the corner of Fetter Lane. It is often said that this has been spoiled by the London, Chatham, and Dover Railway bridge over Ludgate Hill ; I think, however, the effect is more imposing now than it was before the bridge was built. Time has already softened it ; it does not obtrude itself ; it adds greatly to the sense of size, and makes us doubly aware of the movement of life, the colossal circulation to which London owes so much of its impressiveness. We gain more by this than we lose by the infraction of some pedant's canon about the artistically correct intersection of right lines. Vast as is the world below the bridge, there is a vaster still on high, and when trains are passing, the steam from the engine will throw the dome of St. Paul's into the clouds, and make it seem as though there were a commingling of earth and some far-off mysterious palace in dreamland. I am not very fond of Milton, but I admit that he does at times put me in mind of Fleet Street.

While on the subject of Fleet Street, I would put in a word in favour of the much-abused griffin. The whole monument is one of the handsomest in London. As for its being an obstruction, I have discoursed with a large number of omnibus conductors on the subject, and am satisfied that the obstruction is imaginary.

When, again, I think of Waterloo Bridge, and the huge wide-opened jaws of those two Behemoths, the Cannon Street and Charing Cross railway stations, I am not sure that the prospect here is not even finer than in Fleet Street. See how they belch forth puffing trains as the breath of their nostrils, gorging and disgorging incessantly those human atoms whose movement is the life of the city. How like it all is to some great bodily mechanism of which the people are the blood. And then, above all, see the ineffable St. Paul's. I was once on Waterloo Bridge after a heavy thunderstorm in summer. A thick darkness was upon the river and the buildings upon the north side, but just below I could see the water hurrying onward as in an abyss, dark, gloomy, and mysterious. On a level with the eye there was an absolute blank, but above, the sky was clear, and out of the gloom the dome and towers of St. Paul's rose up sharply, looking higher than they actually were, and as though they rested upon space.

Then as for the neighbourhood within, we will say, a radius of thirty miles. It is one of the main businesses of my life to explore this district. I have walked several thousands of miles in doing so, and I mark where I have been in red upon the Ordnance map, so that I may see at a glance what parts I know least well, and direct my attention to them as soon as possible. For ten months in the year I continue my walks in the home counties, every week adding some new village or farmhouse to my list of things worth seeing ; and no matter where else I may have been, I find a charm in the villages of Kent, Surrey, and Sussex, which in its way I know not where to rival.

I have ventured to say the above, because during the remainder of my book I shall be occupied almost exclusively with Italy, and wish to make it clear that my Italian rambles are taken not because I prefer Italy to England, but as by way of *parergon*, or by-work, as every man should have both his profession and his hobby. I have chosen Italy as my second country, and would dedicate this book to her as a thank-offering for the happiness she has afforded me.

Chapter II

Faido

FOR some years past I have paid a visit of greater or less length to Faido in the Canton Ticino, which though politically Swiss is as much Italian in character as any part of Italy. I was attracted to this place, in the first instance, chiefly because it is one of the easiest places on the Italian side of the Alps to reach from England. This merit it will soon possess in a still greater degree, for when the St. Gothard tunnel is open, it will be possible to leave London, we will say, on a Monday morning and be at Faido by six or seven o'clock the next evening, just as one can now do with S. Ambrogio on the line between Susa and Turin, of which more hereafter.

True, by making use of the tunnel one will miss the St. Gothard scenery, but I would not, if I were the reader, lay this too much to heart. Mountain scenery, when one is staying right in the middle of it, or when one is on foot, is one thing, and mountain scenery as seen from the top of a diligence very likely smothered in dust is another. Besides I do not think he will like the St. Gothard scenery very much.

It is a pity there is no mental microscope to show us our likes and dislikes while they are yet too vague to be made out easily. We are so apt to let imaginary likings run away with us, as a person at the far end of Cannon Street railway platform, if he expects a friend to join him, will see that friend in half the impossible people who are coming through the wicket. I once began an essay on "The Art of Knowing what gives one Pleasure," but soon found myself out of the diatonic with it, in all manner of strange keys, amid a maze of metaphysical accidentals and double and treble flats, so I left it alone as a question not worth the trouble it seemed likely to take in answering. It is like everything else, if we much want to know our own mind on any particular point, we may be trusted to develop the faculty which will reveal it to us, and if we do not greatly care about knowing, it does not much matter if we remain in ignorance. But in few cases can we get at our permanent liking without at least as much experience as a fishmonger must have had before he can choose at once the best bloater out of twenty which, to inexperienced eyes, seem one as good as the other. Lord Beaconsfield was a thorough Erasmus Darwinian when he said so well in "Endymion" : "There is nothing like will ; everybody can do exactly what they like in this world, provided they really like it. Sometimes they think they do, but in general it's a mistake."* If this is as true as I believe it to be, "the longing after immortality," though not indeed much of an argument in favour of our being immortal at the present moment, is perfectly sound as a reason for concluding that we shall one day develop immortality, if our desire is deep enough and lasting enough. As for knowing whether or not one likes a picture, which under the present æsthetic reign of terror is *de rigueur*, I once heard a man say the only test was to ask one's self whether one would care to look at it if one was quite sure that one was alone ; I have never been able to get beyond this test with the St. Gothard scenery, and applying it to the Devil's Bridge,

* Vol. iii. p. 300.

I should say a stay of about thirty seconds would be enough for me. I daresay Mendelssohn would have stayed at least two hours at the Devil's Bridge, but then he did stay such a long while before things.

The coming out from the short tunnel on to the plain of Andermatt does certainly give the pleasure of a surprise. I shall never forget coming out of this tunnel one day late in November, and finding the whole Andermatt valley in brilliant sunshine, though from Flüelen up to the Devil's Bridge the clouds had hung heavy and low. It was one of the most striking transformation scenes imaginable. The top of the pass is good, and the Hotel Prosa a comfortable inn to stay at. I do not know whether this house will be discontinued when the railway is opened, but understand that the proprietor has taken the large hotel at Piora, which I will speak of later on. The descent on the Italian side is impressive, and so is the point where sight is first caught of the valley below Airolo, but on the whole I cannot see that the St. Gothard is better than the S. Bernardino on the Italian side, or the Lukmanier, near the top, on the German ; this last is one of the most beautiful things imaginable, but it should be seen by one who is travelling towards German Switzerland, and in a fine summer's evening light. I was never more impressed by the St. Gothard than on the occasion already referred to when I crossed it in winter. We went in sledges from Hospenthal to Airolo, and I remember thinking what splendid fellows the postillions and guards and men who helped to shift the luggage on to the sledges, looked ; they were so ruddy and strong and full of health, as indeed they might well be—living an active outdoor life in such an air ; besides, they were picked men, for the passage in winter is never without possible dangers. It was delightful travelling in the sledge. The sky was of

a deep blue ; there was not a single cloud either in sky or
on mountain, but the snow was already deep, and had
covered everything beneath its smooth and heaving
bosom. There was no breath of air, but the cold was intense ; presently the sun set upon all except the higher
peaks, and the broad shadows stole upwards. Then
there was a rich crimson flush upon the mountain tops,
and after this a pallor cold and ghastly as death. If he
is fortunate in his day, I do not think any one will be
sorry to have crossed the St. Gothard in mid-winter ; but
one pass will do as well as another.

Airolo, at the foot of the pass on the Italian side,
was, till lately, a quiet and beautiful village, rising
from among great green slopes, which in early summer
are covered with innumerable flowers. The place,
however, is now quite changed. The railway has turned
the whole Val Leventina topsy-turvy, and altered it
almost beyond recognition. When the line is finished
and the workmen have gone elsewhere, things will get
right again ; but just now there is an explosiveness
about the valley which puzzles one who has been familiar
with its former quietness. Airolo has been especially
revolutionised, being the headquarters for the works
upon the Italian side of the great St. Gothard tunnel, as
Göschenen is for those on the German side ; besides this,
it was burnt down two or three years ago, hardly one of
the houses being left standing, so that it is now a new
town, and has lost its former picturesqueness, but it will
be not a bad place to stay at as soon as the bustle of the
works has subsided, and there is a good hotel—the Hotel
Airolo. It lies nearly 4000 feet above the sea, so that even
in summer the air is cool. There are plenty of delightful
walks—to Piora, for example, up the Val Canaria, and to
Bedretto.

After leaving Airolo the road descends rapidly for a few hundred feet and then more slowly for four or five kilometres to Piotta. Here the first signs of the Italian spirit appear in the wood carving of some of the houses. It is with these houses that I always consider myself as in Italy again. Then come Ronco on the mountain side to the left, and Quinto ; all the way the pastures are thickly covered with cowslips, even finer than those that grow on Salisbury Plain. A few kilometres farther on and sight is caught of a beautiful green hill with a few natural terraces

PRATO FROM NEAR DAZIO

upon it and a flat top—rising from amid pastures, and backed by higher hills as green as itself. On the top of this hill there stands a white church with an elegant Lombard *campanile*—the *campanile* left unwhitewashed. The whole forms a lovely little bit of landscape such as some old Venetian painter might have chosen as a background for a Madonna.

This place is called Prato. After it is passed the road enters at once upon the Monte Piottino gorge, which is better than the Devil's Bridge, but not so much to my taste as the auriculas and rhododendrons which grow upon the rocks that flank it. The peep, however, at the hamlet of Vigera, caught through the opening of the gorge, is very nice. Soon after crossing the second of the Monte Piottino bridges the first chestnuts are reached, or rather were so till a year ago, when they were all cut down to make room for some construction in connection with the railway. A couple of kilometres farther on and mulberries and occasional fig-trees begin to appear. On this we find ourselves at Faido, the first place upon the Italian side which can be called a town, but which after all is hardly more than a village.

Faido is a picturesque old place. It has several houses dated the middle of the sixteenth century; and there is one, formerly a convent, close to the Hotel dell' Angelo, which must be still older. There is a brewery where excellent beer is made, as good as that of Chiavenna—and a monastery where a few monks still continue to reside. The town is 2365 feet above the sea, and is never too hot even in the height of summer. The Angelo is the principal hotel of the town, and will be found thoroughly comfortable and in all respects a desirable place to stay at. I have stayed there so often, and consider the whole family of its proprietor so much among the number of my friends, that I have no hesitation in cordially recommending the house.

Other attractions I do not know that the actual town possesses, but the neighbourhood is rich. Years ago, in travelling by the St. Gothard road, I had noticed the many little villages perched high up on the sides of the mountain, from one to two thousand feet above the river, and had wondered what sort of places they would be. I resolved, therefore, after a time to make a stay at Faido and go up to all of them. I carried out my intention, and there is not a village nor fraction of a village in the Val Leventina from Airolo to Biasca which I have not inspected. I never tire of them, and the only regret I feel concerning them is, that the greater number are inaccessible except on foot, so that I do not see how I shall be able to reach them if I live to be old. These are the places of which I do find myself continually thinking when I am away from them. I may add that the Val Leventina is much the same as every other subalpine valley on the Italian side of the Alps that I have yet seen.

I had no particular aversion to German Switzerland before I knew the Italian side of the Alps. On the contrary, I was under the impression that I liked German Switzerland almost as much as I liked Italy itself, but now I can look at German Switzerland no longer. As soon as I see the water going down Rhinewards I hurry back to London. I was unwillingly compelled to take pleasure in the first hour and a half of the descent from the top of the Lukmanier towards Disentis, but this is only a lipping over of the brimfulness of Italy on to the Swiss side.

The first place I tried from Faido was Mairengo—where there is the oldest church in the valley—a church older even than the church of St. Nicolao of Giornico. There is little of the original structure, but the rare peculiarity remains that there are two high altars side by side.

There is a fine half-covered timber porch to the church. These porches are rare, the only others like it I know of being at Prato, Rossura, and to some extent Cornone. In each of these cases the arrangement is different, the only agreement being in the having an outer sheltered place, from which the church is entered instead of opening directly on to the churchyard. Mairengo is full of good bits, and nestles among magnificent chestnut-trees. From hence I went to Osco, about 3800 feet above the sea, and 1430 above Faido. It was here I first came to

understand the purpose of certain high poles with cross
bars to them which I had already seen elsewhere. They
are for drying the barley on ; as soon as it is cut it is
hung up on the cross bars and secured in this way from
the rain, but it is obvious this can only be done when
cultivation is on a small scale. These *rascane*, as they are
called, are a feature of the Val Leventina, and look very
well when they are full of barley.

TICINESE BARLEY-STACKS

From Osco I tried to coast along to Calpiognia, but was
warned that the path was dangerous, and found it to be
so. I therefore again descended to Mairengo, and re-
ascended by a path which went straight up behind the
village. After a time I got up to the level of Calpiognia,
or nearly so, and found a path through pine woods which
led me across a torrent in a ravine to Calpiognia itself.
This path is very beautiful. While on it I caught sight
of a lovely village nestling on a plateau that now showed
itself high up on the other side the valley of the Ticino,

perhaps a couple of miles off as the crow flies. This I found upon inquiry to be Dalpe ; above Dalpe rose pine woods and pastures ; then the loftier *alpi*, then rugged precipices, and above all the Dalpe glacier roseate with sunset. I was enchanted, and it was only because night was coming on, and I had a long way to descend before getting back to Faido, that I could get myself away. I

CAMPO SANTO AT CALPIOGNIA

passed through Calpiognia, and though the dusk was deepening, I could not forbear from pausing at the Campo Santo just outside the village. I give a sketch taken by daylight, but neither sketch nor words can give any idea of the pathos of the place. When I saw it first it was in the month of June, and the rank dandelions were in seed. Wild roses in full bloom, great daisies,

and the never-failing salvia ran riot among the graves.
Looking over the churchyard itself there were the purple
mountains of Biasca and the valley of the Ticino some
couple of thousand feet below. There was no sound save
the subdued but ceaseless roar of the Ticino, and the
Piumogna. Involuntarily I found the following passage
from the " Messiah " sounding in my ears, and felt as
though Handel, who in his travels as a young man doubtless saw such places, might have had one of them in his
mind when he wrote the divine music which he has
wedded to the words " of them that sleep."*

* " I know that my Redeemer liveth."—" Messiah."

Or again : *

From Calpiognia I came down to Primadengo, and
thence to Faido.

* Suites de Pièces, set i., prelude to No. 8.

Chapter III

Primadengo, Calpiognia, Dalpe, Cornone, and Prato

NEXT morning I thought I would go up to Calpiognia again. It was Sunday. When I got up to Primadengo I saw no one, and heard nothing, save always the sound of distant waterfalls ; all was spacious and full of what Mr. Ruskin has called a " great peacefulness of light." The village was so quiet that it seemed as though it were deserted ; after a minute or so, however, I heard a cherry fall, and looking up, saw the trees were full of people. There they were, crawling and lolling about on the boughs like caterpillars, and gorging themselves with cherries. They spoke not a word either to me or to one another. They were too happy and goodly to make a noise ; but they lay about on the large branches, and ate and sighed for content and ate till they could eat no longer. Lotus eating was a rough nerve-jarring business in comparison. They were like saints and evangelists by Filippo Lippi. Again the rendering of Handel came into my mind, and I thought of how the goodly fellowship of prophets praised God.*

* Dettingen Te Deum.

And how again in some such another quiet ecstasy the muses sing about Jove's altar in the "Allegro and Penseroso."

Here is a sketch of Primadengo Church—looking over it on to the other side the Ticino, but I could not get the cherry-trees nor cherry-eaters.

On leaving Primadengo I went on to Calpiognia, and there too I found the children's faces all purple with cherry juice ; thence I ascended till I got to a *monte*, or collection of chalets, about 5680 feet above the sea. It was deserted

PRIMADENGO

at this season. I mounted farther and reached an *alpe*, where a man and a boy were tending a mob of calves. Going still higher, I at last came upon a small lake close to the top of the range : I find this lake given in the map as about 7400 feet above the sea. Here, being more than 5000 feet above Faido, I stopped and dined.

I have spoken of a *monte* and of an *alpe*. An *alpe*, or alp, is not, as so many people in England think, a snowy mountain. Mont Blanc and the Jungfrau, for example, are not alps. They are mountains with alps upon them.

An *alpe* is a tract of the highest summer pasturage just below the snow-line, and only capable of being grazed for two or three months in every year. It is held as common land by one or more villages in the immediate neighbourhood, and sometimes by a single individual to whom the village has sold it. A few men and boys attend the whole herd, whether of cattle or goats, and make the cheese, which is apportioned out among the owners of the cattle later on. The pigs go up to be fattened on whey. The cheese is not commonly made at the *alpe*, but as soon as the curd has been pressed clear of whey, it is sent down on men's backs to the village to be made into cheese. Sometimes there will be a little hay grown on an *alpe*, as at Gribbio and in Piora; in this case there will be some chalets built, which will be inhabited for a few weeks and left empty the rest of the year.

The *monte* is the pasture land immediately above the highest enclosed meadows and below the *alpe*. The cattle are kept here in spring and autumn before and after their visit to the *alpe*. The *monte* has many houses, dairies, and cowhouses,—being almost the *paese*, or village, in miniature. It will always have its chapel, and is inhabited by so considerable a number of the villagers, for so long a time both in spring and autumn, that they find it worth while to make themselves more comfortable than is necessary for the few who make the short summer visit to the *alpe*.

Every inch of the ascent was good, but the descent was even better on account of the views of the Dalpe glacier on the other side the Ticino, towards which

one's back is turned as one ascends. All day long the
villages of Dalpe and Cornone had been tempting me,
so I resolved to take them next day. This I did, crossing
the Ticino and following a broad well-beaten path which
ascends the mountains in a southerly direction. I found
the rare English fern *Woodsia hyperborea* growing in great

DALPE

luxuriance on the rocks between the path and the river.
I saw some fronds fully six inches in length. I also found
one specimen of *Asplenium alternifolium*, which, however,
is abundant on the other side the valley, on the walls that
flank the path between Primadengo and Calpiognia, and
elsewhere. *Woodsia* also grows on the roadside walls near
Airolo, but not so fine as at Faido. I have often looked
for it in other subalpine valleys of North Italy and the
Canton Ticino, but have never happened to light upon it.

About three or four hundred feet above the river, under some pines, I saw a string of ants crossing and re-crossing the road ; I have since seen these ants every year in the same place. In one part I almost think the stone is a little worn with the daily passage and repassage of so many thousands of tiny feet, but for the most part it certainly is not. Half-an-hour or so after crossing the string of ants, one passes from under the pine-trees into a grassy meadow, which in spring is decked with all manner of Alpine flowers ; after crossing this, the old St. Gothard road is reached, which passed by Prato and Dalpe, so as to avoid the gorge of the Monte Piottino. This road is of very great antiquity, and has been long disused, except for local purposes ; for even before the carriage road over the St. Gothard was finished in 1827, there was a horse track through the Monte Piottino. In another twenty minutes or so, on coming out from a wood of willows and alders, Dalpe is seen close at hand after a walk of from an hour-and-a-half to two hours from Faido.

Dalpe is rather more than 1500 feet above Faido, and is therefore nearly 4000 feet above the sea. It is reckoned a *bel paese*, inasmuch as it has a little tolerably level pasture and tillable land near it, and a fine *alpe*. This is how the wealth of a village is reckoned. The Italians set great store by a little bit of *bella pianura*, or level ground ; to them it is as precious as a hill or rock is to a Londoner out for a holiday. The peasantry are as blind to the beauties of rough unmanageable land as Peter Bell was to those of the primrose with a yellow brim (I quote from memory). The people complain of the climate of Dalpe, the snow not going off before the end of March or beginning of April. No climate, they say, should be colder than that of Faido ; barley, however, and potatoes do very well at Dalpe, and nothing can exceed the hay crops. A good deal of the hay is sent down to Faido on men's backs or rather on their heads, for the road is impracticable even for sledges. It is astonishing what a weight the men will bear upon their heads, and the rate at which they will come down while loaded. An average load is four hundredweight. The man is hardly visible beneath his burden, which looks like a good big part of an ordinary English haystack. With this weight on his head he will go down rough places almost at a run and never miss his footing. The men generally carry the hay down in threes and fours together for company. They look distressed, as well they may : every muscle is strained, and it is easy to see that their powers are being taxed to their utmost limit ; it is better not even to say good-day to them when they are thus loaded ; they have enough to attend to just then ; nevertheless, as soon as they have deposited their load at Faido they will go up to Dalpe again or Calpiognia, or wherever it may be, for another, and bring it down without resting. Two such journeys are reckoned enough for one day. This is how the people get their *corpo di legno e gamba di ferro*— "their bodies of wood and legs of iron." But I think they rather overdo it.

Talking of legs, as I went through the main street of Dalpe an old lady of about sixty-five stopped me, and told me that while gathering her winter store of firewood she had had the misfortune to hurt her leg. I was very sorry, but I failed to satisfy her ; the more I sympathised in general terms, the more I felt that something further was expected of me. I went on trying to do the civil thing, when the old lady cut me short by saying it would be much better if I were to see the leg at once ; so she showed it me in the street, and there, sure enough, close

to the groin there was a swelling. Again I said how sorry
I was; and added that perhaps she ought to show it to a
medical man. " But aren't *you* a medical man ? " said
she in an alarmed manner. " Certainly not," replied I.
" Then why did you let me show you my leg ? " said she
indignantly, and pulling her clothes down, the poor old
woman began to hobble off; presently two others joined
her, and I heard hearty peals of laughter as she recounted
her story. A stranger visiting these out-of-the-way villages
is almost certain to be mistaken for a doctor. What
business, they say to themselves, can any one else have
there, and who in his senses would dream of visiting them
for pleasure ? This old lady had rushed to the usual
conclusion, and had been trying to get a little advice
gratis.

Above Dalpe there is a path through the upper valley
of the Piumogna, which leads to the glacier whence the
river comes. The highest peak above this upper valley
just turns the 10,000 feet, but I was never able to find out
that it has a name, nor is there a name marked in the
Ordnance map of the Canton Ticino. The valley promises
well, but I have not been to its head, where at about 7400
feet there is a small lake. Great quantities of crystals are
found in the mountains above Dalpe. Some people make
a living by collecting these from the higher parts of the
ranges where none but born mountaineers and chamois
can venture ; many, again, emigrate to Paris, London,
America, or elsewhere, and return either for a month
or two, or sometimes for a permanency, having become
rich. In Cornone there is one large white new house
belonging to a man who has made his fortune near Como,
and in all these villages there are similar houses. From
the Val Leventina and the Val Blenio, but more especially
from this last, very large numbers come to London, while

hardly fewer go to America. Signor Gatti, the great ice merchant, came from the Val Blenio.

I once found the words, " Tommy, make room for your uncle," on a chapel outside the walls of one very quiet little upland hamlet. The writing was in a child's scrawl, and in like fashion with all else that was written on the same wall. I should have been much surprised, if I had not already found out how many families return to these parts with children to whom English is the native language. Many as are the villages in the Canton Ticino in which I have sat sketching for hours together, I have rarely done so without being accosted sooner or later by some one who could speak English, either with an American accent or without it. It is curious at some out-of-the-way place high up among the mountains, to see a lot of children at play, and to hear one of them shout out, " Marietta, if you do that again, I'll go and tell mother." One English word has become universally adopted by the *Ticinesi* themselves. They say " waitee " just as we should say " wait," to stop some one from going away. It is abhorrent to them to end a word with a consonant, so they have added " ee," but there can be no doubt about the origin of the word.*

When we bear in mind the tendency of any language, if it once attains a certain predominance, to supplant

---

* In the index that Butler prepared in view of a possible second edition of *Alps and Sanctuaries* occurs the following entry under the heading " Waitee ": " All wrong ; ' waitee ' is ' ohè, ti.' " He was subsequently compelled to abandon this eminently plausible etymology, for his friend the Avvocato Negri of Casale - Monferrato told him that the mysterious " waitee " is actually a word in the Ticinese dialect, and, if it were written, would appear as " vuaitee." It means " stop " or " look here," and is used to attract attention. Butler used to couple this little mistake of his with another that he made in *The Authoress of the Odyssey*, when he said, " Scheria means Jutland—a piece of land jutting out into the sea." Jutland, on the contrary, means the land of the Jutes, and has no more to do with jutting than " waitee " has to do with waiting.—R. A. S.

all others, and when we look at the map of the world and see the extent now in the hands of the two English-speaking nations, I think it may be prophesied that the language in which this book is written will one day be almost as familiar to the greater number of *Ticinesi* as their own.

I may mention one other expression which, though not derived from English, has a curious analogy to an English usage. When the beautiful children with names like Handel's operas come round one while one is sketching, some one of them will assuredly before long be heard to whisper the words " Tira giù," or as children say when they come round one in England, " He is drawing it down." The fundamental idea is, of course, that the draughtsman drags the object which he is drawing away from its position, and " transfers " it, as we say by the same metaphor, to his paper, as St. Cecilia " drew an angel down " in " Alexander's Feast."

A good walk from Dalpe is to the Alpe di Campolungo and Fusio, but it is better taken from Fusio. A very favourite path with me is the one leading conjointly from Cornone and Dalpe to Prato. The view up the valley of the St. Gothard looking down on Prato is fine ; I give a sketch of it taken five years ago before the railway had been begun.

The little objects looking like sentry boxes that go all round the church contain rough modern frescoes, representing, if I remember rightly, the events attendant upon the Crucifixion. These are on a small scale what the chapels on the sacred mountain of Varallo are on a large one. Small single oratories are scattered about all over the Canton Ticino, and indeed everywhere in North Italy by the roadside, at all halting-places, and especially at the crest of any more marked ascent, where the tired wayfarer,

probably heavy laden, might be inclined to say a naughty
word or two if not checked. The people like them, and
miss them when they come to England. They sometimes
do what the lower animals do in confinement when pre-
cluded from habits they are accustomed to, and put up
with strange makeshifts by way of substitute. I once
saw a poor Ticinese woman kneeling in prayer before a

PRATO, AND VALLEY OF ST. GOTHARD

dentist's show-case in the Hampstead Road; she doubtless mistook the teeth for the relics of some saint. I am
afraid she was a little like a hen sitting upon a chalk egg,
but she seemed quite contented.

Which of us, indeed, does not sit contentedly enough
upon chalk eggs at times? And what would life be but
for the power to do so? We do not sufficiently realise
the part which illusion has played in our development.

One of the prime requisites for evolution is a certain power for adaptation to varying circumstances, that is to say, of plasticity, bodily and mental. But the power of adaptation is mainly dependent on the power of thinking certain new things sufficiently like certain others to which we have been accustomed for us not to be too much incommoded by the change—upon the power, in fact, of mistaking the new for the old. The power of fusing ideas (and through ideas, structures) depends upon the power of *con*fusing them ; the power to confuse ideas that are not very unlike, and that are presented to us in immediate sequence, is mainly due to the fact of the impetus, so to speak, which the mind has upon it. We always, I believe, make an effort to see every new object as a repetition of the object last before us. Objects are so varied, and present themselves so rapidly, that as a general rule we renounce this effort too promptly to notice it, but it is always there, and it is because of it that we are able to mistake, and hence to evolve new mental and bodily developments. Where the effort is successful, there is illusion ; where nearly successful but not quite, there is a shock and a sense of being puzzled— more or less, as the case may be ; where it is so obviously impossible as not to be pursued, there is no perception of the effort at all.

Mr. Locke has been greatly praised for his essay upon human understanding. An essay on human misunderstanding should be no less interesting and important. Illusion to a small extent is one of the main causes, if indeed it is not the main cause, of progress, but it must be upon a small scale. All abortive speculation, whether commercial or philosophical, is based upon it, and much as we may abuse such speculation, we are, all of us, its debtors.

Leonardo da Vinci says that Sandro Botticelli spoke slightingly of landscape-painting, and called it " but a vain study, since by throwing a sponge impregnated with various colours against a wall, it leaves some spots upon it, which may appear like a landscape." Leonardo da Vinci continues : " It is true that a variety of com-

PRATO CHURCH PORCH, NO. I

positions may be seen in such spots according to the disposition of mind with which they are considered ; such as heads of men, various animals, battles, rocky scenes, seas, clouds, words, and the like. It may be compared to the sound of bells which may seem to say whatever we choose to imagine. In the same manner these spots may furnish hints for composition, though

they do not teach us how to finish any particular part."*
No one can hate drunkenness more than I do, but I am
confident the human intellect owes its superiority over
that of the lower animals in great measure to the stimulus
which alcohol has given to imagination—imagination
being little else than another name for illusion. As for
wayside chapels, mine, when I am in London, are the
shop windows with pretty things in them.

The flowers on the slopes above Prato are wonderful,
and the village is full of nice bits for sketching, but the
best thing, to my fancy, is the church, and the way it
stands, and the lovely covered porch through which it
is entered. This porch is not striking from the outside,
but I took two sketches of it from within. There is, also,
a fresco, half finished, of St. George and the Dragon,
probably of the fifteenth century, and not without feeling.
There is not much inside the church, which is modernised
and more recent than the tower. The tower is very good,
and only second, if second, in the upper Leventina to
that of Quinto, which, however, is not nearly so well
placed.

The people of Prato are just as fond of cherries as those
of Primadengo, but I did not see any men in the trees.
The children in these parts are the most beautiful and
most fascinating that I know anywhere ; they have black
mouths all through the month of July from the quantities
of cherries that they devour. I can bear witness that
they are irresistible, for one kind old gentleman, seeing
me painting near his house, used to bring me daily a
branch of a cherry-tree with all the cherries on it. " Son
piccole," he would say, " ma son gustose "—" They are
small, but tasty," which indeed they were. Seeing I ate

* Treatise on Painting, chap. cccxlix.

all he gave me—for there was no stopping short as long
as a single cherry was left—he, day by day, increased
the size of the branch, but no matter how many he
brought I was always even with him. I did my best to
stop him from bringing them, or myself from eating all of
them, but it was no use.

Trolinda Del Pietro

Here is the autograph of one of the little black-mouthed
folk. I watch them growing up from year to year in
many a village. I was sketching at Primadengo, and a
little girl of about three years came up with her brother,
a boy of perhaps eight. Before long the smaller child
began to set her cap at me, smiling, ogling, and showing
all her tricks like an accomplished little flirt. Her brother
said, " She always goes on like that to strangers." I
said, " What's her name ? " " Forolinda." The name
being new to me, I made the boy write it, and here it
is. He has forgotten to cross his F, but the writing is
wonderfully good for a boy of his age. The child's name,
doubtless, is Florinda.

More than once at Prato, and often elsewhere, people
have wanted to buy my sketches : if I had not required
them for my own use I might have sold a good many.
I do not think my patrons intended giving more than
four or five francs a sketch, but a quick worker, who
could cover his three or four Fortuny panels a day, might
pay his expenses. It often happens that people who are
doing well in London or Paris are paying a visit to their
native village, and like to take back something to remind
them of it in the winter.

From Prato, there are two ways to Faido, one past an old castle, built to defend the northern entrance of the Monte Piottino, and so over a small pass which will avoid the gorge ; and the other, by Dazio and the Monte Piottino gorge. Both are good.

PRATO CHURCH PORCH, NO. II

Chapter IV

Rossura, Calonico

ANOTHER day I went up to Rossura, a village that can be seen from the windows of the Hotel dell' Angelo, and which stands about 3500 feet above the sea, or a little more than 1100 feet above Faido. The path to it passes along some meadows, from which the church of Calonico can be seen on the top of its rocks some few miles off. By and by a torrent is reached, and the ascent begins in earnest. When the level of Rossura has been nearly attained, the path turns off into meadows to the right, and continues— occasionally under magnificent chestnuts — till one comes to Rossura.

ROSSURA CHURCH

The church has been a good deal restored during the last few years, and an interesting old chapel—with an altar in it—at which mass was said during a time of

49

plague, while the people stood some way off in a meadow, has just been entirely renovated; but as with some English churches, the more closely a piece of old work is copied the more palpably does the modern spirit show

ROSSURA CHURCH PORCH

through it, so here the opposite occurs, for the old-worldliness of the place has not been impaired by much renovation, though the intention has been to make everything as modern as possible.

I know few things more touching in their way than

the porch of Rossura church. It is dated early in the
last century, and is absolutely without ornament ; the
flight of steps inside it lead up to the level of the floor
of the church. One lovely summer Sunday morning,
passing the church betimes, I saw the people kneeling
upon these steps, the church within being crammed. In
the darker light of the porch, they told out against the
sky that showed through the open arch beyond them ;
far away the eye rested on the mountains—deep blue
save where the snow still lingered. I never saw anything
more beautiful—and these forsooth are the people whom
so many of us think to better by distributing tracts about
Protestantism among them !

While I was looking, there came a sound of music
through the open door—the people lifting up their
voices and singing, as near as I can remember, something
which on the piano would come thus :—

I liked the porch almost best under an aspect which
it no longer presents. One summer an opening was
made in the west wall, which was afterwards closed
because the wind blew through it too much and made
the church too cold. While it was open, one could sit
on the church steps and look down through it on to the
bottom of the Ticino valley; and through the windows
one could see the slopes about Dalpe and Cornone. Between the two windows there is a picture of austere old
S. Carlo Borromeo with his hands joined in prayer.

It was at Rossura that I made the acquaintance of
a word which I have since found very largely used
throughout North Italy. It is pronounced "chow"
pure and simple, but is written, if written at all, "ciau,"
or "ciao," the "à" being kept very broad. I believe
the word is derived from "schiavo," a slave, which
became corrupted into "schiao," and "ciao." It is
used with two meanings, both of which, however, are
deducible from the word slave. In its first and more
common use it is simply a salute, either on greeting or
taking leave, and means, "I am your very obedient
servant." Thus, if one has been talking to a small child,
its mother will tell it to say "chow" before it goes away,
and will then nod her head and say "chow" herself.
The other use is a kind of pious expletive, intending "I
must endure it," "I am the slave of a higher power." It

was in this sense I first heard it at Rossura. A woman was washing at a fountain while I was eating my lunch. She said she had lost her daughter in Paris a few weeks earlier. "She was a beautiful woman," said the bereaved

ROSSURA CHURCH PORCH IN 1879

mother, "but—chow. She had great talents—chow. I had her educated by the nuns of Bellinzona—chow. Her knowledge of geography was consummáte—chow, chow," &c. Here "chow" means "pazienza," "I have done and said all that I can, and must now bear it as best I may."

I tried to comfort her, but could do nothing, till at last it occurred to me to say " chow " too. I did so, and was astonished at the soothing effect it had upon her. How subtle are the laws that govern consolation! I suppose they must ultimately be connected with reproduction—the consoling idea being a kind of small cross which *re-generates* or *re-creates* the sufferer. It is important, therefore, that the new ideas with which the old are to be crossed should differ from these last sufficiently to divert the attention, and yet not so much as to cause a painful shock.

There should be a little shock, or there will be no variation in the new ideas that are generated, but they will resemble those that preceded them, and grief will be continued ; there must not be too great a shock or there will be no illusion—no confusion and fusion between the new set of ideas and the old, and in consequence, there will be no result at all, or, if any, an increase in mental discord. We know very little, however, upon this subject, and are continually shown to be at fault by finding an unexpectedly small cross produce a wide diversion of the mental images, while in other cases a wide one will produce hardly any result. Sometimes again, a cross which we should have said was much too wide will have an excellent effect. I did not anticipate, for example, that my saying " chow " would have done much for the poor woman who had lost her daughter ; the cross did not seem wide enough ; she was already, as I thought, saturated with " chow." I can only account for the effect my application of it produced by supposing the word to have derived some element of strangeness and novelty as coming from a foreigner—

just as land which will give a poor crop, if planted with sets from potatoes that have been grown for three or four years on this same soil, will yet yield excellently if similar sets be brought from twenty miles off. For the potato, so far as I have studied it, is a good-tempered, frivolous plant, easily amused and easily bored, and one, moreover, which if bored, yawns horribly.

As an example of a cross proving satisfactory which I had expected would be too wide, I would quote the following, which came under my notice when I was in America. A young man called upon me in a flood of tears over the loss of his grandmother, of whose death at the age of ninety-three he had just heard. I could do nothing with him ; I tried all the ordinary panaceas without effect, and was giving him up in despair, when I thought of crossing him with the well-known ballad of Wednesbury Cocking.* He brightened up instantly, and left me in as cheerful a state as he had been before in a desponding one. " Chow " seems to do for the Italians what Wednesbury Cocking did for my American friend ; it is a kind of small spiritual pick-me-up, or cup of tea.

From Rossura I went on to Tengia, about a hundred and fifty feet higher than Rossura. From Tengia the path to Calonico, the next village, is a little hard to find, and a boy had better be taken for ten minutes or so beyond Tengia. Calonico church shows well for some time before it is actually reached. The pastures here are very rich in flowers, the tiger lilies being more abundant before the hay is mown, than perhaps even at Fusio itself. The whole walk is lovely, and the Gribbiasca waterfall, the most graceful in the Val Leventina, is just opposite.

* See Appendix A.

How often have I not sat about here in the shade
sketching, and watched the blue upon the mountains
which Titian watched from under the chestnuts of
Cadore. No sound except the distant water, or the

TENGIA, NO. 1

croak of a raven, or the booming of the great guns in
that battle which is being fought out between man and
nature on the Biaschina and the Monte Piottino. It is
always a pleasure to me to feel that I have known the

Val Leventina intimately before the great change in it which the railway will effect, and that I may hope to see it after the present turmoil is over. Our descendants a hundred years hence will not think of the inces-

TENGIA, NO. II

sant noise as though of cannonading with which we were so familiar. From nowhere was it more striking than from Calonico, the Monte Piottino having no sooner become silent than the Biaschina would open

fire, and sometimes both would be firing at once.
Posterity may care to know that another and less
agreeable feature of the present time was the quantity
of stones that would come flying about in places which
one would have thought were out of range. All along
the road, for example, between Giornico and Lavorgo,
there was incessant blasting going on, and it was sur-
prising to see the height to which stones were sometimes carried. The dwellers in houses near the blasting would cover their roofs with boughs and leaves to
soften the fall of the stones. A few people were hurt,
but much less damage was done than might have been
expected. I may mention for the benefit of English
readers that the tunnels through Monte Piottino and
the Biaschina are marvels of engineering skill, being
both of them spiral ; the road describes a complete
circle, and descends rapidly all the while, so that the
point of egress as one goes from Airolo towards Faido
is at a much lower level than that of ingress.

If an accident does happen, they call it a *disgrazia*,
thus confirming the soundness of a philosophy which
I put forward in an earlier work. Every misfortune
they hold (and quite rightly) to be a disgrace to the
person who suffers it ; " Son disgraziato " is the Italian
for " I have been unfortunate." I was once going to
give a penny to a poor woman by the roadside, when
two other women stopped me. " Non merita," they
said ; " She is no deserving object for charity "—the
fact being that she was an idiot. Nevertheless they
were very kind to her.

Chapter V

Calonico (*continued*) and Giornico

OUR inventions increase in geometrical ratio. They are like living beings, each one of which may become parent of a dozen others—some good and some ne'er-do-weels ; but they differ from animals and vegetables inasmuch as they not only increase in a geometrical ratio, but the period of their gestation decreases in geometrical ratio also. Take this matter of Alpine roads for example. For how many millions of years was there no approach to a road over the St. Gothard, save the untutored watercourses of the Ticino and the Reuss, and the track of the bouquetin or the chamois ? For how many more ages after this was there not a mere shepherd's or huntsman's path by the river side— without so much as a log thrown over so as to form a rude bridge ? No one would probably have ever thought of making a bridge out of his own unaided imagination, more than any monkey that we know of has done so. But an avalanche or a flood once swept a pine into position and left it there ; on this a genius, who was doubtless thought to be doing something very infamous, ventured to make use of it. Another time a pine was found nearly across the stream, but not quite, and not quite, again, in the place where it was wanted. A second genius, to the horror of his fellow-tribesmen—who declared that this time the world really would come to an end—shifted

the pine a few feet so as to bring it across the stream
and into the place where it was wanted. This man
was the inventor of bridges—his family repudiated
him, and he came to a bad end. From this to cutting
down the pine and bringing it from some distance is
an easy step. To avoid detail, let us come to the old
Roman horse road over the Alps. The time between
the shepherd's path and the Roman road is probably
short in comparison with that between the mere chamois
track and the first thing that can be called a path of men.
From the Roman we go on to the mediæval road with
more frequent stone bridges, and from the mediæval to
the Napoleonic carriage road.

The close of the last century and the first quarter
of this present one was the great era for the making of
carriage roads. Fifty years have hardly passed and
here we are already in the age of tunnelling and rail-
roads. The first period, from the chamois track to the
foot road, was one of millions of years ; the second,
from the first foot road to the Roman military way,
was one of many thousands ; the third, from the Roman
to the mediæval, was perhaps a thousand ; from the
mediæval to the Napoleonic, five hundred ; from the
Napoleonic to the railroad, fifty. What will come next
we know not, but it should come within twenty years,
and will probably have something to do with electricity.

It follows by an easy process of reasoning that, after
another couple of hundred years or so, great sweeping
changes should be made several times in an hour, or
indeed in a second, or fraction of a second, till they
pass unnoticed as the revolutions we undergo in the
embryonic stages, or are felt simply as vibrations. This
would undoubtedly be the case but for the existence of
a friction which interferes between theory and practice.

This friction is caused partly by the disturbance of vested interests which every invention involves, and which will be found intolerable when men become millionaires and paupers alternately once a fortnight— living one week in a palace and the next in a workhouse, and having perpetually to be sold up, and then to buy a new house and refurnish, &c.—so that artificial means for stopping inventions will be adopted ; and partly by the fact that though all inventions breed in geometrical ratio, yet some multiply more rapidly than others, and the backwardness of one art will impede the forwardness of another. At any rate, so far as I can see, the present is about the only comfortable time for a man to live in, that either ever has been or ever will be. The past was too slow, and the future will be much too fast.

Another thing which we do not bear in mind when thinking of the Alps is their narrowness, and the small extent of ground they really cover. From Göschenen, for example, to Airolo seems a very long distance. One must go up to the Devil's Bridge, and then to Andermatt. From here by Hospenthal to the top of the pass seems a long way, and again it is a long way down to Airolo ; but all this would easily go on to the ground between Kensington and Stratford. From Göschenen to Andermatt is about as far as from Holland House to Hyde Park Corner. From Andermatt to Hospenthal is much the same distance as from Hyde Park Corner to the Oxford Street end of Tottenham Court Road. From Hospenthal to the hospice on the top of the pass is about equal to the space between Tottenham Court Road and Bow ; and from Bow you must go down three thousand feet of zig-zags into Stratford, for Airolo. I have made the deviation from the straight line about the same in one case as in the other ; in each, the direct distance is nine

and a half miles. The whole distance from Flüelen,
on the Lake of Lucerne, to Biasca, which is almost on the
same level with the Lago Maggiore, is only forty miles,
and could be all got in between London and Lewes, while
from Lucerne to Locarno, actually on the Lago Maggiore
itself, would go, with a good large margin to spare,
between London and Dover. We can hardly fancy,
however, people going backwards and forwards to business
daily between Flüelen and Biasca, as some doubtless do
between London and Lewes.

But how small all Europe is. We seem almost able to
take it in at a single *coup d'œil*. From Mont Blanc we can
see the mountains on the Paris side of Dijon on the one
hand, and those above Florence and Bologna on the
other. What a hole would not be made in Europe if this
great eyeful were scooped out of it.

The fact is (but it is so obvious that I am ashamed
to say anything about it), science is rapidly reducing
space to the same unsatisfactory state that it has already
reduced time. Take lamb : we can get lamb all the year
round. This is perpetual spring ; but perpetual spring is
no spring at all ; it is not a season ; there are no more
seasons, and being no seasons, there is no time. Take
rhubarb, again. Rhubarb to the philosopher is the
beginning of autumn, if indeed, the philosopher can see
anything as the beginning of anything. If any one asks
why, I suppose the philosopher would say that rhubarb is
the beginning of the fruit season, which is clearly autumnal, according to our present classification. From
rhubarb to the green gooseberry the step is so small as to
require no bridging—with one's eyes shut, and plenty of
cream and sugar, they are almost indistinguishable—
but the gooseberry is quite an autumnal fruit, and only a
little earlier than apples and plums, which last are almost

winter ; clearly, therefore, for scientific purposes rhubarb is autumnal.

As soon as we can find gradations, or a sufficient number of uniting links between two things, they become united or made one thing, and any classification of them must be illusory. Classification is only possible where there is a shock given to the senses by reason of a perceived difference, which, if it is considerable, can be expressed in words. When the world was younger and less experienced, people were shocked at what appeared great differences between living forms ; but species, whether of animals or plants, are now seen to be so united, either inferentially or by actual finding of the links, that all classification is felt to be arbitrary. The seasons are like species—they were at one time thought to be clearly marked, and capable of being classified with some approach to satisfaction. It is now seen that they blend either in the present or the past insensibly into one another, and cannot be classified except by cutting Gordian knots in a way which none but plain sensible people can tolerate. Strictly speaking, there is only one place, one time, one action, and one individual or thing ; of this thing or individual each one of us is a part. It is perplexing, but it is philosophy ; and modern philosophy like modern music is nothing if it is not perplexing.

A simple verification of the autumnal character of rhubarb may, at first sight, appear to be found in Covent Garden Market, where we can actually see the rhubarb towards the end of October. But this way of looking at the matter argues a fatal ineptitude for the pursuit of true philosophy. It would be a most serious error to regard the rhubarb that will appear in Covent Garden Market next October as belonging to the autumn then supposed to be current. Practically, no doubt, it does so, but theoretically it must be considered as the first-fruits of the autumn (if any) of the following year, which begins before the preceding summer (or, perhaps, more strictly, the preceding summer but one—and hence, but any number), has well ended. Whether this, however, is so or no, the rhubarb can be seen in Covent Garden, and I am afraid it must be admitted that to the philosophically

CALONICO CHURCH, NO. 1

minded there lurks within it a theory of evolution, and even Pantheism, as surely as Theism was lurking in Bishop Berkeley's tar water.

To return, however, to Calonico. The church is built on the extreme edge of a cliff that has been formed by the breaking away of a large fragment of the mountain. This fragment may be seen lying down below shattered into countless pieces. There is a fissure in the cliff which suggests that at no very distant day some more will follow, and I am afraid carry the church too. My favourite view of the church is from the other side of the small valley which separates it from the village, (see preceding page). Another very good view is from closer up to the church.

The *curato* of Calonico was very kind to me. We had long talks together. I could see it pained him that

CALONICO CHURCH, NO. II

I was not a Catholic. He could never quite get over this, but he was very good and tolerant. He was anxious to be assured that I was not one of those English who went about distributing tracts, and trying to convert people. This of course was the last thing I should have wished to do ; and when I told him so, he viewed me with sorrow, but henceforth without alarm.

All the time I was with him I felt how much I wished I could be a Catholic in Catholic countries, and a Protestant in Protestant ones. Surely there are some things

which, like politics, are too serious to be taken quite
seriously. *Surtout point de zèle* is not the saying of a
cynic, but the conclusion of a sensible man ; and the
more deep our feeling is about any matter, the more
occasion have we to be on our guard against *zèle* in this
particular respect. There is but one step from the
" earnest " to the " intense." When St. Paul told us to
be all things to all men he let in the thin end of the wedge,
nor did he mark it to say how far it was to be driven.

I have Italian friends whom I greatly value, and who
tell me they think I flirt just a trifle too much with *il partito
nero* when I am in Italy, for they know that in the main
I think as they do. " These people," they say, " make
themselves very agreeable to you, and show you their
smooth side ; we, who see more of them, know their
rough one. Knuckle under to them, and they will perhaps condescend to patronise you ; have any individuality of your own, and they know neither scruple nor
remorse in their attempts to get you out of their way.
" Il prete," they say, with a significant look, " è sempre
prete. For the future let us have professors and men of
science instead of priests." I smile to myself at this last,
and reply, that I am a foreigner come among them for
recreation, and anxious to keep clear of their internal dis-
cords. I do not wish to cut myself off from one side of
their national character—a side which, in some respects,
is no less interesting than the one with which I suppose
I am on the whole more sympathetic. If I were an
Italian, I should feel bound to take a side ; as it is, I wish
to leave all quarrelling behind me, having as much of
that in England as suffices to keep me in good health
and temper.

In old times people gave their spiritual and intel-
lectual sop to Nemesis. Even when most positive,

they admitted a percentage of doubt. Mr. Tennyson
has said well, " There lives more doubt "—I quote
from memory—" in honest faith, believe me, than in
half the " systems of philosophy, or words to that effect.
The victor had a slave at his ear during his triumph ;
the slaves during the Roman Saturnalia dressed in
their masters' clothes, sat at meat with them, told them
of their faults, and blacked their faces for them.
They made their masters wait upon them. In the
ages of faith, an ass dressed in sacerdotal robes was
gravely conducted to the cathedral choir at a certain
season, and mass was said before him, and hymns chanted
discordantly. The elder D'Israeli, from whom I am
quoting, writes : " On other occasions, they put burnt
old shoes to fume in the censers ; ran about the church
leaping, singing, dancing, and playing at dice upon the
altar, while a *boy bishop* or *pope of fools* burlesqued the
divine service ; " and later on he says : " So late as 1645,
a pupil of Gassendi, writing to his master what he himself
witnessed at Aix on the feast of Innocents, says—' I have
seen in some monasteries in this province extravagances
solemnised, which pagans would not have practised.
Neither the clergy nor the guardians indeed go to the
choir on this day, but all is given up to the lay brethren,
the cabbage cutters, errand boys, cooks, scullions, and
gardeners ; in a word, all the menials fill their places
in the church, and insist that they perform the offices
proper for the day. They dress themselves with all
the sacerdotal ornaments, but torn to rags, or wear them
inside out ; they hold in their hands the books reversed
or sideways, which they pretend to read with large
spectacles without glasses, and to which they fix the
rinds of scooped oranges . . . ; particularly while
dangling the censers they keep shaking them in derision,

and letting the ashes fly about their heads and faces, one against the other. In this equipage they neither sing hymns nor psalms nor masses, but mumble a certain gibberish as shrill and squeaking as a herd of pigs whipped on to market. The nonsense verses they chant are singularly barbarous :—

> Hæc est clara dies, clararum clara dierum,
> Hæc est festa dies festarum festa dierum.' " *

Faith was far more assured in the times when the spiritual saturnalia were allowed than now. The irreverence which was not dangerous then, is now intolerable. It is a bad sign for a man's peace in his own convictions when he cannot stand turning the canvas of his life occasionally upside down, or reversing it in a mirror, as painters do with their pictures that they may judge the better concerning them. I would persuade all Jews, Mohammedans, Comtists, and freethinkers to turn high Anglicans, or better still, downright Catholics for a week in every year, and I would send people like Mr. Gladstone to attend Mr. Bradlaugh's lectures in the forenoon, and the Grecian pantomime in the evening, two or three times every winter. I should perhaps tell them that the Grecian pantomime has nothing to do with Greek plays. They little know how much more keenly they would relish their normal opinions during the rest of the year for the little spiritual outing which I would prescribe for them, which, after all, is but another phase of the wise saying—*Surtout point de zèle*. St. Paul attempted an obviously hopeless task (as the Church of Rome very well understands) when he tried to put down seasonarianism. People must and will go to church to be a little better, to the theatre to be a little naughtier, to the Royal Institution to be a

* Curiosities of Literature, Lond. 1866, Routledge & Co., p. 272.

little more scientific, than they are in actual life. It is only by pulsations of goodness, naughtiness, and whatever else we affect that we can get on at all. I grant that when in his office, a man should be exact and precise, but our holidays are our garden, and too much precision here is a mistake.

Surely truces, without even an *arrière pensée* of difference of opinion, between those who are compelled to take widely different sides during the greater part of their lives, must be of infinite service to those who can enter on them. There are few merely spiritual pleasures comparable to that derived from the temporary laying down of a quarrel, even though we may know that it must be renewed shortly. It is a great grief to me that there is no place where I can go among Mr. Darwin, Professors Huxley, Tyndall, and Ray Lankester, Miss Buckley, Mr. Romanes, Mr. Allen, and others whom I cannot call to mind at this moment, as I can go among the Italian priests. I remember in one monastery (but this was not in the Canton Ticino) the novice taught me how to make sacramental wafers, and I played him Handel on the organ as well as I could. I told him that Handel was a Catholic ; he said he could tell that by his music at once. There is no chance of getting among our scientists in this way.

Some friends say I was telling a lie when I told the novice Handel was a Catholic, and ought not to have done so. I make it a rule to swallow a few gnats a day, lest I should come to strain at them, and so bolt camels ; but the whole question of lying is difficult. What *is* " lying " ? Turning for moral guidance to my cousins the lower animals, whose unsophisticated nature proclaims what God has taught them with a directness we may sometimes study, I find the plover lying when she lures us

from her young ones under the fiction of a broken wing. Is
God angry, think you, with this pretty deviation from the
letter of strict accuracy ? or was it not He who whispered
to her to tell the falsehood—to tell it with a circumstance,
without conscientious scruple, not once only, but to make
a practice of it, so as to be a plausible, habitual, and professional liar for some six weeks or so in the year ? I
imagine so. When I was young I used to read in good
books that it was God who taught the bird to make her
nest, and if so He probably taught each species the other
domestic arrangements best suited to it. Or did the nest-
building information come from God, and was there an evil
one among the birds also who taught them at any rate
to steer clear of priggishness ?

Think of the spider again—an ugly creature, but I
suppose God likes it. What a mean and odious lie is that
web which naturalists extol as such a marvel of ingenuity !

Once on a summer afternoon in a far country I met
one of those orchids who make it their business to imitate
a fly with their petals. This lie they dispose so cunningly
that real flies, thinking the honey is being already plun-
dered, pass them without molesting them. Watching in-
tently and keeping very still, methought I heard this
orchid speaking to the offspring which she felt within her,
though I saw them not. " My children," she exclaimed,
" I must soon leave you ; think upon the fly, my loved
ones, for this is truth ; cling to this great thought in your
passage through life, for it is the one thing needful ; once
lose sight of it and you are lost ! " Over and over again
she sang this burden in a small still voice, and so I left her.
Then straightway I came upon some butterflies whose
profession it was to pretend to believe in all manner of
vital truths which in their inner practice they rejected ;
thus, asserting themselves to be certain other and hateful

butterflies which no bird will eat by reason of their abominable smell, these cunning ones conceal their own sweetness, and live long in the land and see good days. No : lying is so deeply rooted in nature that we may expel it with a fork, and yet it will always come back again : it is like the poor, we must have it always with us ; we must all eat a peck of moral dirt before we die.

All depends upon who it is that is lying. One man may steal a horse when another may not look over a hedge. The good man who tells no lies wittingly to himself and is never unkindly, may lie and lie and lie whenever he chooses to other people, and he will not be false to any man : his lies become truths as they pass into the hearers' ear. If a man deceives himself and is unkind, the truth is not in him, it turns to falsehood while yet in his mouth, like the quails in the Wilderness of Sinai. How this is so or why, I know not, but that the Lord hath mercy on whom He will have mercy and whom He willeth He hardeneth.

My Italian friends are doubtless in the main right about the priests, but there are many exceptions, as they themselves gladly admit. For my own part I have found the *curato* in the small subalpine villages of North Italy to be more often than not a kindly excellent man to whom I am attracted by sympathies deeper than any mere superficial differences of opinion can counteract. With monks, however, as a general rule I am less able to get on : nevertheless, I have received much courtesy at the hands of some.

My young friend the novice was delightful—only it was so sad to think of the future that is before him. He wanted to know all about England, and when I told him it was an island, clasped his hands and said, " Oh che Provvidenza ! " He told me how the other young men

of his own age plagued him as he trudged his rounds
high up among the most distant hamlets begging alms
for the poor. " Be a good fellow," they would say to
him, " drop all this nonsense and come back to us,
and we will never plague you again." Then he would
turn upon them and put their words from him. Of course
my sympathies were with the other young men rather
than with him, but it was impossible not to be sorry for
the manner in which he had been humbugged from the
day of his birth, till he was now incapable of seeing things
from any other standpoint than that of authority.

What he said to me about knowing that Handel
was a Catholic by his music, put me in mind of what
another good Catholic once said to me about a picture.
He was a Frenchman and very nice, but a *dévot*, and
anxious to convert me. He paid a few days' visit to
London, so I showed him the National Gallery. While
there I pointed out to him Sebastian del Piombo's picture
of the raising of Lazarus as one of the supposed masterpieces of our collection. He had the proper orthodox fit
of admiration over it, and then we went through the
other rooms. After a while we found ourselves before
West's picture of " Christ healing the sick." My French
friend did not, I suppose, examine it very carefully, at
any rate he believed he was again before the raising of
Lazarus by Sebastian del Piombo ; he paused before it
and had his fit of admiration over again : then turning to
me he said, " Ah ! you would understand this picture
better if you were a Catholic." I did not tell him of the
mistake he had made, but I thought even a Protestant
after a certain amount of experience would learn to see
some difference between Benjamin West and Sebastian
del Piombo.

From Calonico I went down into the main road and

walked to Giornico, taking the right bank of the river
from the bridge at the top of the Biaschina. Not a sod of
the railway was as yet turned. At Giornico I visited the
grand old church of S. Nicolao, which, though a later foundation than the church at Mairengo, retains its original condition, and appears, therefore, to be much the older of the
two. The stones are very massive, and
the courses are here and there irregular
as in Cyclopean walls; the end wall is not
bonded into the side walls but simply
built between them; the main door is
very fine, and there is a side door also
very good. There are two altars one
above the other, as in the churches of
S. Abbondio and S. Cristoforo at Como,
but I could not make the lower altar
intelligible in my sketch, and indeed
could hardly see it, so was obliged to
leave it out. The remains of some very
early frescoes can be seen, but I did
not think them remarkable. Altogether,
however, the church is one which no one
should miss seeing who takes an interest
in early architecture.

MAIN DOORWAY,
S. NICOLAO

While painting the study from which the following
sketch is taken, I was struck with the wonderfully vivid
green which the whitewashed vault of the chancel and
the arch dividing the chancel from the body of the church
took by way of reflection from the grass and trees outside.
It is not easy at first to see how the green manages to
find its way inside the church, but the grass seems to
get in everywhere. I had already often seen green reflected from brilliant pasturage on to the shadow under
the eaves of whitewashed houses, but I never saw it

suffuse a whole interior as it does on a fine summer's day at Giornico. I do not remember to have seen this effect in England.

Looking up again against the mountain through the open door of the church when the sun was in a certain position, I could see an infinity of insect life swarming

INTERIOR OF OLD CHURCH, GIORNICO

throughout the air. No one could have suspected its existence, till the sun's rays fell on the wings of these small creatures at a proper angle ; on this they became revealed against the darkness of the mountain behind them. The swallows that were flying among them cannot have to hunt them, they need only fly with their mouths wide open and they must run against as many as

will be good for them. I saw this incredibly multitudinous
swarm extending to a great height, and am satisfied that
it was no more than what is always present during the
summer months, though it is only visible in certain lights.
To these minute creatures the space between the mountains on the two sides of the Ticino valley must be as
great as that between England and America to a codfish.
Many, doubtless, live in the mid-air, and never touch the
bottom or sides of the valley, except at birth and death,
if then. No doubt some atmospheric effects of haze on a
summer's afternoon are due to nothing but these insects.
What, again, do the smaller of them live upon ? On
germs, which to them are comfortable mouthfuls, though
to us invisible even with a microscope ?

I find nothing more in my notes about Giornico except
that the people are very handsome, and, as I thought, of a
Roman type. The place was a Roman military station,
but it does not follow that the soldiers were Romans ;
nevertheless, there is a strain of bullet-headed blood in
the place. Also I remember being told in 1869 that two
bears had been killed in the mountains above Giornico
the preceding year. At Giornico the vine begins to grow
lustily, and wine is made. The vines are trellised, and
looking down upon them one would think one could walk
upon them as upon a solid surface, so closely and luxuri-
antly do they grow.

From Giornico I began to turn my steps homeward
in company with an engineer who was also about to walk
back to Faido, but we resolved to take Chironico on our
way, and kept therefore to the right bank of the river.
After about three or four kilometres from Giornico we
reached Chironico, which is well placed upon a filled-up
lake and envied as a *paese ricco*, but is not so captivating
as some others. Hence we ascended till at last we reached

Gribbio (3960 ft.), a collection of chalets inhabited only for a short time in the year, but a nice place in summer, rich in gentians and sulphur-coloured anemones. From Gribbio there is a path to Dalpe, offering no difficulty whatever and perfect in its way. On this occasion, however, we went straight back to Faido by a rather shorter way than the ordinary path, and this certainly was a little difficult, or as my companion called it, " un tantino difficoltoso," in one or two places ; I at least did not quite like them.

Another day I went to Lavorgo, below Calonico, and thence up to Anzonico. The church and-churchyard at Anzonico are very good ; from Anzonico there is a path to Cavagnago—which is also full of good bits for sketching —and Sobrio. The highest villages in the immediate neighbourhood of Faido are Campello and Molare ; they can be seen from the market-place of the town, and are well worth the trouble of a climb.

Chapter VI

Piora

AN excursion which may be very well made from Faido
is to the Val Piora, which I have already more than
once mentioned. There is a large hotel here which has
been opened some years, but has not hitherto proved
the success which it was hoped it would be. I have
stayed there two or three times and found it very comfortable; doubtless, now that Signor Lombardi of the
Hotel Prosa has taken it, it will become a more popular
place of resort.

I took a trap from Faido to Ambri, and thence walked
over to Quinto; here the path begins to ascend, and
after an hour Ronco is reached. There is a house at
Ronco where refreshments and excellent Faido beer
can be had. The old lady who keeps the house would
make a perfect Fate; I saw her sitting at her window
spinning, and looking down over the Ticino valley as
though it were the world and she were spinning its
destiny. She had a somewhat stern expression, thin
lips, iron-grey eyes, and an aquiline nose; her scanty
locks straggled from under the handkerchief which she
wore round her head. Her employment and the wistful
far-away look she cast upon the expanse below made a
very fine *ensemble*. " She would have afforded," as
Sir Walter Scott says, " a study for a Rembrandt,

77

had that celebrated painter existed at the period," * but
she must have been a smart-looking handsome girl once.

She brightened up in conversation. I talked about
Piora, which I already knew, and the Lago Tom, the
highest of the three lakes. She said she knew the Lago
Tom. I said laughingly, " Oh, I have no doubt you do.
We've had many a good day at the Lago Tom, I know."
She looked down at once.

In spite of her nearly eighty years she was active
as a woman of forty, and altogether she was a very grand
old lady. Her house is scrupulously clean. While I
watched her spinning, I thought of what must so often
occur to summer visitors. I mean what sort of a look-out
the old woman must have in winter, when the wind roars
and whistles, and the snow drives down the valley with a
fury of which we in England can have little conception.
What a place to see a snowstorm from ! and what a place
from which to survey the landscape next morning after
the storm is over and the air is calm and brilliant. There
are such mornings : I saw one once, but I was at the
bottom of the valley and not high up, as at Ronco.
Ronco would take a little sun even in midwinter, but at
the bottom of the valley there is no sun for weeks and
weeks together ; all is in deep shadow below, though the
upper hillsides may be seen to have the sun upon them.
I walked once on a frosty winter's morning from Airolo to
Giornico, and can call to mind nothing in its way more
beautiful : everything was locked in frost—there was
not a waterwheel but was sheeted and coated with ice :
the road was hard as granite—all was quiet and seen as
through a dark but incredibly transparent medium. Near
Piotta I met the whole village dragging a large tree ;
there were many men and women dragging at it, but

* Ivanhoe, chap. xxiii., near the beginning.

they had to pull hard and they were silent ; as I passed
them I thought what comely, well-begotten people they
were. Then, looking up, there was a sky, cloudless and
of the deepest blue, against which the snow-clad mountains stood out splendidly. No one will regret a walk in
these valleys during the depth of winter. But I should
have liked to have looked down from the sun into the
sunlessness, as the old Fate woman at Ronco can do when
she sits in winter at her window ; or again, I should like
to see how things would look from this same window on a
leaden morning in midwinter after snow has fallen heavily
and the sky is murky and much darker than the earth.
When the storm is at its height, the snow must search
and search and search even through the double windows
with which the houses are protected. It must rest upon
the frames of the pictures of saints, and of the sister's
" grab," and of the last hours of Count Ugolino, which
adorn the walls of the parlour. No wonder there is a
S. Maria della Neve—a " St. Mary of the Snow " ; but I
do wonder that she has not been painted.

From Ronco the path keeps level and then descends
a little so as to cross the stream that comes down from
Piora. This is near the village of Altanca, the church
of which looks remarkably well from here. Then there
is an hour and a half's rapid ascent, and at last all on a
sudden one finds one's self on the Lago Ritom, close to
the hotel.

The lake is about a mile, or a mile and a half, long,
and half a mile broad. It is 6000 feet above the sea,
very deep at the lower end, and does not freeze where
the stream issues from it, so that the magnificent trout
in the lake can get air and live through the winter.
In many other lakes, as for example the Lago di Tremorgio, they cannot do this, and hence perish, though

the lakes have been repeatedly stocked. The trout in the Lago Ritom are said to be the finest in the world, and certainly I know none so fine myself. They grow to be as large as moderate-sized salmon, and have a deep red flesh, very firm and full of flavour. I had two cutlets off one for breakfast and should have said they were salmon unless I had known otherwise. In winter, when the lake is frozen over, the people bring their hay from the farther Lake of Cadagno in sledges across the Lake Ritom. Here, again, winter must be worth seeing, but on a rough snowy day Piora must be an awful place. There are a few stunted pines near the hotel, but the hillsides are for the most part bare and green. Piora in fact is a fine breezy open upland valley of singular beauty, and with a sweet atmosphere of cow about it ; it is rich in rhododendrons, and all manner of Alpine flowers, just a trifle bleak, but as bracing as the Engadine itself.

The first night I was ever in Piora there was a brilliant moon, and the unruffled surface of the lake took the reflection of the mountains. I could see the cattle a mile off, and hear the tinkling of their bells which danced multitudinously before the ear as fireflies come and go before the eyes ; for all through a fine summer's night the cattle will feed as though it were day. A little above the lake I came upon a man in a cave before a furnace, burning lime, and he sat looking into the fire with his back to the moonlight. He was a quiet moody man, and I am afraid I bored him, for I could get hardly anything out of him but " Oh altro "—polite but not communicative. So after a while I left him with his face burnished as with gold from the fire, and his back silver with the moonbeams ; behind him were the pastures and the reflections in the lake and the mountains ; and the distant cowbells were ringing.

Then I wandered on till I came to the chapel of
S. Carlo; and in a few minutes found myself on the
Lago di Cadagno. Here I heard that there were people,
and the people were not so much asleep as the simple
peasantry of these upland valleys are expected to be by
nine o'clock in the evening. For now was the time

CHAPEL OF S. CARLO, PIORA

when they had moved up from Ronco, Altanca, and other
villages in some numbers to cut the hay, and were living
for a fortnight or three weeks in the chalets upon the
Lago di Cadagno. As I have said, there is a chapel, but
I doubt whether it is attended during this season with
the regularity with which the parish churches of Ronco,
Altanca, &c., are attended during the rest of the year
The young people, I am sure, like these annual visits to

the high places, and will be hardly weaned from them. Happily the hay will be always there, and will have to be cut by some one, and the old people will send the young ones.

As I was thinking of these things, I found myself going off into a doze, and thought the burnished man from the furnace came up and sat beside me, and laid his hand upon my shoulder. Then I saw the green slopes that rise all round the lake were much higher than I had thought ; they went up thousands of feet, and there were pine forests upon them, while two large glaciers came down in streams that ended in a precipice of ice, falling sheer into the lake. The edges of the mountains against the sky were rugged and full of clefts, through which I saw thick clouds of dust being blown by the wind as though from the other side of the mountains.

And as I looked, I saw that this was not dust, but people coming in crowds from the other side, but so small as to be visible at first only as dust. And the people became musicians, and the mountainous amphitheatre a huge orchestra, and the glaciers were two noble armies of women-singers in white robes, ranged tier above tier behind each other, and the pines became orchestral players, while the thick dust-like cloud of chorus-singers kept pouring in through the clefts in the precipices in inconceivable numbers. When I turned my telescope upon them I saw they were crowded up to the extreme edge of the mountains, so that I could see underneath the soles of their boots as their legs dangled in the air. In the midst of all, a precipice that rose from out of the glaciers shaped itself suddenly into an organ, and there was one whose face I well knew sitting at the keyboard, smiling and pluming himself like a bird as he

thundered forth a giant fugue by way of overture. I
heard the great pedal notes in the bass stalk majesti-
cally up and down, like the rays of the Aurora that go
about upon the face of the heavens off the coast of
Labrador. Then presently the people rose and sang
the chorus " Venus laughing from the skies ; " but ere
the sound had well died away, I awoke, and all was
changed ; a light fleecy cloud had filled the whole basin,
but I still thought I heard a sound of music, and a
scampering-off of great crowds from the part where the
precipices should be. The music went thus :—*

* Handel's third set of organ concertos, No. 6.

By and by the cantering, galloping movement became a trotting one, thus :—

After that I heard no more but a little singing from the chalets, and turned homewards. When I got to the chapel of S. Carlo, I was in the moonlight again, and when near the hotel, I passed the man at the mouth of the furnace with the moon still gleaming upon his back, and the fire upon his face, and he was very grave and quiet.

Next morning I went along the lake till I came to a good-sized streamlet on the north side. If this is followed for half-an-hour or so—and the walk is a very good one—Lake Tom is reached, about 7500 feet above the sea. The lake is not large, and there are not so many chalets as at Cadagno ; still there are some. The view of the mountain tops on the other side the Ticino valley, as seen from across the lake, is very fine. I tried to sketch, but was fairly driven back by a cloud of black gnats. The ridges immediately at the back of the lake, and no great height above it, are the main dividing line of the watershed ; so are those that rise from the Lago di Cadagno ; in fact, about 600 feet above this lake is the top of a pass which goes through the Piano dei Porci, and leads down to S. Maria Maggiore, on the German side of the Lukmanier. I do not know the short piece between the Lago di Cadagno and S. Maria, but it is sure to be good. It is a pity there is no place at S. Maria where one can put up for a night or two. There is a small inn there, but it did not look tempting.

Before leaving the Val Leventina, I would call attention to the beautiful old parish church at Biasca, where there is now an excellent inn, the Hotel Biasca. This church is not so old as the one at Giornico, but it is a good though plain example of early Lombard architecture.

Chapter VII

S. Michele and the Monte Pirchiriano

SOME time after the traveller from Paris to Turin has passed through the Mont Cenis tunnel, and shortly before he arrives at Bussoleno station, the line turns eastward, and a view is obtained of the valley of the Dora, with the hills beyond Turin, and the Superga, in the distance. On the right-hand side of the valley and

S. MICHELE FROM NEAR BUSSOLENO

S. MICHELE

about half-way between Susa and Turin the eye is struck by an abruptly-descending mountain with a large building like a castle upon the top of it, and the nearer it is approached the more imposing does it prove to be. Presently the mountain is seen more edgeways, and the shape changes. In half-an-hour or so from this point, S. Ambrogio is reached, once a thriving town, where

carriages used to break the journey between Turin and
Susa, but left stranded since the opening of the railway.
Here we are at the very foot of the Monte Pirchiriano,
for so the mountain is called, and can see the front of
the building—which is none other than the famous
sanctuary of S. Michele, commonly called " della Chiusa,"
from the wall built here by Desiderius, king of the Lom-
bards, to protect his kingdom from Charlemagne.

The history of the sanctuary is briefly as follows :—

At the close of the tenth century, when Otho III was
Emperor of Germany, a certain Hugh de Montboissier,
a noble of Auvergne, commonly called "Hugh the
Unsewn " (*lo sdruscito*), was commanded by the Pope to
found a monastery in expiation of some grave offence.
He chose for his site the summit of the Monte Pirchiriano
in the valley of Susa, being attracted partly by the fame
of a church already built there by a recluse of Ravenna,
Giovanni Vincenzo by name, and partly by the striking
nature of the situation. Hugh de Montboissier when
returning from Rome to France with Isengarde his wife,
would, as a matter of course, pass through the valley of
Susa. The two—perhaps when stopping to dine at
S. Ambrogio—would look up and observe the church
founded by Giovanni Vincenzo : they had got to build a
monastery somewhere ; it would very likely, therefore,
occur to them that they could not perpetuate their names
better than by choosing this site, which was on a much
travelled road, and on which a fine building would show
to advantage. If my view is correct, we have here an
illustration of a fact which is continually observable—
namely, that all things which come to much, whether
they be books, buildings, pictures, music, or living
beings, are suggested by others of their own kind. It
is always the most successful, like Handel and Shake-

speare, who owe most to their forerunners, in spite of the modifications with which their works descend.

Giovanni Vincenzo had built his church about the year 987. It is maintained by some that he had been Bishop of Ravenna, but Claretta gives sufficient reason for thinking otherwise. In the " Cronaca Clusina " it is said that he had for some years previously lived as a recluse on the Monte Caprasio, to the north of the present Monte Pirchiriano ; but that one night he had a vision, in which he saw the summit of Monte Pirchiriano enveloped in heaven-descended flames, and on this founded a church there, and dedicated it to St. Michael. This is the origin of the name Pirchiriano, which means πῦρ κυρίανον, or the Lord's fire.

The fame of the heavenly flames and the piety of pilgrims brought in enough money to complete the building—which, to judge from the remains of it embodied in the later work, must have been small, but still a church, and more than a mere chapel or oratory. It was, as I have already suggested, probably imposing enough to fire the imagination of Hugh de Montboissier, and make him feel the capabilities of the situation, which a mere ordinary wayside chapel might perhaps have failed to do. Having built his church, Giovanni Vincenzo returned to his solitude on the top of Monte Caprasio, and thenceforth went backwards and forwards from one place of abode to the other.

Avogadro is among those who make Giovanni Bishop, or rather Archbishop, of Ravenna, and gives the following account of the circumstances which led to his resigning his diocese and going to live at the top of the inhospitable Monte Caprasio. It seems there had been a confirmation at Ravenna, during which he had accidentally forgotten to confirm the child of a certain widow.

The child, being in weakly health, died before Giovanni could repair his oversight, and this preyed upon his mind. In answer, however, to his earnest prayers, it pleased the Almighty to give him power to raise the dead child to life again : this he did, and having immediately performed the rite of confirmation, restored the boy to his overjoyed mother. He now became so much revered that he began to be alarmed lest pride should obtain dominion over him ; he felt, therefore, that his only course was to resign his diocese, and go and live the life of a recluse on the top of some high mountain. It is said that he suffered agonies of doubt as to whether it was not selfish of him to take such care of his own eternal welfare, at the expense of that of his flock, whom no successor could so well guide and guard from evil ; but in the end he took a reasonable view of the matter, and concluded that his first duty was to secure his own spiritual position. Nothing short of the top of a very uncomfortable mountain could do this, so he at once resigned his bishopric and chose Monte Caprasio as on the whole the most comfortable uncomfortable mountain he could find.

The latter part of the story will seem strange to Englishmen. We can hardly fancy the Archbishop of Canterbury or York resigning his diocese and settling down quietly on the top of Scafell or Cader Idris to secure his eternal welfare. They would hardly do so even on the top of Primrose Hill. But nine hundred years ago human nature was not the same as nowadays.

The valley of Susa, then little else than marsh and forest, was held by a marquis of the name of Arduin, a descendant of a French or Norman adventurer Roger, who, with a brother, also named Arduin, had come to seek his fortune in Italy at the beginning of the tenth century. Roger had a son, Arduin Glabrio, who recovered the valley of Susa from the Saracens, and established himself at Susa, at the junction of the roads that come down from Mont Cenis and the Mont Genèvre. He built a castle here which commanded the valley, and was his base of operations as Lord of the Marches and Warden of the Alps.

Hugh de Montboissier applied to Arduin for leave to build upon the Monte Pirchiriano. Arduin was then holding his court at Avigliana, a small town near S. Ambrogio, even now singularly little altered, and full of mediæval remains; he not only gave his consent, but volunteered to sell a site to the monastery, so as to ensure it against future disturbance.

The first church of Giovanni Vincenzo had been built upon whatever little space could be found upon the top of the mountain, without, so far as I can gather, enlarging the ground artificially. The present church —the one, that is to say, built by Hugh de Montboissier about A.D. 1000—rests almost entirely upon stone piers and masonry. The rock has been masked by a lofty granite wall of several feet in thickness, which presents something of a keep-like appearance. The spectator naturally imagines that there are rooms, &c., behind this wall, whereas in point of fact there is nothing but the staircase leading up to the floor of the church. Arches spring from this masking wall, and are continued thence until the rock is reached; it is on the level surface thus obtained that the church rests. The true floor, therefore, does not begin till near what appears from the outside to be the top of the building.

There is some uncertainty as to the exact date of the foundation of the monastery, but Claretta* inclines

* "Storia diplomatica dell' antica abbazia di S. Michele della Chiusa," by Gaudenzio Claretta. Turin, 1870. Pp. 8, 9.

decidedly to the date 999, as against 966, the one assigned by Mabillon and Torraneo. Claretta relies on the discovery, by Provana, of a document in the royal archives which seems to place the matter beyond dispute. The first abbot was undoubtedly Avverto or Arveo, who established the rules of the Benedictine Order in his monastery. "In the seven hours of daily work prescribed by the Benedictine rule," writes Cesare Balbo, "innumerable were the fields they ploughed, and the houses they built in deserts, while in more frequented places men were laying cultivated ground waste, and destroying buildings : innumerable, again, were the works of the holy fathers and of ancient authors which were copied and preserved."[*]

From this time forward the monastery received gifts in land and privileges, and became in a few years the most important religious establishment in that part of Italy.

There have been several fires—one, among others, in the year 1340, which destroyed a great part of the monastery, and some of the deeds under which it held valuable grants ; but though the part inhabited by the monks may have been rebuilt or added to, the church is certainly untouched.

[*] " Storia diplomatica dell' antica abbazia di S. Michele della Chiusa," by Gaudenzio Claretta. Turin, 1870. P. 14.

Chapter VIII

S. Michele (*continued*)

I HAD often seen this wonderful pile of buildings, and had marvelled at it, as all must do who pass from Susa to Turin, but I never went actually up to it till last summer, in company with my friend and *collaborateur*, Mr. H. F. Jones. We reached S. Ambrogio station one sultry evening in July, and, before many minutes were over, were on the path that leads to San Pietro, a little more than an hour's walk above S. Ambrogio.

In spite of what I have said about Kent, Surrey, and Sussex, we found ourselves thinking how thin and wanting, as it were, in adipose cushion is every other country in comparison with Italy ; but the charm is enhanced in these days by the feeling that it can be reached so easily. Wednesday morning, Fleet Street ; Thursday evening, a path upon the quiet mountain side, under the overspreading chestnuts, with Lombardy at one's feet.

Some twenty minutes after we had begun to climb, the sanctuary became lost to sight, large drops of thunder-rain began to fall, and by the time we reached San Pietro it was pouring heavily, and had become quite dark. An hour or so later the sky had cleared, and there was a splendid moon : opening the windows, we found ourselves looking over the tops of trees on to some lovely upland pastures, on a winding path through which we could almost fancy we saw a youth led by an angel,

and there was a dog with him, and he held a fish in his
hand. Far below were lights from villages in the valley
of the Dora. Above us rose the mountains, bathed in
shadow, or glittering in the moonbeams, and there came
from them the pleasant murmuring of streamlets that
had been swollen by the storm.

Next morning the sky was cloudless and the air in-
vigorating. S. Ambrogio, at the foot of the mountain,

S. MICHELE FROM S. PIETRO

must be some 800 feet above the sea, and San Pietro
about 1500 feet above S. Ambrogio. The sanctuary at the
top of the mountain is 2800 feet above the sea-level, or
about 500 feet above San Pietro. A situation more delightful than that of San Pietro it is impossible to conceive. It contains some 200 inhabitants, and lies on a
ledge of level land, which is, of course, covered with the
most beautifully green grass, and in spring carpeted with

wild-flowers ; great broad-leaved chestnuts rise from out the meadows, and beneath their shade are strewn masses of sober mulberry-coloured rock ; but above all these rises the great feature of the place, from which, when it is in sight, the eyes can hardly be diverted,—I mean the sanctuary of S. Michele itself.

A sketch gives but little idea of the place. In nature it appears as one of those fascinating things like the smoke from Vesuvius, or the town on the Sacro Monte at Varese, which take possession of one to the exclusion of all else, as long as they are in sight. From each point of view it becomes more and more striking. Climbing up to it from San Pietro and getting at last nearly on a level with the lower parts of the building, or again keeping to a pathway along the side of the mountain towards Avigliana, it will come as on the following page.

There is a very beautiful view from near the spot where the first of these sketches is taken. We are then on the very ridge or crest of the mountain, and look down on the one hand upon the valley of the Dora going up to Susa, with the glaciers of the Mont Cenis in the background, and on the other upon the plains near Turin, with the *colline* bounding the horizon. Immediately beneath is seen the glaring white straight line of the old Mont Cenis road, looking much more important than the dingy narrow little strip of railroad that has super-seded it. The trains that pass along the line look no bigger than caterpillars, but even at this distance they make a great roar. If the path from which the second view is taken is followed for a quarter of an hour or so, another no less beautiful point is reached from which one can look down upon the two small lakes of Avigliana. These lakes supply Turin with water, and, I may add,

S. MICHELE, NEAR VIEW

S MICHELE, FROM PATH TO AVIGLIANA

with the best water that I know of as supplied to any town.

We will now return to the place from which the first of the sketches on p. 95 was taken, and proceed to the

MAIN ENTRANCE TO THE SANCTUARY

sanctuary itself. Passing the small but very massive circular ruin shown on the right hand of the sketch, about which nothing whatever is known either as regards its date or object, we ascend by a gentle incline to the outer gate of the sanctuary. The battered plates of iron that cover the wooden doors are marked with many a bullet. Then we keep under cover for a short space, after which we find ourselves at the foot of a long flight of steps. Close by there is a little terrace with a wall round it, where one can stand and enjoy a view over the valley of the Dora to Turin.

Having ascended the steps, we are at the main entrance to the building—a massive Lombard doorway, evidently the original one. In the space above the door there have been two frescoes, an earlier and a later one, one painted over the other, but nothing now remains save the signature of the second painter, signed in Gothic characters. On entering, more steps must be at once climbed, and then the staircase turns at right angles and tends towards the rock.

At the head of the flight shown p. 98, the natural rock appears. The arch above it forms a recess filled with desiccated corpses. The great pier to the left, and, indeed, all the masonry that can be seen, has no other object than to obtain space for, and to support, the floor·of the church itself. My drawing was taken from about the level of the top of the archway through which the building is entered. There comes in at this point a third small staircase from behind ; ascending this, one finds one's self in the window above the door, from the balcony of which there is a marvellous panorama. I took advantage of the window to measure the thickness of the walls, and found them a little over seven feet thick and built of massive granite blocks. The stones on the inside are so sharp and clean cut that they look as if they were not more than fifty years old. On the outside, the granite, hard as it is, is much weathered, which, indeed, considering the exposed situation, is hardly to be wondered at.

Here again how the wind must howl and whistle, and how the snow must beat in winter ! No one who has not seen snow falling during a time when the thermometer is about at zero can know how searching a thing

STEPS LEADING TO THE CHURCH. NO I

it is. How softly would it not lie upon the skulls and shoulders of the skeletons. Fancy a dull dark January afternoon's twilight upon this staircase, after a heavy snow, when the soft fleece clings to the walls, having drifted in through many an opening. Or fancy a brilliant

winter's moonlight, with the moon falling upon the
skeletons after snow. And then let there be a burst of
music from an organ in the church above (I am sorry to
say they have only a harmonium ; I wish some one would
give them a fine organ). I should like the following for
example :—*

How this would sound upon these stairs, if they would
leave the church-door open. It is said in Murray's handbook that formerly the corpses which are now under the

* Handel ; slow movement in the fifth grand concerto.

arch, used to be placed in a sitting position upon the stairs,
and the peasants would crown them with flowers. Fancy
twilight or moonlight on these stairs, with the corpses

STEPS LEADING TO THE CHURCH.   NO. 2

sitting among the withered flowers and snow, and the
pealing of a great organ.

After ascending the steps that lead towards the
skeletons, we turn again sharp round to the left, and

come upon another noble flight—broad and lofty, and cut in great measure from the living rock.

At the top of this flight there are two sets of Lombard portals, both of them very fine, but in such darkness and so placed that it was impossible to get a drawing of them in detail. After passing through them, the staircase turns again, and, as far as I can remember, some twenty or thirty steps bring one up to the level of the top of the arch which forms the recess where the corpses are. Here there is another beautiful Lombard doorway, with a small arcade on either side which I thought English, rather than Italian, in character. An impression was produced upon both of us that this doorway and the arcade on either side were by a different architect from the two lower archways, and from the inside of the church ; or at any rate, that the details of the enrichment were cut by a different mason, or gang of masons. I think, however, the whole doorway is in a later style, and must have been put in after some fire had destroyed the earlier one.

Opening the door, which by day is always unlocked, we found ourselves in the church itself. As I have said, it is of pure Lombard architecture, and very good of its kind ; I do not think it has been touched since the beginning of the eleventh century, except that it has been re-roofed and the pitch of the roof altered. At the base of the most westerly of the three piers that divide the nave from the aisles, there crops out a small piece of the living rock ; this is at the end farthest from the choir. It is not likely that Giovanni Vincenzo's church reached east of this point, for from this point onwards towards the choir the floor is artificially supported, and the supporting structure is due entirely to Hugo de Mont-boissier. The part of the original church which still remains is perhaps the wall, which forms the western limit of the present church. This wall is not external. It forms the eastern wall of a large chamber with frescoes. I am not sure that this chamber does not occupy the whole space of the original church.

There are a few nice votive pictures in the church, and one or two very early frescoes, which are not without interest ; but the main charm of the place is in the architecture, and the sense at once of age and strength which it produces. The stock things to see are the vaults in which many of the members of the royal house of Savoy, legitimate and illegitimate, lie buried ; they need not, however, be seen.

I have said that the whole building is of much about the same date, and, unless perhaps in the residential parts, about which I can say little, has not been altered. This is not the view taken by the author of Murray's Handbook for North Italy, who says that " injudicious repairs have marred the effect of the building ; " but this writer has fallen into several errors. He talks, for example, of the " open Lombard gallery of small circular arches " as being " one of the oldest and most curious features of the building," whereas it is obviously no older than the rest of the church, nor than the keep-like construction upon which it rests. Again, he is clearly in error when he says that the " extremely beautiful circular arch by which we pass from the staircase to the corridor leading to the church, is a vestige of the original building." The double round arched portals through which we pass from the main staircase to the corridor are of exactly the same date as the staircase itself, and as the rest of the church. They certainly formed no part of Giovanni Vincenzo's edifice ; for, besides being far too rich, they are not on a level with what remains of that building, but

several feet below it. It is hard to know what the writer
means by " the original building ; " he appears to think
it extended to the present choir, which, he says, " retains
traces of an earlier age." The choir retains no such
traces. The only remains of the original church are at the
back of the west end, invisible from the inside of the
church, and at the opposite end to the choir. As for the
church being " in a plain Gothic style," it is an extremely
beautiful example of pure Lombard, of the first few years
of the eleventh century. True, the middle arch of the

GARDEN AT THE SANCTUARY OF S. MICHELE

three which divide the nave from the aisles is pointed,
whereas the two others are round, but this is evidently
done to economise space, which was here unusually
costly. There was room for more than two round arches,
but not room enough for three, so it was decided to dock
the middle arch a little. It is a she-arch—that is to say,
it has no keystone, but is formed simply by propping
two segments of a circle one against the other. It
certainly is not a Gothic arch ; it is a Lombard arch,
modified in an unusual manner, owing to its having been
built under unusual conditions.

The visitor should on no account omit to ring the bell and ask to be shown the open Lombard gallery already referred to as running round the outside of the choir. It is well worth walking round this, if only for the view.

The official who showed us round was very kind, and as a personal favour we were allowed to visit the fathers' private garden. The large arm-chairs are made out of clipped box-trees. While on our way to the garden we passed a spot where there was an alarming buzzing, and found ourselves surrounded by what appeared to be an angry swarm of bees; closer inspection showed that the host was a medley one, composed of wasps, huge hornets, hive-bees, humble-bees, flies, dragon-flies, butter-flies, and all kinds of insects, flying about a single patch of ivy in full blossom, which attracted them so strongly that they neglected everything else. I think some of them were intoxicated. If this was so, then perhaps Bacchus is called " ivy-crowned " because ivy-blossoms intoxicate insects, but I never remember to have before observed that ivy-blossoms had any special attraction for insects.

I have forgotten to say anything about a beam of wood which may be seen standing out at right angles from the tower to the right of the main building. This I believe to have been the gallows. Another like it may be seen at S. Giorio, but I have not got it in my sketch of that place. The attendant who took us round S. Michele denied that it was the gallows, but I think it must have been. Also, the attendant showed us one place which is called *Il Salto della bella Alda.* Alda was being pursued by a soldier; to preserve her honour, she leaped from a window and fell over a precipice some hundreds of feet below; by the intercession of the Virgin she was saved, but became so much elated that she determined to repeat the feat. She jumped a second time from the window, but was dashed to pieces. We were told this as being unworthy of actual credence, but as a legend of the place. We said we found no great difficulty in believing the first half of the story, but could hardly believe that any one would jump from that window twice.*

* For documents relating to the sanctuary, see Appendix B, p. 309.

Chapter IX

The North Italian Priesthood

THERE is now a school in the sanctuary ; we met the boys several times. They seemed well cared for and contented. The priests who reside in the sanctuary were courtesy itself ; they took a warm interest in England, and were anxious for any information I could give them about the monastery near Loughborough—a name which they had much difficulty in pronouncing. They were perfectly tolerant, and ready to extend to others the consideration they expected for themselves. This should not be saying much, but as things go it is saying a good deal. What indeed more can be wished for ?

The faces of such priests as these—and I should say such priests form a full half of the North Italian priesthood—are perfectly free from that bad furtive expression which we associate with priestcraft, and which, when seen, cannot be mistaken : their faces are those of our own best English country clergy, with perhaps a trifle less flesh about them and a trifle more of a not unkindly asceticism.

Comparing our own clergy with the best North Italian and Ticinese priests, I should say there was little to choose between them. The latter are in a logically stronger position, and this gives them greater courage in their opinions ; the former have the advantage in respect

of money, and the more varied knowledge of the world
which money will command.   When I say Catholics have
logically the advantage over Protestants, I mean that
starting from premises which both sides admit, a merely
logical Protestant will find himself driven to the Church
of Rome.   Most men as they grow older will, I think, feel
this, and they will see in it the explanation of the comparatively narrow area over which the Reformation extended, and of the gain which Catholicism has made of
late years here in England.   On the other hand, reasonable
people will look with distrust upon too much reason.
The foundations of action lie deeper than reason can
reach.   They rest on faith—for there is no absolutely
certain incontrovertible premise which can be laid by
man, any more than there is any investment for money
or security in the daily affairs of life which is absolutely
unimpeachable.   The funds are not absolutely safe ;
a volcano might break out under the Bank of England.
A railway journey is not absolutely safe ; one person,
at least, in several millions gets killed.   We invest our
money upon faith mainly.   We choose our doctor upon
faith, for how little independent judgment can we form
concerning his capacity ?   We choose schools for our
children chiefly upon faith.   The most important things
a man has are his body, his soul, and his money.   It is
generally better for him to commit these interests to the
care of others of whom he can know little, rather than be
his own medical man, or invest his money on his own
judgment ; and this is nothing else than making a faith
which lies deeper than reason can reach, the basis of our
action in those respects which touch us most nearly.

On the other hand, as good a case could be made out
for placing reason as the foundation, inasmuch as it
would be easy to show that a faith, to be worth anything,

must be a reasonable one—one, that is to say, which is based upon reason. The fact is, that faith and reason are like desire and power, or demand and supply ; it is impossible to say which comes first : they come up hand in hand, and are so small when we can first descry them, that it is impossible to say which we first caught sight of. All we can now see is that each has a tendency continually to outstrip the other by a little, but by a very little only. Strictly they are not two things, but two aspects of one thing ; for convenience sake, however, we classify them separately.

It follows, therefore—but whether it follows or no, it is certainly true—that neither faith alone nor reason alone is a sufficient guide : a man's safety lies neither in faith nor reason, but in temper—in the power of fusing faith and reason, even when they appear most mutually destructive. A man of temper will be certain in spite of uncertainty, and at the same time uncertain in spite of certainty ; reasonable in spite of his resting mainly upon faith rather than reason, and full of faith even when appealing most strongly to reason. If it is asked, In what should a man have faith ? To what faith should he turn when reason has led him to a conclusion which he distrusts ? the answer is, To the current feeling among those whom he most looks up to—looking upon himself with suspicion if he is either among the foremost or the laggers. In the rough, homely common sense of the community to which we belong we have as firm ground as can be got. This, though not absolutely infallible, is secure enough for practical purposes.

As I have said, Catholic priests have rather a fascination for me—when they are not Englishmen. I should say that the best North Italian priests are more openly tolerant than our English clergy generally are. I remember picking up one who was walking along a road, and giving him a lift in my trap. Of course we fell to talking, and it came out that I was a member of the Church of England. " Ebbene, caro Signore," said he when we shook hands at parting ; " mi rincresce che Lei non crede come me, ma in questi tempi non possiamo avere tutti i medesimi principii."*

I travelled another day from Susa to S. Ambrogio with a priest, who told me he took in " The Catholic Times," and who was well up to date on English matters. Being myself a Conservative, I found his opinions sound on all points but one—I refer to the Irish question : he had no sympathy with the obstructionists in Parliament, but nevertheless thought the Irish were harshly treated. I explained matters as well as I could, and found him very willing to listen to our side of the question.

The one thing, he said, which shocked him with the English, was the manner in which they went about distributing tracts upon the Continent. I said no one could deplore the practice more profoundly than myself, but that there were stupid and conceited people in every country, who would insist upon thrusting their opinions upon people who did not want them. He replied that the Italians travelled not a little in England, but that he was sure not one of them would dream of offering Catholic tracts to people, for example, in the streets of London. Certainly I have never seen an Italian to be guilty of such rudeness. It seems to me that it is not only toleration that is a duty ; we ought to go beyond this now ; we should conform, when we are among a sufficient number of those who would not understand our refusal to do so ; any other course is to attach too much importance at once to

* " Well, my dear sir, I am sorry you do not think as I do, but in hese days we cannot all of us start with the same principles."

our own opinions and to those of our opponents. By all means let a man stand by his convictions when the occasion requires, but let him reserve his strength, unless it is imperatively called for. Do not let him exaggerate trifles, and let him remember that everything is a trifle in comparison with the not giving offence to a large number of kindly, simple-minded people. Evolution, as we all know, is the great doctrine of modern times; the very essence of evolution consists in the not shocking anything too violently, but enabling it to mistake a new action for an old one, without " making believe " too much.

One day when I was eating my lunch near a fountain, there came up a moody, meditative hen, crooning plaintively after her wont. I threw her a crumb of bread while she was still a good way off, and then threw more, getting her to come a little closer and a little closer each time; at last she actually took a piece from my hand. She did not quite like it, but she did it. This is the evolution principle; and if we wish those who differ from us to understand us, it is the only method to proceed upon. I have sometimes thought that some of my friends among the priests have been treating me as I treated the meditative hen. But what of that ? They will not kill and eat me, nor take my eggs. Whatever, therefore, promotes a more friendly feeling between us must be pure gain.

The mistake our advanced Liberals make is that of flinging much too large pieces of bread at a time, and flinging them at their hen, instead of a little way off her. Of course the hen is fluttered and driven away. Sometimes, too, they do not sufficiently distinguish between bread and stones.

As a general rule, the common people treat the priests

respectfully, but once I heard several attacking one warmly on the score of eternal punishment. " Sarà," said one, " per cento anni, per cinque cento, per mille o forse per dieci mille anni, ma non sarà eterna ; perchè il Dio è un uomo forte—grande, generoso, di buon cuore."* An Italian told me once that if ever I came upon a priest whom I wanted to tease, I was to ask him if he knew a place called La Torre Pellice. I have never yet had the chance of doing this ; for, though I am fairly quick at seeing whether I am likely to get on with a priest or no, I find the priest is generally fairly quick too ; and I am no sooner in a diligence or railway carriage with an unsympathetic priest, than he curls himself round into a moral ball and prays horribly—bristling out with collects all over like a cross-grained spiritual hedgehog. Partly, therefore, from having no wish to go out of my way to make myself obnoxious, and partly through the opposite party being determined that I shall not get the chance, the question about La Torre Pellice has never come off, and I do not know what a priest would say if the subject were introduced,—but I did get a talking about La Torre Pellice all the same.

I was going from Turin to Pinerolo, and found myself seated opposite a fine-looking elderly gentleman who was reading a paper headed, " Le Témoin, Echo des Vallées Vaudoises " : for the Vaudois, or Waldenses, though on the Italian side of the Alps, are French in language and perhaps in origin. I fell to talking with this gentleman, and found he was on his way to La Torre Pellice, the headquarters of indigenous Italian evangelicism. He told me there were about 25,000 inhabitants

---

* " It may be for a hundred, or for five hundred years, or for a thousand, or even ten thousand, but it will not be eternal ; for God is a strong man—great, generous, and of large heart."

of these valleys, and that they were without exception
Protestant, or rather that they had never accepted
Catholicism, but had retained the primitive Apostolic
faith in its original purity. He hinted to me that they
were descendants of some one or more of the lost ten
tribes of Israel. The English, he told me (meaning, I
gather, the English of the England that affects Exeter
Hall), had done great things for the inhabitants of La
Torre at different times, and there were streets called the
Via Williams and Via Beckwith. They were, he said, a
very growing sect, and had missionaries and establishments in all the principal cities in North Italy ; in
fact, so far as I could gather, they were as aggressive as
malcontents generally are, and, Italians though they were,
would give away tracts just as readily as we do. I did
not, therefore, go to La Torre.

Sometimes priests say things, as a matter of course,
which would make any English clergyman's hair stand
on end. At one town there is a remarkable fourteenth-
century bridge, commonly known as "The Devil's
Bridge." I was sketching near this when a jolly old
priest with a red nose came up and began a conversation
with me. He was evidently a popular character, for every
one who passed greeted him. He told me that the devil
did not really build the bridge. I said I presumed not,
for he was not in the habit of spending his time so well.

" I wish he had built it," said my friend ; " for then
perhaps he would build us some more."

" Or we might even get a church out of him," said I, a
little slyly.

" Ha, ha, ha ! we will convert him, and make a good
Christian of him in the end."

When will our Protestantism, or Rationalism, or whatever it may be, sit as lightly upon ourselves ?

Chapter X

S. Ambrogio and Neighbourhood

SINCE the opening of the railway, the old inn where the diligences and private carriages used to stop has been closed ; but I was made, in a homely way, ex-

INN AT S. AMBROGIO

tremely comfortable at the Scudo di Francia, kept by Signor Bonaudo and his wife. I stayed here over a fortnight, during which I made several excursions.

One day I went to San Giorio, as it is always written, though San Giorgio is evidently intended. Here there is a ruined castle, beautifully placed upon a hill; this castle shows well from the railway shortly after leaving Bussoleno station, on the right hand going towards Turin. Having been struck with it, I went by train to Bussoleno (where there is much that I was unwillingly compelled to neglect), and walked back to San Giorio. On my way, however, I saw a patch of Cima-da-Conegli-ano-looking meadow-land on a hill some way above me, and on this there rose from among the chestnuts what looked like a castellated mansion. I thought it well to make a digression to this, and when I got there, after a lovely walk, knocked at the door, having been told by peasants that there would be no difficulty about my taking a look round. The place is called the Castel Burrello, and is tenanted by an old priest who has retired hither to end his days. I sent in my card and business by his servant, and by-and-by he came out to me himself.

" Vous êtes Anglais, monsieur ? " said he in French.

" Oui, monsieur."

" Vous êtes Catholique ? "

" Monsieur, je suis de la religion de mes pères."

" Pardon, monsieur, vos ancêtres étaient Catholiques jusqu'au temps de Henri VIII."

" Mais il y a trois cent ans depuis le temps de Henri VIII."

" Eh bien ! chacun a ses convictions ; vous ne parlez pas contre la religion ? "

" Jamais, jamais, monsieur ; j'ai un respect énorme pour l'Eglise Catholique."

" Monsieur, faites comme chez vous ; allez où vous voulez ; vous trouverez toutes les portes ouvertes. Amusez-vous bien."

He then explained to me that the castle had never been a properly fortified place, being intended only as a summer residence for the barons of Bussoleno, who used to resort hither during the extreme heat, if times were tolerably quiet. After this he left me. Taking him at his word, I walked all round, but there was only a shell remaining; the rest of the building had evidently been burnt, even the wing in which the present proprietor

S. GIORIO—COMBA DI SUSA

resides being, if I remember rightly, modernised. The site, however, and the sloping meadows which the castle crowns, are of extreme beauty.

I now walked down to San Giorio, and found a small inn where I could get bread, butter, eggs, and good wine. I was waited upon by a good-natured boy, the son of the landlord, who was accompanied by a hawk that sat always either upon his hand or shoulder. As I looked at the pair I thought they were very much alike, and certainly they were very much in love with one another. After dinner I sketched the castle. While I was doing so, a gentleman told me that a large breach in the wall was made a few years ago, and a part of the wall found to be hollow ; the bottom of the hollow part being unwittingly removed, there fell through a skeleton in a full suit of armour. Others, whom I asked, had heard nothing of this.

Talking of hawks, I saw a good many boys with tame young hawks in the villages round about. There was a tame hawk at the station of S. Ambrogio. The station-master said it used to go now and again to the church-steeple to catch sparrows, but would always return in an hour or two. Before my stay was over it got in the way of a passing train and was run over.

Young birds are much eaten in this neighbourhood. The houses and barns, not to say the steeples of the churches, are to be seen stuck about with what look like terra-cotta water-bottles with the necks outwards. Two or three may be seen in the illustration on p. 113 outside the window that comes out of the roof, on the left-hand side of the picture. I have seen some outside an Italian restaurant near Lewisham. They are artificial bird's-nests for the sparrows to build in : as soon as the young are old enough they are taken and made into a pie. The church-tower near the Hotel de la Poste at Lanzo is more stuck about with them than any other building that I have seen.

Swallows and hawks are about the only birds whose young are not eaten. One afternoon I met a boy with a jay on his finger : having imprudently made advances to this young gentleman in the hopes of getting acquainted with the bird, he said he thought I had better buy it and have it for my dinner ; but I did not fancy it. Another day I saw the *padrona* at the inn-door talking to a lad, who pulled open his shirt-front and showed some twenty or thirty nestlings in the simple pocket formed by his shirt on the one side and his skin upon the other. The *padrona* wanted me to say I should like to eat them, in which case she would have bought them; but one cannot get all the nonsense one hears at home out of one's head in a moment, and I am afraid I preached a little. The *padrona*, who is one of the most fascinating women in the world, and at sixty is still handsome, looked a little vexed and puzzled: she admitted the truth of what I said, but pleaded that the boys found it very hard to gain a few *soldi*, and if people didn't kill and eat one thing, they would another. The result of it all was that I determined for the future to leave young birds to their fate; they and the boys must settle that matter between themselves. If the young bird was a boy, and the boy a young bird, it would have been the boy who was taken ruthlessly from his nest and eaten. An old bird has no right to have a homestead, and a young bird has no right to exist at all, unless they can keep both homestead and existence out of the way of boys who are in want of half-pence. It is all perfectly right, and when we go and stay among these charming people, let us do so as learners, not as teachers.

I watched the *padrona* getting my supper ready. With what art do not these people manage their fire. The New Zealand Maoris say the white man is a fool: " He makes a large fire, and then has to sit away from it; the Maori makes a small fire, and sits over it." The scheme of an Italian kitchen-fire is that there shall always be one stout log smouldering on the hearth, from which a few live coals may be chipped off if wanted, and put into the small square gratings which are used for stewing or roasting. Any warming up, or shorter boiling, is done on the Maori principle of making a small fire of light dry wood, and feeding it frequently. They economise everything. Thus I saw the *padrona* wash some hen's eggs well in cold water ; I did not see why she should wash them before boiling them, but presently the soup which I was to have for my supper began to boil. Then she put the eggs into the soup and boiled them in it.

After supper I had a talk with the *padrone*, who told me I was working too hard. " Totam noctem," said he in Latin, " lavoravimus et nihil incepimus." (" We have laboured all night and taken nothing." " Oh ! " he continued, " I have eyes and ears in my head." And as he spoke, with his right hand he drew down his lower eyelid, and with his left pinched the pig of his ear. " You will be ill if you go on like this." Then he laid his hand along his cheek, put his head on one side, and shut his eyes, to imitate a sick man in bed. On this I arranged to go an excursion with him on the day following to a farm he had a few miles off, and to which he went every Friday.

We went to Borgone station, and walked across the valley to a village called Villar Fochiardo. Thence we began gently to ascend, passing under some noble chestnuts. Signor Bonaudo said that this is one of the best chestnut-growing districts in Italy. A good tree, he told me, would give its forty francs a year. This seems as though chestnut-growing must be lucrative, for an acre should carry some five or six trees, and there is no outlay to speak of. Besides the chestnuts, the land gives a still further return by way of the grass that grows beneath them. Walnuts do not yield nearly so much per tree as chestnuts do. In three-quarters of an hour or so we reached Signor Bonaudo's farm, which was called the

Casina di Banda. The buildings had once been a monastery, founded at the beginning of the seventeenth century and secularised by the first Napoleon, but had been purchased from the state a few years ago by Signor Bonaudo, in partnership with three others, after the passing of the Church Property Act. It is beautifully situated some hundreds of feet above the valley, and commands a lovely view of the *Comba,* as it is called, or *Combe* of Susa. The accompanying sketch will give an idea of the view looking towards Turin. The large building on the hill is, of course, S. Michele. The very distant dome is the Superga on the other side of Turin.

CASINA DI BANDA

The first thing Signor Bonaudo did when he got to his farm was to see whether the water had been duly turned on to his own portion of the estate. Each of the four purchasers had his separate portion, and each had a right to the water for thirty-six hours per week. Signor Bonaudo went round with his hind at once, and saw that the dams in the ducts were so opened or closed that his own land was being irrigated.

Nothing can exceed the ingenuity with which the little canals are arranged so that each part of a meadow, however undulating, shall be saturated equally. The people are very jealous of their water rights, and indeed not unnaturally, for the yield of grass depends in very great measure upon the amount of irrigation which the land can get.

The matter of the water having been seen to, we went to the monastery, or, as it now is, the homestead. As we entered the farmyard we found two cows fighting, and a great strapping wench belabouring them in order to separate them. " Let them alone," said the *padrone ;* " let them fight it out here on the level ground." Then he explained to me that he wished them to find out which was mistress, and fall each of them into her proper place, for if they fought on the rough hillsides they might easily break each other's necks.

We walked all over the monastery. The day was steamy with frequent showers, and thunderstorms in the air. The rooms were dark and mouldy, and smelt rather of rancid cheese, but it was not a bad sort of rambling old place, and if thoroughly done up would make a delightful inn. There is a report that there is hidden treasure here. I do not know a single old castle or monastery in North Italy about which no such report is current, but in the present case there seems more than usual ground (so the hind told me) for believing the story to be well founded, for the monks did certainly smelt the quartz in the neighbourhood, and as no gold was ever known to leave the monastery, it is most likely that all the enormous quantity which they must have made in the course of some two centuries is still upon the premises, if one could only lay one's hands upon it. So reasonable did this seem, that about two years ago it was resolved to call in a somnambulist or clairvoyant from Turin, who, when he arrived at the spot, became seized

with convulsions, betokening of course that there was
treasure not far off : these convulsions increased till he
reached the choir of the chapel, and here he swooned—
falling down as if dead, and being resuscitated with
apparent difficulty. He afterwards declared that it was
in this chapel that the treasure was hidden. In spite of
all this, however, the chapel has not been turned upside
down and ransacked, perhaps from fear of offending the
saint to whom it is dedicated.

VOTIVE PICTURE

In the chapel there are a few votive pictures, but not
very striking ones. I hurriedly sketched one, but have
failed to do it justice. The hind saw me copying the
little girl in bed, and I had an impression as though he
did not quite understand my motive. I told him I had a
dear little girl of my own at home, who had been alarm-
ingly ill in the spring, and that this picture reminded me
of her. This made everything quite comfortable.

We had brought up our dinner from S. Ambrogio,

and ate it in what had been the refectory of the monastery. The windows were broken, and the swallows, who had built upon the ceiling inside the room, kept flying close to us all the time we were eating. Great mallows and hollyhocks peered in at the window, and beyond them there was a pretty Devonshire-looking orchard. The noontide sun streamed in at intervals between the showers.

After dinner we went " al cresto della collina "—to the crest of the hill—to use Signor Bonaudo's words, and looked down upon S. Giorio, and the other villages of the *Combe* of Susa. Nothing could be more delightful. Then, getting under the chestnuts, I made the sketch which I have already given. While making it I was accosted by an underjawed man (there is an unusually large percentage of underjawed people in the neighbourhood of S. Ambrogio), who asked whether my taking this sketch must not be considered as a sign that war was imminent. The people in this valley have bitter and comparatively recent experience of war, and are alarmed at anything which they fancy may indicate its recurrence. Talking further with him, he said, " Here we have no signori ; we need not take off our hats to any one except the priest. We grow all we eat, we spin and weave all we wear ; if all the world except our own valley were blotted out, it would make no difference, so long as we remain as we are and unmolested." He was a wild, weird, St. John the Baptist looking person, with shaggy hair, and an Andrea Mantegnesque feeling about him. I gave him a pipe of English tobacco, which he seemed to relish, and so we parted.

I stayed a week or so at another place not a hundred miles from Susa, but I will not name it, for fear of causing offence. It was situated high, above the valley of the

Dora, among the pastures, and just about the upper limit
of the chestnuts. It offers a summer retreat, of which the
people in Turin avail themselves in considerable numbers.
The inn was a more sophisticated one than Signor
Bonaudo's house at S. Ambrogio, and there were several
Turin people staying there as well as myself, but there
were no English. During the whole time I was in that
neighbourhood I saw not a single English, French, or
German tourist. The ways of the inn, therefore, were
exclusively Italian, and I had a better opportunity of
seeing the Italians as they are among themselves than
I ever had before.

Nothing struck me more than the easy terms on which
every one, including the waiter, appeared to be with every
one else. This, which in England would be impossible,
is here not only possible but a matter of course, because
the general standard of good breeding is distinctly higher
than it is among ourselves. I do not mean to say that
there are no rude or unmannerly Italians, but that
there are fewer in proportion than there are in any other
nation with which I have acquaintance. This is not to be
wondered at, for the Italians have had a civilisation for
now some three or four thousand years, whereas all other
nations are, comparatively speaking, new countries, with
a something even yet of colonial roughness pervading
them. As the colonies to England, so is England to Italy
in respect of the average standard of courtesy and good
manners. In a new country everything has a tendency to
go wild again, man included ; and the longer civilisation
has existed in any country the more trustworthy and
agreeable will its inhabitants be. This preface is necessary, as explaining how it is possible that things can be
done in Italy without offence which would be intolerable
elsewhere ; but I confess to feeling rather hopeless of

being able to describe what I actually saw without giving a wrong impression concerning it.

Among the visitors was the head confidential clerk of a well-known Milanese house, with his wife and sister. The sister was an invalid, and so also was the husband, but the wife was a very pretty woman and a very merry one. The waiter was a good-looking young fellow of about five-and-twenty, and between him and Signora Bonvicino—for we will say this was the clerk's name— there sprang up a violent flirtation, all open and above board. The waiter was evidently very fond of her, but said the most atrociously impudent things to her from time to time. Dining under the veranda at the next table, I heard the Signora complain that the cutlets were burnt. So they were—very badly burnt. The waiter looked at them for a moment—threw her a con- temptuous glance, clearly intended to provoke war— " Chi non ha appetito* . . ." he exclaimed, and was moving off with a shrug of the shoulders. The Signora recognising a challenge, rose instantly from the table, and catching him by the nape of his neck, kicked him deftly downstairs into the kitchen, both laughing heartily, and the husband and sister joining. I never saw anything more neatly done. Of course, in a few minutes some fresh and quite unexceptionable cutlets made their appearance.

Another morning, when I came down to breakfast, I found an altercation going on between the same pair as to whether the lady's nose was too large or not. It was not at all too large. It was a very pretty little nose. The waiter was maintaining that it was too large, and the lady that it was not.

* " If a person has not got an appetite . . ."

One evening Signor Bonvicino told me that his employer had a very large connection in England, and that though he had never been in London, he knew all about it almost as well as if he had. The great centre of business, he said, was in Red Lion Square. It was here his employer's agent resided, and this was a more important part than even the city proper. I threw a drop or two of cold water on this, but without avail. Presently I asked what the waiter's name was, not having been able to catch it. I asked this of the Signora, and saw a little look on her face as though she were not quite prepared to reply. Not understanding this, I repeated my question.

" Oh ! his name is Cesare," was the answer.

" Cesare ! but that is not the name I hear you call him by."

" Well, perhaps not ; we generally call him Cricco,"* and she looked as if she had suddenly remembered having been told that there were such things as prigs, and might, for aught she knew, be in the presence of one of these creatures now.

Her husband came to the rescue. " Yes," said he, " his real name is Julius Cæsar, but we call him Cricco. Cricco è un nome di paese ; parlando così non si offende la religione."†

The Roman Catholic religion, if left to itself and not compelled to be introspective, is more kindly and less given to taking offence than outsiders generally believe. At the Sacro Monte of Varese they sell little round tin boxes that look like medals, and contain pictures of all the chapels. In the lid of the box there is a short printed account of the Sacro Monte, which winds up with the

---

* The waiter's nickname no doubt was Cristo, which was softened into Cricco for the reason put forward below.—R. A. S.

† " Cricco is a rustic appellation, and thus religion is not offended."

words, " La religione *e lo stupendo panorama* tirano numerosi ed allegri visitatori."*

Our people are much too earnest to allow that a view could have anything to do with taking people up to the top of a hill where there was a cathedral, or that people could be " merry " while on an errand connected with religion.

On leaving this place I wanted to say good-bye to Signora Bonvicino, and could not find her ; after a time I heard she was at the fountain, so I went and found her on her knees washing her husband's and her own clothes, with her pretty round arms bare nearly to the shoulder. It never so much as occurred to her to mind being caught at this work.

Some months later, shortly before winter, I returned to the same inn for a few days, and found it somewhat demoralised. There had been grand doings of some sort, and, though the doings were over, the moral and material débris were not yet quite removed. The *famiglia* Bonvicino was gone, and so was Cricco. The cook, the new waiter, and the landlord (who sings a good comic song upon occasion) had all drunk as much wine as they could carry ; and later on I found Veneranda, the one-eyed old chambermaid, lying upon my bed fast asleep. I afterwards heard that, in spite of the autumnal weather, the landlord spent his night on the grass under the chestnuts, while the cook was found at four o'clock in the morning lying at full length upon a table under the veranda. Next day, however, all had become normal again.

Among our fellow-guests during this visit was a fiery-faced eructive butcher from Turin. A difference of

* " Religion and the magnificent panorama attract numerous and merry visitors."

opinion having arisen between him and his wife, I told the Signora that I would rather be wrong with her than right with her husband. The lady was delighted.

" Do you hear that, my dear ? " said she. " He says he had rather be wrong with me than right with you. Isn't he a naughty man ? "

She said that if she died her husband was going to marry a girl of fifteen. I said : " And if your husband dies, ma'am, send me a dispatch to London, and I will come and marry you myself." They were both delighted at this.

She told us the thunder had upset her and frightened her.

" Has it given you a headache ? "

She replied : No ; but it had upset her stomach. No doubt the thunder had shaken her stomach's confidence in the soundness of its opinions, so as to weaken its proselytising power. By and by, seeing that she ate a pretty good dinner, I inquired :

" Is your stomach better now, ma'am ? "

And she said it was. Next day my stomach was bad too.

I told her I had been married, but had lost my wife and had determined never to marry again till I could find a widow whom I had admired as a married woman.

Giovanni, the new waiter, explained to me that the butcher was not really bad or cruel at all. I shook my head at him and said I wished I could think so, but that his poor wife looked very ill and unhappy.

The housemaid's name was La Rosa Mistica.

The landlord was a favourite with all the guests. Every one patted him on the cheeks or the head, or chucked him under the chin, or did something nice and friendly at him. He was a little man with a face like a russet pippin apple, about sixty-five years old, but made of iron. He was going to marry a third wife, and six young women had already come up from S. Ambrogio to be looked at. I saw one of them. She was a Visigoth-looking sort of person and wore a large wobbly-brimmed straw hat; she was about forty, and gave me the impression of being familiar with labour of all kinds. He pressed me to give my opinion of her, but I sneaked out of it by declaring that I must see a good deal more of the lady than I was ever likely to see before I could form an opinion at all.

On coming down from the sanctuary one afternoon I heard the landlord's comic song, of which I have spoken above. It was about the musical instruments in a band : the trumpet did this, the clarinet did that, the flute went tootle, tootle, tootle, and there was an appropriate motion of the hand for every instrument. I was a little disappointed with it, but the landlord said I was too serious and the only thing that would cure me was to learn the song myself. He said the butcher had learned it already, so it was not hard, which indeed it was not. It was about as hard as :

> The battle of the Nile
> I was there all the while
> At the battle of the Nile.

I had to learn it and sing it (Heaven help me, for I have no more voice than a mouse !), and the landlord said that the motion of my little finger was very promising.

The chestnuts are never better than after harvest, when they are heavy-laden with their pale green hedgehog-like fruit and alive with people swarming among their branches, pruning them while the leaves are still good winter food for cattle. Why, I wonder, is there such an

especial charm about the pruning of trees ? Who does
not feel it ? No matter what the tree is, the poplar of
France, or the brookside willow or oak coppice of England,
or the chestnuts or mulberries of Italy, all are interesting
when being pruned, or when pruned just lately. A
friend once consulted me casually about a picture on
which he was at work, and complained that a row of
trees in it was without sufficient interest. I was fortunate
enough to be able to help him by saying : " Prune them
freely and put a magpie's nest in one of them," and the
trees became interesting at once. People in trees always
look well, or rather, I should say, trees always look
well with people in them, or indeed with any living thing
in them, especially when it is of a kind that is not commonly seen in them ; and the measured lop of the bill-
hook and, by and by, the click as a bough breaks and
the lazy crash as it falls over on to the ground, are as
pleasing to the ear as is the bough-bestrewn herbage to
the eye.

To what height and to what slender boughs do not
these hardy climbers trust themselves. It is said that the
coming man is to be toeless. I will venture for it that he
will not be toeless if these chestnut-pruning men and
women have much to do with his development. Let the
race prune chestnuts for a couple of hundred generations
or so, and it will have little trouble with its toes. Of
course, the pruners fall sometimes, but very rarely. I
remember in the Val Mastallone seeing a votive picture
of a poor lady in a short petticoat and trousers trimmed
with red round the bottom who was falling head foremost
from the top of a high tree, whose leaves she had been
picking, and was being saved by the intervention of two
saints who caught her upon two gridirons. Such acci-
dents, however, and, I should think, such interventions,

are exceedingly rare, and as a rule the peasants venture freely into places which in England no one but a sailor or a steeple-jack would attempt.

And so we left this part of Italy, wishing that more Hugo de Montboissiers had committed more crimes and had had to expiate them by building more sanctuaries.

Chapter XI

Lanzo

FROM S. Ambrogio we went to Turin, a city so well known that I need not describe it. The Hotel Europa is the best, and, indeed, one of the best hotels on the continent. Nothing can exceed it for comfort and good cookery. The gallery of old masters contains some great gems. Especially remarkable are two pictures of Tobias and the angel, by Antonio Pollaiuolo and Sandro Botticelli; and a magnificent tempera painting of the Crucifixion, by Gaudenzio Ferrari—one of his very finest works. There are also several other pictures by the same master, but the Crucifixion is the best.

From Turin I went alone to Lanzo, about an hour and a half's railway journey from Turin, and found a comfortable inn, the Hotel de la Poste. There is a fine fourteenth-century tower here, and the general effect of the town is good.

One morning while I was getting my breakfast, English fashion, with some cutlets to accompany my bread and butter, I saw an elderly Italian gentleman, with his hand up to his chin, eyeing me with thoughtful interest. After a time he broke silence.

"Ed il latte," he said, "serve per la suppa."*

I said that that was the view we took of it. He thought it over a while, and then feelingly exclaimed—

* "And the milk [in your coffee] does for you instead of soup."

131

" Oh bel ! "

Soon afterwards he left me with the words—

" Là ! dunque ! cerrea ! chow ! stia bene."

MEDIÆVAL TOWER AT LANZO

" Là " is a very common close to an Italian conversation. I used to be a little afraid of it at first. It sounds
rather like saying, " There, that's that. Please to bear

in mind that I talked to you very nicely, and let you bore
me for a long time; I think I have now done the thing
handsomely, so you'll be good enough to score me one and
let me go." But I soon found out that it was quite a
friendly and civil way of saying good-bye.

PIAZZA AT LANZO

The " dunque " is softer; it seems to say, " I cannot
bring myself to say so sad a word as ' farewell,' but we
must both of us know that the time has come for us to
part, and so "——

" Cerrea " is an abbreviation and corruption of " di
sua Signoria,"—" by your highness's leave." " Chow "

I have explained already. "Stia bene" is simply "farewell."

The principal piazza of Lanzo is nice. In the upper part of the town there is a large school or college. One can see into the school through a grating from the road. I looked down, and saw that the boys had cut their names all over the desks, just as English boys would do. They were very merry and noisy, and though there was a priest standing at one end of the room, he let them do much as they liked, and they seemed quite happy. I heard one boy shout out to another, " Non c' è pericolo," in answer to something the other had said. This is exactly the "no fear" of America and the colonies. Near the school there is a field on the slope of the hill which commands a view over the plain. A woman was mowing there, and, by way of making myself agreeable, I remarked that the view was fine. "Yes, it is," she answered ; "you can see all the trains."

The baskets with which the people carry things in this neighbourhood are of a different construction from any I have seen elsewhere. They are made to fit all round the head like something between a saddle and a helmet, and at the same time to rest upon the shoulders—the head being, as it were, ensaddled by the basket, and the weight being supported by the shoulders as well as by the head. Why is it that such contrivances as this should prevail in one valley and not in another ? If, one is tempted to argue, the plan is a convenient one, why does it not spread further ? If inconvenient, why has it spread so far ? If it is good in the valley of the Stura, why is it not also good in the contiguous valley of the Dora ? There must be places where people using helmet-made baskets live next door to people who use baskets that are borne entirely by back and shoulders. Why do not the people in one or other of these houses adopt their neighbour's basket ? Not because people are not amenable to conviction, for within a certain radius from the source of the invention they are convinced to a man. Nor again is it from any insuperable objection to a change of habit. The Stura people have changed their habit— possibly for the worse ; but if they have changed it for the worse, how is it they do not find it out and change again ?

Take, again, the *pane Grissino*, from which the neighbourhood of Turin has derived its nickname of *il Grissinotto*. It is made in long sticks, rather thicker than a tobacco pipe, and eats crisp like toast. It is almost universally preferred to ordinary bread by the inhabitants of what was formerly Piedmont, but beyond these limits it is rarely seen. Why so ? Either it is good or not good. If not good, how has it prevailed over so large an area ? If good, why does it not extend its empire ? The Reformation is another case in point : granted that Protestantism is illogical, how is it that so few within a given area can perceive it to be so ? The same question arises in respect of the distribution of many plants and animals ; the reason of the limits which some of them cannot pass, being, indeed, perfectly clear, but as regards perhaps the greater number of them, undiscoverable. The upshot of it is that things do not in practice find their perfect level any more than water does so, but are liable to disturbance by way of tides and local currents, or storms. It is in his power to perceive and profit by these irregularities that the strength or weakness of a commercial man will be apparent.

One day I made an excursion from Lanzo to a place, the name of which I cannot remember, but which is not far from the Groscavallo glacier. Here I found several

Italians staying to take the air, and among them one young gentleman, who told me he was writing a book upon this neighbourhood, and was going to illustrate it with his own drawings. This naturally interested me, and I encouraged him to tell me more, which he was nothing loth to do. He said he had a passion for drawing, and was making rapid progress; but there was one thing that held him back—the not having any Conté

STUDY BY AN ITALIAN AMATEUR. NO. I

chalk : if he had but this, all his difficulties would vanish. Unfortunately I had no Conté chalk with me, but I asked to see the drawings, and was shown about twenty, all of which greatly pleased me. I at once proposed an exchange, and have thus become possessed of the two which I reproduce here. Being pencil drawings, and not done with a view to Mr. Dawson's process, they have suffered somewhat in reproduction, but I decided to let them suffer rather than attempt to copy them. What can be more absolutely in the spirit of the fourteenth century than the drawings given above? They seem as though done by some fourteenth-century painter who had risen from the dead. And to show that they are no rare accident, I will give another (p. 138), also done by an entirely self-taught Italian, and intended to represent the castle of Laurenzana in the neighbourhood of Potenza.

If the reader will pardon a digression, I will refer to a

STUDY BY AN ITALIAN AMATEUR. NO. 2

more important example of an old master born out of due time. One day, in the cathedral at Varallo, I saw a picture painted on linen of which I could make nothing. It was not old and it was not modern. The expression of the Virgin's face was lovely, and there was more individuality than is commonly found in modern Italian work. Modern Italian colour is generally either cold and dirty, or else staring. The colour here was tender, and reminded me of fifteenth-century Florentine work. The

folds of the drapery were not modern ; there was a sense
of effort about them, as though the painter had tried to
do them better, but had been unable to get them as free
and flowing as he had wished.   Yet the picture was not
old ; to all appearance it might have been painted a
matter of ten years ; nor again was it an echo—it was a
sound : the archaism was not affected ; on the contrary,

STUDY BY A SELF-TAUGHT ITALIAN

there was something which said, as plainly as though the
living painter had spoken it, that his somewhat con-
strained treatment was due simply to his having been
puzzled with the intricacy of what he saw, and giving
as much as he could with a hand which was less advanced
than his judgment. By some strange law it comes about
that the imperfection of men who are at this stage of any
art is the only true perfection ; for the wisdom of the wise

is set at naught, and the foolishness of the simple is chosen, and it is out of the mouths of babes and sucklings that strength is ordained.

Unable to arrive at any conclusion, I asked the sacristan, and was told it was by a certain Dedomenici of Rossa, in the Val Sesia, and that it had been painted some forty or fifty years ago. I expressed my surprise, and the sacristan continued : " Yes, but what is most wonderful about him is that he never left his native valley, and never had any instruction, but picked up his art for himself as best he could."

I have been twice to Varallo since, to see whether I should change my mind, but have not done so. If Dedomenici had been a Florentine or Venetian in the best times, he would have done as well as the best ; as it is, his work is remarkable. He died about 1840, very old, and he kept on improving to the last. His last work—at least I was told upon the spot that it was his last—is in a little roadside chapel perched high upon a rock, and dedicated, if I remember rightly, to S. Michele, on the path from Fobello in the Val Mastallone to Taponaccio. It is a Madonna and child in clouds, with two full-length saints standing beneath—all the figures life-size. I came upon this chapel quite accidentally one evening, and, looking in, recognised the altar-piece as a Dedomenici. I inquired at the next village who had painted it, and was told, " un certo Dedomenici da Rossa." I was also told that he was nearly eighty years old when he painted this picture. I went a couple of years ago to reconsider it, and found that I remained much of my original opinion. I do not think that any of my readers who care about the history of Italian art will regret having paid it a visit.

Such men are more common in Italy than is believed.

There is a fresco of the Crucifixion outside the Campo Santo at Fusio, in the Canton Ticino, done by a local artist, which, though far inferior to the work of Dedomenici, is still remarkable. The painter evidently knows nothing of the rules of his art, but he has made Christ on the cross bowing His head towards the souls in purgatory, instead of in the conventional fine frenzy to which we are accustomed. There is a storm which has caught and is sweeping the drapery round Christ's body. The angel's wings are no longer white, but many coloured as in old times, and there is a touch of humour in the fact that of the six souls in purgatory, four are women and only two men. The expression on Christ's face is very fine, but otherwise the drawing could not well be more imperfect than it is.

Chapter XII

Considerations on the Decline of Italian Art

THOSE who know the Italians will see no sign of decay about them. They are the quickest witted people in the world, and at the same time have much more of the old Roman steadiness than they are generally credited with. Not only is there no sign of degeneration, but, as regards practical matters, there is every sign of health and vigorous development. The North Italians are more like Englishmen, both in body and mind, than any other people whom I know; I am continually meeting Italians whom I should take for Englishmen if I did not know their nationality. They have all our strong points, but they have more grace and elasticity of mind than we have.

Priggishness is the sin which doth most easily beset middle-class and so-called educated Englishmen: we call it purity and culture, but it does not much matter what we call it. It is the almost inevitable outcome of a university education, and will last as long as Oxford and Cambridge do, but not much longer.

Lord Beaconsfield sent Lothair to Oxford; it is with great pleasure that I see he did not send Endymion. My friend Jones called my attention to this, and we noted that the growth observable throughout Lord Beaconsfield's life was continued to the end. He was one of those who, no matter how long he lived, would have been always growing : this is what makes his later novels so much better than those of Thackeray or Dickens. There was something of the child about him to the last. Earnestness was his greatest danger, but if he did not quite overcome it (as who indeed can ? It is the last enemy that shall be subdued), he managed to veil it with a fair amount of success. As for Endymion, of course if Lord Beaconsfield had thought Oxford would be good for him, he could, as Jones pointed out to me, just as well have killed Mr. Ferrars a year or two later. We feel satisfied, therefore, that Endymion's exclusion from a university was carefully considered, and are glad.

I will not say that priggishness is absolutely unknown among the North Italians ; sometimes one comes upon a young Italian who wants to learn German, but not often. Priggism, or whatever the substantive is, is as essentially a Teutonic vice as holiness is a Semitic characteristic ; and if an Italian happens to be a prig, he will, like Tacitus, invariably show a hankering after German institutions. The idea, however, that the Italians were ever a finer people than they are now, will not pass muster with those who know them.

At the same time, there can be no doubt that modern Italian art is in many respects as bad as it was once good. I will confine myself to painting only. The modern Italian painters, with very few exceptions, paint as badly as we do, or even worse, and their motives are as poor as is their painting. At an exhibition of modern Italian pictures, I generally feel that there is hardly a picture on the walls but is a sham—that is to say, painted not from love of this particular subject and an irresistible desire to paint it, but from a wish to paint an academy picture, and win money or applause.

The same holds good in England, and in all other countries that I know of. There is very little tolerable painting anywhere. In some kinds, indeed, of black and white work the present age is strong. The illustrations to " Punch," for example, are often as good as anything that can be imagined. We know of nothing like them in any past age or country. This is the one kind of art—and it is a very good one—in which we excel as distinctly as the age of Phidias excelled in sculpture. Leonardo da Vinci would never have succeeded in getting his drawings accepted at 85 Fleet Street, any more than one of the artists on the staff of " Punch " could paint a fresco which should hold its own against Da Vinci's Last Supper. Michael Angelo again and Titian would have failed disastrously at modern illustration. They had no more sense of humour than a Hebrew prophet ; they had no eye for the more trivial side of anything round about them. This aspect went in at one eye and out at the other—and they lost more than ever poor Peter Bell lost in the matter of primroses. I never can see what there was to find fault with in that young man.

Fancy a street-Arab by Michael Angelo. Fancy even the result which would have ensued if he had tried to put the figures into the illustrations of this book. I should have been very sorry to let him try his hand at it. To him a priest chucking a small boy under the chin was simply non-existent. He did not care for it, and had therefore no eye for it. If the reader will turn to the copy of a fresco of St. Christopher on p. 209, he will see the conventional treatment of the rocks on either side the saint. This was the best thing the artist could do, and probably cost him no little trouble. Yet there were rocks all around him—little, in fact, else than rock in those

days ; and the artist could have drawn them well enough
if it had occurred to him to try and do so. If he could
draw St. Christopher, he could have drawn a rock ; but
he had an interest in the one, and saw nothing in the
other which made him think it worth while to pay
attention to it. What rocks were to him, the common
occurrences of everyday life were to those who are generally held to be the giants of painting. The result of
this neglect to kiss the soil—of this attempt to be always
soaring—is that these giants are for the most part now
very uninteresting, while the smaller men who preceded
them grow fresher and more delightful yearly. It was
not so with Handel and Shakespeare. Handel's

"Ploughman near at hand, whistling o'er the furrowed land,"

is intensely sympathetic, and his humour is admirable
whenever he has occasion for it.

Leonardo da Vinci is the only one of the giant Italian
masters who ever tried to be humorous, and he failed
completely : so, indeed, must any one if he tries to be
humorous. We do not want this ; we only want them
not to shut their eyes to by-play when it comes in their
way, and if they are giving us an account of what they
have seen, to tell us something about this too. I believe
the older the world grows, the better it enjoys a joke.
The mediæval joke generally was a heavy, lumbering
old thing, only a little better than the classical one.
Perhaps in those days life was harder than it is now, and
people if they looked at it at all closely dwelt upon its
soberer side. Certainly in humorous art, we may claim
to be not only *principes*, but *facile principes*. Nevertheless, the Italian comic journals are, some of them, admirably illustrated, though in a style quite different from
our own ; sometimes, also, they are beautifully coloured.

As regards painting, the last rays of the sunset of
genuine art are to be found in the votive pictures at
Locarno or Oropa, and in many a wayside chapel. In
these, religious art still lingers as a living language,
however rudely spoken. In these alone is the story told,
not as in the Latin and Greek verses of the scholar, who
thinks he has succeeded best when he has most concealed
his natural manner of expressing himself, but by one who
knows what he wants to say, and says it in his mother-
tongue, shortly, and without
caring whether or not his words
are in accordance with academic rules. I regret to see
photography being introduced
for votive purposes, and also
to detect in some places a
disposition on the part of the
authorities to be a little
ashamed of these pictures and
to place them rather out of
sight.

Sometimes in a little country
village, as at Doera near
Mesocco, there is a modern

PARADISO! PARADISO!

fresco on a chapel in which the old spirit appears, with
its absolute indifference as to whether it was ridiculous
or no, but such examples are rare.

Sometimes, again, I have even thought I have detected
a ray of sunset upon a milkman's window-blind in
London, and once upon an undertaker's, but it was too
faint a ray to read by. The best thing of the kind
that I have seen in London is the picture of the lady
who is cleaning knives with Mr. Spong's patent knife-
cleaner, in his shop window nearly opposite Day &

Martin's in Holborn. It falls a long way short, however, of a good Italian votive picture ; but it has the advantage of moving.

I knew of a little girl once, rather less than four years old, whose uncle had promised to take her for a drive in a carriage with him, and had failed to do so. The child was found soon afterwards on the stairs weeping, and being asked what was the matter, replied, "Mans is all alike." This is Giottesque. I often think of it as I look upon Italian votive pictures. The meaning is so sound in spite of the expression being so defective—if, indeed, expression can be defective when it has so well conveyed the meaning.

I knew, again, an old lady whose education had been neglected in her youth. She came into a large fortune, and at some forty years of age put herself under the best masters. She once said to me as follows, speaking very slowly and allowing a long time between each part of the sentence ;—"You see," she said, "the world, and all that it contains, is wrapped up in such curious forms, that it is only by a knowledge of human nature, that we can rightly tell what to say, to do, or to admire." I copied the sentence into my note-book immediately on taking my leave. It is like an academy picture.

But to return to the Italians. The question is, how has the deplorable falling-off in Italian painting been caused ? And by doing what may we again get Bellinis and Andrea Mantegnas as in old time ? The fault does not lie in any want of raw material : the drawings I have already given prove this. Nor, again, does it lie in want of taking pains. The modern Italian painter frets himself to the full as much as his predecessor did—if the truth were known, probably a great deal more. It does not lie in want of schooling or art education. For the last three hundred years, ever since the Carracci opened their academy at Bologna, there has been no lack of art education in Italy. Curiously enough, the date of the opening of the Bolognese Academy coincides as nearly as may be with the complete decadence of Italian painting.

BY AN ITALIAN SCHOOLBOY

This is an example of the way in which Italian boys begin their art education now. The drawing which I reproduce here was given me by the eminent sculptor, Professor Vela, as the work of a lad of twelve years old, and as doing credit alike to the school where the lad was taught and to the pupil himself.*

* Butler said of this drawing that it was " the hieroglyph of a lost soul."—R. A. S.

So it undoubtedly does. It shows as plainly the receptiveness and docility of the modern Italian, as the illustrations given above show his freshness and naïveté when left to himself. The drawing is just such as we try to get our own young people to do, and few English elementary schools in a small country town would succeed in turning out so good a one. I have nothing, therefore, but praise both for the pupil and the teacher ; but about the system which makes such teachers and such pupils commendable, I am more sceptical. That system trains boys to study other people's works rather than nature, and, as Leonardo da Vinci so well says, it makes them nature's grandchildren and not her children. The boy who did the drawing given above is not likely to produce good work in later life. He has been taught to see nature with an old man's eyes at once, without going through the embryonic stages. He has never said his " mans is all alike," and by twenty will be painting like my old friend's long academic sentence. All his individuality has been crushed out of him.

I will now give a reproduction of the frontispiece to Avogadro's work on the sanctuary of S. Michele, from which I have already quoted ; it is a very pretty and effective piece of work, but those who are good enough to turn back to p. 93, and to believe that I have drawn carefully, will see how disappointing Avogadro's frontispiece must be to those who hold, as most of us will, that a draughtsman's first business is to put down what he sees, and to let prettiness take care of itself. The main features, indeed, can still be traced, but they have become as transformed and lifeless as rudimentary organs. Such a frontispiece, however, is the almost inevitable consequence of the system of training that will make boys of twelve do drawings like the one given on p. 147.

If half a dozen young Italians could be got together
with a taste for drawing like that shown by the authors
of the sketches on pp. 136, 137, 138 ; if they had power
to add to their number ; if they were allowed to see
paintings and drawings done up to the year A.D. 1510,
and votive pictures and the comic papers ; if they were
left with no other assistance than this, absolutely free to
please themselves, and could be persuaded not to try
and please any one else, I believe that in fifty years we

AVOGADRO'S VIEW OF S. MICHELE

should have all that was ever done repeated with fresh
naïveté, and as much more delightfully than even by the
best old masters, as these are more delightful than anything we know of in classic painting. The young plants
keep growing up abundantly every day—look at Bas-
tianini, dead not ten years since—but they are browsed
down by the academies. I remember there came out a
book many years ago with the title, " What becomes of all
the clever little children ? " I never saw the book, but
the title is pertinent.

Any man who can write, can draw to a not incon-
siderable extent. Look at the Bayeux tapestry; yet
Matilda probably never had a drawing lesson in her life.
See how well prisoner after prisoner in the Tower of
London has cut this or that out in the stone of his prison
wall, without, in all probability, having ever tried his
hand at drawing before. Look at my friend Jones, who
has several illustrations in this book. The first year he
went abroad with me he could hardly draw at all. He
was no year away from England more than three weeks.
How did he learn? On the old principle, if I am not
mistaken. The old principle was for a man to be doing
something which he was pretty strongly bent on doing,
and to get a much younger one to help him. The younger
paid nothing for instruction, but the elder took the work,
as long as the relation of master and pupil existed between
them. I, then, was making illustrations for this book,
and got Jones to help me. I let him see what I was doing,
and derive an idea of the sort of thing I wanted, and then
left him alone—beyond giving him the same kind of small
criticism that I expected from himself—but I appropriated
his work. That is the way to teach, and the result was
that in an incredibly short time Jones could draw.
The taking the work is a *sine quâ non*. If I had not been
going to have his work, Jones, in spite of all his quick-
ness, would probably have been rather slower in learning to draw. Being paid in money is nothing like so
good.

This is the system of apprenticeship *versus* the academic
system. The academic system consists in giving people
the rules for doing things. The apprenticeship system
consists in letting them do it, with just a trifle of super-
vision. " For all a rhetorician's rules," says my great
namesake, " teach nothing, but to name his tools ; "

and academic rules generally are much the same as the rhetorician's. Some men can pass through academies unscathed, but they are very few, and in the main the academic influence is a baleful one, whether exerted in a university or a school. While young men at universities are being prepared for their entry into life, their rivals have already entered it. The most university and examination ridden people in the world are the Chinese, and they are the least progressive.

Men should learn to draw as they learn conveyancing : they should go into a painter's studio and paint on his pictures. I am told that half the conveyances in the country are drawn by pupils ; there is no more mystery about painting than about conveyancing—not half in fact, I should think, so much. One may ask, How can the beginner paint, or draw conveyances, till he has learnt how to do so ? The answer is, How can he learn, without at any rate trying to do ? If he likes his subject, he will try : if he tries, he will soon succeed in doing something which shall open a door. It does not matter what a man does ; so long as he does it with the attention which affection engenders, he will come to see his way to something else. After long waiting he will certainly find one door open, and go through it. He will say to himself that he can never find another. He has found this, more by luck than cunning, but now he is done. Yet by and by he will see that there is *one* more small, unimportant door which he had overlooked, and he proceeds through this too. If he remains now for a long while and sees no other, do not let him fret ; doors are like the kingdom of heaven, they come not by observation, least of all do they come by forcing : let them just go on doing what comes nearest, but doing it attentively, and a great wide door will one day spring into existence where there had been no sign of one but a little time previously. Only let him be always doing something, and let him cross himself now and again, for belief in the wondrous efficacy of crosses and crossing is the corner-stone of the creed of the evolutionist. Then after years—but not probably till after a great many—doors will open up all round, so many and so wide that the difficulty will not be to find a door, but rather to obtain the means of even hurriedly surveying a portion of those that stand invitingly open.

I know that just as good a case can be made out for the other side. It may be said as truly that unless a student is incessantly on the watch for doors he will never see them, and that unless he is incessantly pressing forward to the kingdom of heaven he will never find it—so that the kingdom does come by observation. It is with this as with everything else—there must be a harmonious fusing of two principles which are in flat contradiction to one another.

The question whether it is better to abide quiet and take advantage of opportunities that come, or to go further afield in search of them, is one of the oldest which living beings have had to deal with. It was on this that the first great schism or heresy arose in what was heretofore the catholic faith of protoplasm. The schism still lasts, and has resulted in two great sects—animals and plants. The opinion that it is better to go in search of prey is formulated in animals ; the other—that it is better on the whole to stay at home and profit by what comes—in plants. Some intermediate forms still record to us the long struggle during which the schism was not yet complete.

If I may be pardoned for pursuing this digression further, I would say that it is the plants and not we who are the heretics. There can be no question about this ; we are perfectly justified, therefore, in devouring them. Ours is the original and orthodox belief, for protoplasm is much more animal than vegetable ; it is much more true to say that plants have descended from animals than animals from plants. Nevertheless, like many other heretics, plants have thriven very fairly well. There are a great many of them, and as regards beauty, if not wit—of a limited kind indeed, but still wit— it is hard to say that the animal kingdom has the advantage. The views of plants are sadly narrow ; all dissenters are narrow-minded ; but within their own bounds they know the details of their business sufficiently well—as well as though they kept the most nicely-balanced system of accounts to show them their position. They are eaten, it is true ; to eat them is our bigoted and intolerant way of trying to convert them : eating is only a violent mode of proselytising or converting ; and we do convert them—to good animal substance, of our own way of thinking. But then, animals are eaten too. They convert one another, almost as much as they convert plants. And an animal is no sooner dead than a plant will convert it back again. It is obvious, however, that no schism could have been so long successful, without having a good deal to say for itself.

Neither party has been quite consistent. Who ever is or can be ? Every extreme—every opinion carried to its logical end—will prove to be an absurdity. Plants throw out roots and boughs and leaves ; this is a kind of locomotion ; and as Dr. Erasmus Darwin long since pointed out, they do sometimes approach nearly to what may be called travelling ; a man of consistent character will never look at a bough, a root, or a tendril without egarrding it as a melancholy and unprincipled compromise. On the other hand, many animals are sessile, and some singularly successful genera, as spiders, are in the main liers-in-wait. It may appear, however, on the whole, like reopening a settled question to uphold the principle of being busy and attentive over a small area, rather than going to and fro over a larger one, for a mammal like man, but I think most readers will be with me in thinking that, at any rate as regards art and litera-ture, it is he who does his small immediate work most carefully who will find doors open most certainly to him, that will conduct him into the richest chambers.

Many years ago, in New Zealand, I used sometimes to accompany a dray and team of bullocks who would have to be turned loose at night that they might feed. There were no hedges or fences then, so sometimes I could not find my team in the morning, and had no clue to the direction in which they had gone. At first I used to try and throw my soul into the bullocks' souls, so as to divine if possible what they would be likely to have done, and would then ride off ten miles in the wrong direction. People used in those days to lose their bullocks sometimes for a week or fortnight—when they perhaps were all the time hiding in a gully hard by the place where they were turned out. After some time I changed my tactics. On losing my bullocks I would go to the nearest accommodation house, and stand occasional drinks to travellers. Some one would ere long, as a general rule, turn up who had seen the bullocks. This case does not go quite on all fours with what I have been saying above, inasmuch as I was not very industrious in my limited area ; but the standing drinks and inquiring was being as industrious as the circumstances would allow.

To return, universities and academies are an obstacle

to the finding of doors in later life ; partly because they push their young men too fast through doorways that the universities have provided, and so discourage the habit of being on the look-out for others ; and partly because they do not take pains enough to make sure that their doors are *bonâ fide* ones. If, to change the metaphor, an academy has taken a bad shilling, it is seldom very scrupulous about trying to pass it on. It will stick to it that the shilling is a good one as long as the police will let it. I was very happy at Cambridge ; when I left it I thought I never again could be so happy anywhere else ; I shall ever retain a most kindly recollection both of Cambridge and of the school where I passed my boyhood ; but I feel, as I think most others must in middle life, that I have spent as much of my maturer years in unlearning as in learning.

The proper course is for a boy to begin the practical business of life many years earlier than he now commonly does. He should begin at the very bottom of a profession ; if possible of one which his family has pursued before him —for the professions will assuredly one day become hereditary. The ideal railway director will have begun at fourteen as a railway porter. He need not be a porter for more than a week or ten days, any more than he need have been a tadpole more than a short time ; but he should take a turn in practice, though briefly, at each of the lower branches in the profession. The painter should do just the same. He should begin by setting his employer's palette and cleaning his brushes. As for the good side of universities, the proper preservative of this is to be found in the club.

If, then, we are to have a renaissance of art, there must be a complete standing aloof from the academic system. That system has had time enough. Where

and who are its men ? Can it point to one painter who
can hold his own with the men of, say, from 1450 to
1550 ? Academies will bring out men who can paint
hair very like hair, and eyes very like eyes, but this is
not enough. This is grammar and deportment ; we want
wit and a kindly nature, and these cannot be got from
academies. As far as mere *technique* is concerned, almost
every one now can paint as well as is in the least desirable.
The same *mutatis mutandis* holds good with writing as
with painting. We want less word-painting and fine
phrases, and more observation at first-hand. Let us
have a periodical illustrated by people who cannot draw,
and written by people who cannot write (perhaps,
however, after all, we have some), but who look and
think for themselves, and express themselves just as they
please,—and this we certainly have not. Every con-
tributor should be at once turned out if he or she is
generally believed to have tried to do something which
he or she did not care about trying to do, and anything
should be admitted which is the outcome of a genuine
liking. People are always good company when they are
doing what they really enjoy. A cat is good company
when it is purring, or a dog when it is wagging its tail.

The sketching clubs up and down the country might
form the nucleus of such a society, provided all professional men were rigorously excluded. As for the old
masters, the better plan would be never even to look at
one of them, and to consign Raffaelle, along with Plato,
Marcus Aurelius Antoninus, Dante, Goethe, and two
others, neither of them Englishmen, to limbo, as the
Seven Humbugs of Christendom.

While we are about it, let us leave off talking about
" art for art's sake." Who is art, that it should have a
sake ? A work of art should be produced for the pleasure

it gives the producer, and the pleasure he thinks it will give to a few of whom he is fond ; but neither money nor people whom he does not know personally should be thought of. Of course such a society as I have proposed would not remain incorrupt long. "Everything that grows, holds in perfection but a little moment." The members would try to imitate professional men in spite of their rules, or, if they escaped this and after a while got to paint well, they would become dogmatic, and a rebellion against their authority would be as necessary ere long as it was against that of their predecessors : but the balance on the whole would be to the good.

Professional men should be excluded, if for no other reason yet for this, that they know too much for the beginner to be *en rapport* with them. It is the beginner who can help the beginner, as it is the child who is the most instructive companion for another child. The beginner can understand the beginner, but the cross between him and the proficient performer is too wide for fertility. It savours of impatience, and is in flat contradiction to the first principles of biology. It does a beginner positive harm to look at the masterpieces of the great executionists, such as Rembrandt or Turner.

If one is climbing a very high mountain which will tax all one's strength, nothing fatigues so much as casting upward glances to the top ; nothing encourages so much as casting downward glances. The top seems never to draw nearer ; the parts that we have passed retreat rapidly. Let a water-colour student go and see the drawing by Turner, in the basement of our National Gallery, dated 1787. This is the sort of thing for him, not to copy, but to look at for a minute or two now and again. It will show him nothing about painting, but it may serve to teach him not to overtax his strength,

and will prove to him that the greatest masters in painting, as in everything else, begin by doing work which is
no way superior to that of their neighbours. A collection
of the earliest known works of the greatest men would be
much more useful to the student than any number of
their maturer works, for it would show him that he need
not worry himself because his work does not look clever,
or as silly people say, " show power."

The secrets of success are affection for the pursuit
chosen, a flat refusal to be hurried or to pass anything as
understood which is not understood, and an obstinacy
of character which shall make the student's friends
find it less trouble to let him have his own way than to
bend him into theirs. Our schools and academies or
universities are covertly, but essentially, radical institutions and abhorrent to the genius of Conservatism. Their
sin is the true radical sin of being in too great a hurry, and
of believing in short cuts too soon. But it must be
remembered that this proposition, like every other, wants
tempering with a slight infusion of its direct opposite.

I said in an early part of this book that the best test to
know whether or no one likes a picture is to ask one's self
whether one would like to look at it if one was quite sure
one was alone. The best test for a painter as to whether
he likes painting his picture is to ask himself whether he
should like to paint it if he was quite sure that no one
except himself, and the few of whom he was very fond,
would ever see it. If he can answer this question in the
affirmative, he is all right ; if he cannot, he is all wrong. I
will close these remarks with an illustration which will
show how nearly we can approach the early Florentines
even now—when nobody is looking at us. I do not know
who Mr. Pollard is. I never heard of him till I came across
a cheap lithograph of his Funeral of Tom Moody in the

parlour of a village inn. I should not think he ever was an R.A., but he has approached as nearly as the difference between the geniuses of the two countries will allow, to the spirit of the painters who painted in the Campo Santo at Pisa. Look, again, at Garrard, at the close of the

FUNERAL OF TOM MOODY

last century. We generally succeed with sporting or quasi-sporting subjects, and our cheap coloured coaching and hunting subjects are almost always good, and often very good indeed. We like these things: therefore we observe them; therefore we soon become able to express them. Historical and costume pictures we have no genuine love for; we do not, therefore, go beyond re-peating commonplaces concerning them.

I must reserve other remarks upon this subject for another occasion.

Chapter XIII

Viù, Fucine, and S. Ignazio

I MUST now return to my young friend at Groscavallo.
I have published his drawings without his permission,
having unfortunately lost his name and address, and
being unable therefore to apply to him. I hope that,
should they ever meet his eye, he will accept this apology
and the assurance of my most profound consideration.

Delighted as I had been with his proposed illustrations,
I thought I had better hear some of the letterpress, so I
begged him to read me his MS. My time was short, and
he began at once. The few introductory pages were very
nice, but there was nothing particularly noticeable about
them ; when, however, he came to his description of the
place where we now were, he spoke of a beautiful young
lady as attracting his attention on the evening of his
arrival. It seemed that she was as much struck with him
as he with her, and I thought we were going to have a
romance, when he proceeded as follows : " We perceived
that we were sympathetic, and in less than a quarter of
an hour had exchanged the most solemn vows that we
would never marry one another." " What ? " said I,
hardly able to believe my ears, " will you kindly read
those last words over again ? " He did so, slowly and
distinctly ; I caught them beyond all power of mistake,
and they were as I have given them above :—" We
perceived that we were sympathetic, and in less than a

quarter of an hour had exchanged the most solemn vows that we would never marry one another." While I was rubbing my eyes and making up my mind whether I had stumbled upon a great satirist or no, I heard a voice from below — " Signor Butler, Signor Butler, la vettura è pronta." I had therefore to leave my doubt

S. IGNAZIO, NEAR LANZO

unsolved, but all the time as we drove down the valley I had the words above quoted ringing in my head. If ever any of my readers come across the book itself— for I should hope it will be published—I should be

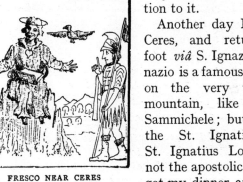

FRESCO NEAR CERES

very grateful to them if they will direct my attention to it.

Another day I went to Ceres, and returned on foot *viâ* S. Ignazio. S. Ignazio is a famous sanctuary on the very top of a mountain, like that of Sammichele ; but it is late, the St. Ignatius being St. Ignatius Loyola, and not the apostolic father. I got my dinner at a village inn at the foot of the mountain, and from the window caught sight of a fresco upon the wall of a chapel a few yards off. There was a companion to it hardly less interesting, but I had not time to sketch it. I do not know what the one I give is intended to represent.

St. Ignatius is upon a rock, and is pleased with something, but there is nothing to show what it is, except his attitude, which seems to say, " Senza far fatica,"—" You see I can do it quite easily," or, " There is no deception." Nor do we easily gather what it is that the Roman

VIÙ CHURCH

centurion is saying to St. Ignatius. I cannot make up my mind whether he is merely warning him to beware of the reaction, or whether he is a little scandalised.

From this village I went up the mountain to the sanctu-ary of S. Ignazio itself, which looks well from the distance,

Viù and Neighbourhood 163

and commands a striking view, but contains nothing of interest, except a few nice votive pictures.

From Lanzo I went to Viù, a summer resort largely frequented by the Turinese, but rarely visited by English people. There is a good inn at Viù—the one close to where the public conveyance stops—and the neighbourhood is enchanting. The little village on the crest of the hill in the distance, to the left of the church, as shown on the preceding page, is called the Colma di S. Giovanni, and is well worth a visit. In spring, before the grass is cut, the pastures must be even better than when I saw them in August, and they were then still of almost incredible beauty.

I went to S. Giovanni by the directest way—descending, that is, to the level of the Stura, crossing it, and then going straight up the mountain. I returned by a slight detour so as to take the village of Fucine, a *frazione* of Viù a little higher up the river. I found many picturesque bits ; among them the one which I give on the next page. It was a grand *festa ;* first they had had mass, then there had been the *funzioni*, which I never quite understand, and thenceforth till sundown there was a public ball on the bowling ground of a little inn on the Viù side of the bridge. The principal inn is on the other side. It was here I went and ordered dinner. The landlady brought me a *minestra*, or hodge-podge soup, full of savoury vegetables, and very good ; a nice cutlet fried in bread-crumbs, bread and butter *ad libitum*, and half a bottle of excellent wine. She brought all together on a tray, and put them down on the table. " It'll come to a franc," said she, " in all, but please to pay first." I did so, of course, and she was satisfied. A day or two afterwards I went to the same inn, hoping to dine as well and cheaply as before ; but I think they must have discovered that I was a *forestiere inglese* in the meantime, for they did not make me pay first, and charged me normal prices.

What pretty words they have ! While eating my dinner

FUCINE, NEAR VIÙ

I wanted a small plate and asked for it. The landlady changed the word I had used, and told a girl to bring me a *tondino*. A *tondino* is an abbreviation of *rotondino*, a

" little round thing." A plate is a *tondo*, a small plate a *tondino*. The delicacy of expression which their diminutives and intensitives give is untranslateable. One day I was asking after a waiter whom I had known in previous years, but who was ill. I said I hoped he was not badly off. " Oh dear, no," was the answer ; " he has a *discreta posizionina* "—" a snug little sum put by." " Is the road to such and such a place difficult ? " I once inquired. " Un tantino," was the answer. " Ever such a very little," I suppose, is as near as we can get to this. At one inn I asked whether I could have my linen back from the wash by a certain time, and was told it was *impossibilissimo*. I have an Italian friend long resident in England who often introduces English words when talking with me in Italian. Thus I have heard him say that such and such a thing is *tanto cheapissimo*. As for their gestures, they are inimitable. To say nothing of the pretty little way in which they say " no," by moving the forefinger backwards and forwards once or twice, they have a hundred movements to save themselves the trouble of speaking, which say what they have to say better than any words can do. It is delightful to see an Italian move his hand in such way as to show you that you have got to go round a corner. Gesture is easier both to make and to understand than speech is. Speech is a late acquisition, and in critical moments is commonly discarded in favour of gesture, which is older and more habitual.

I once saw an Italian explaining something to another and tapping his nose a great deal. He became more and more confidential, and the more confidential he became, the more he tapped, till his finger seemed to become glued to, and almost grow into his nose. At last the supreme moment came. He drew the finger down, pressing it closely against his lower lip, so as to drag it all down and show his gums and the roots of his teeth. " There," he seemed to say, " you now know all : consider me as turned inside out : my mucous membrane is before you."

At Fucine, and indeed in all the valleys hereabout, spinning-wheels are not uncommon. I also saw a woman sitting in her room with the door opening on to the street, weaving linen at a hand-loom. The woman and the hand-loom were both very old and rickety. The first and the last specimens of anything, whether animal or vegetable organism, or machine, or institution, are seldom quite satisfactory. Some five or six years ago I saw an old gentleman sitting outside the St. Lawrence Hall at Montreal, in Canada, and wearing a pigtail, but it was not a good pigtail ; and when the Scotch baron killed the last wolf in Scotland, it was probably a weak, mangy old thing, capable of little further mischief.

Presently I walked a mile or two up the river, and met a godfather coming along with a cradle on his shoulder ; he was followed by two women, one carrying some long wax candles, and the other something wrapped up in a piece of brown paper ; they were going to get the child christened at Fucine. Soon after I met a priest, and bowed, as a matter of course. In towns or places where many foreigners come and go this is unnecessary, but in small out-of-the-way places one should take one's hat off to the priest. I mention this because many Englishmen do not know that it is expected of them, and neglect the accustomed courtesy through ignorance. Surely, even here in England, if one is in a small country village, off one's beat, and meets the clergyman, it is more polite than not to take off one's hat.

Viù is one of the places from which pilgrims ascend

the Rocca Melone at the beginning of August. This is one of the most popular and remarkable pilgrimages of North Italy; the Rocca Melone is 11,000 feet high, and forms a peak so sharp, that there is room for little else than the small wooden chapel which stands at the top of it. There is no accommodation whatever, except at some rough barracks (so I have been told) some thousands of feet below the summit. These, I was informed, are sometimes so crowded that the people doze standing, and the cold at night is intense, unless under the shelter just referred to; yet some five or six thousand pilgrims ascend on the day and night of the *festa*— chiefly from Susa, but also from all parts of the valleys of the Dora and the Stura. They leave Susa early in the morning, camp out or get shelter in the barracks that evening, reaching the chapel at the top of the Rocca Melone next day. I have not made the ascent myself, but it would probably be worth making by one who did not mind the fatigue.

I may mention that thatch is not uncommon in the Stura valley. In the Val Mastallone, and more especially between Civiasco (above Varallo) and Orta, thatch is more common still, and the thatching is often very beautifully done. Thatch in a stone country is an indication of German, or at any rate Cisalpine descent, and is among the many proofs of the extent to which German races crossed the Alps and spread far down over Piedmont and Lombardy. I was more struck with traces of German influence on the path from Pella on the Lago d'Orta, to the Colma on the way to Varallo, than perhaps anywhere else. The churches have a tendency to have pure spires—a thing never seen in Italy proper; clipped yews and box-trees are common; there are lime-trees in the churchyards, and thatch is the rule, not the exception.

At Rimella in the Val Mastallone, not far off, German is still the current language. As I sat sketching, a woman came up to me, and said, " Was machen sie ? " as a matter of course. Rimella is the highest village in its valley, yet if one crosses the saddle at the head of the valley, one does not descend upon a German-speaking district ; one descends on the Val Anzasca, where Italian is universally spoken. Until recently German was the language of many other villages at the heads of valleys, even though these valleys were themselves entirely sur-rounded by Italian-speaking people. At Alagna in the Val Sesia, German is still spoken.

Whatever their origin, however, the people are now thoroughly Italianised. Nevertheless, as I have already said, it is strange what a number of people one meets among them, whom most people would unhesitatingly pronounce to be English if asked to name their nation-ality.

Chapter XIV

Sanctuary of Oropa

FROM Lanzo I went back to Turin, where Jones again joined me, and we resolved to go and see the famous sanctuary of Oropa near Biella. Biella is about three hours' railway journey from Turin. It is reached by a branch line of some twenty miles, that leaves the main line between Turin and Milan at Santhià. Except the view of the Alps, which in clear weather cannot be surpassed, there is nothing of very particular interest between Turin and Santhià, nor need Santhià detain the traveller longer than he can help. Biella we found to consist of an upper and a lower town—the upper, as may be supposed, being the older. It is at the very junction of the plain and the mountains, and is a thriving place, with more of the busy air of an English commercial town than perhaps any other of its size in North Italy. Even in the old town large rambling old *palazzi* have been converted into factories, and the click of the shuttle is heard in unexpected places.

We were unable to find that Biella contains any remarkable pictures or other works of art, though they are doubtless to be found by those who have the time to look for them. There is a very fine *campanile* near the post-office, and an old brick baptistery, also hard by ; but the church to which both *campanile* and baptistery belonged, has, as the author of " Round about London " so well says, been " utterly restored ; " it cannot be uglier than what we sometimes do, but it is quite as ugly. We found an Italian opera company in Biella ; peeping through a grating, as many others were doing, we watched the company rehearsing " La forza del destino," which was to be given later in the week.

The morning after our arrival, we took the daily diligence for Oropa, leaving Biella at eight o'clock. Before we were clear of the town we could see the long line of the hospice, and the chapels dotted about near it, high up in a valley at some distance off ; presently we were shown another fine building some eight or nine miles away, which we were told was the sanctuary of Graglia. About this time the pictures and statuettes of the Madonna began to change their hue and to become black—for the sacred image of Oropa being black, all the Madonnas in her immediate neighbourhood are of the same complexion. Underneath some of them is written, " Nigra sum sed sum formosa," which, as a rule, was more true as regards the first epithet than the second.

It was not market-day, but streams of people were coming to the town. Many of them were pilgrims return-ing from the sanctuary, but more were bringing the produce of their farms, or the work of their hands for sale. We had to face a steady stream of chairs, which were coming to town in baskets upon women's heads. Each basket contained twelve chairs, though whether it is correct to say that the basket contained the chairs— when the chairs were all, so to say, froth running over the top of the basket—is a point I cannot settle. Cer-tainly we had never seen anything like so many chairs before, and felt almost as though we had surprised nature in the laboratory wherefrom she turns out the chair supply of the world. The road continued through a succession of villages almost running into one another for a long way after Biella was passed, but everywhere we noticed the same air of busy thriving industry which we had seen in Biella itself. We noted also that a preponderance of the people had light hair, while that of the children was frequently nearly white, as though the infusion of German blood was here stronger even than usual. Though so thickly peopled, the country was of great beauty. Near at hand were the most exquisite pastures close shaven after their second mowing, gay with autumnal crocuses, and shaded with stately chestnuts ; beyond were rugged mountains, in a combe on one of which we saw Oropa itself now gradually nearing ; behind and below, many villages with vineyards and terraces cultivated to the highest perfection ; further on, Biella already distant, and beyond this a " big stare," as an American might say, over the plains of Lombardy from Turin to Milan, with the Apennines from Genoa to Bologna hemming the horizon. On the road immediately before us, we still faced the same steady stream of chairs flowing ever Biella-ward.

After a couple of hours the houses became more rare ; we got above the sources of the chair-stream ; bits of rough rock began to jut out from the pasture ; here and there the rhododendron began to show itself by the roadside ; the chestnuts left off along a line as level as though cut with a knife ; stone-roofed *cascine* began to abound, with goats and cattle feeding near them ; the booths of the religious trinket-mongers increased ; the blind, halt, and maimed became more importunate, and the foot-passengers were more entirely composed of those whose object was, or had been, a visit to the sanctuary itself. The numbers of these pilgrims—

generally in their Sunday's best, and often comprising the greater part of a family—were so great, though there was no special *festa*, as to testify to the popularity of the institution. They generally walked barefoot, and carried their shoes and stockings; their baggage consisted of a few spare clothes, a little food, and a pot or pan or two to cook with. Many of them looked very tired, and had

FAÇADE OF THE SANCTUARY OF OROPA

evidently tramped from long distances—indeed, we saw costumes belonging to valleys which could not be less than two or three days distant. They were almost invariably quiet, respectable, and decently clad, sometimes a little merry, but never noisy, and none of them tipsy. As we travelled along the road, we must have fallen in with several hundreds of these pilgrims coming and going; nor is this likely to be an extravagant estimate, seeing that the hospice can make up more than five thousand beds. By eleven we were at the sanctuary itself.

Fancy a quiet upland valley, the floor of which is about the same height as the top of Snowdon, shut in by lofty mountains upon three sides, while on the fourth the eye wanders at will over the plains below. Fancy finding a level space in such a valley watered by a beautiful mountain stream, and nearly filled by a pile of collegiate buildings, not less important than those, we will say, of Trinity College, Cambridge. True, Oropa is not in the least like Trinity, except that one of its courts is large, grassy, has a chapel and a fountain in it, and rooms all round it ; but I do not know how better to give a rough description of Oropa than by comparing it with one of our largest English colleges.

The buildings consist of two main courts. The first comprises a couple of modern wings, connected by the magnificent façade of what is now the second or inner court. This façade dates from about the middle of the seventeenth century ; its lowest storey is formed by an open colonnade, and the whole stands upon a raised terrace from which a noble flight of steps descends into the outer court.

Ascending the steps and passing under the colonnade, we found ourselves in the second or inner court, which is a complete quadrangle, and is, we were told, of rather older date than the façade. This is the quadrangle which gives its collegiate character to Oropa. It is surrounded by cloisters on three sides, on to which the rooms in which the pilgrims are lodged open—those at least that are on the ground-floor, for there are three storeys. The chapel, which was dedicated in the year 1600, juts out into the court upon the north-east side. On the north-west and south-west sides are entrances

through which one may pass to the open country. The
grass, at the time of our visit, was for the most part
covered with sheets spread out to dry. They looked
very nice, and, dried on such grass and in such an air,
they must be delicious to sleep on. There is, indeed,
rather an appearance as though it were a perpetual

INNER COURT OF SANCTUARY OF OROPA

washing-day at Oropa, but this is not to be wondered at
considering the numbers of comers and goers; besides,
people in Italy do not make so much fuss about trifles
as we do. If they want to wash their sheets and dry
them, they do not send them to Ealing, but lay them out
in the first place that comes handy, and nobody's bones
are broken.

Chapter XV

Oropa (*continued*)

ON the east side of the main block of buildings there is a grassy slope adorned with chapels that contain figures illustrating scenes in the history of the Virgin. These figures are of terra-cotta, for the most part life-size, and painted up to nature. In some cases, if I remember rightly, they have hemp or flax for hair, as at Varallo, and throughout realism is aimed at as far as possible, not only in the figures, but in the accessories. We have very little of the same kind in England. In the Tower of London there is an effigy of Queen Elizabeth going to the city to give thanks for the defeat of the Spanish Armada. This looks as if it might have been the work of some one of the Valsesian sculptors.

CHAPELS AT OROPA

There are also the figures that strike the quarters of Sir John Bennett's city clock in Cheapside. The automatic movements of these last-named figures would have struck the originators of the Varallo chapels with envy. They aimed at realism so closely that they would assuredly have had recourse to clockwork in some one or two of their chapels ; I cannot doubt, for example, that they would have eagerly welcomed the idea of making the cock crow to Peter by a cuckoo-clock arrangement, if it had been presented to them. This opens up the whole question of realism *versus* conventionalism in art—a subject much too large to be treated here.

As I have said, the founders of these Italian chapels aimed at realism. Each chapel was intended as an illustration, and the desire was to bring the whole scene more vividly before the faithful by combining the picture, the statue, and the effect of a scene upon the stage in a single work of art. The attempt would be an ambitious one, though made once only in a neighbourhood, but in most of the places in North Italy where anything of the kind has been done, the people have not been content with a single illustration ; it has been their scheme to take a mountain as though it had been a book or wall and cover it with illustrations. In some cases—as at Orta, whose Sacro Monte is perhaps the most beautiful of all as regards the site itself—the failure is complete, but in some of the chapels at Varese and in many of those at Varallo, great works have been produced which have not yet attracted as much attention as they deserve. It may be doubted, indeed, whether there is a more remarkable work of art in North Italy than the Crucifixion chapel at Varallo, where the twenty-five statues, as well as the frescoes behind them, are (with the exception of the figure of Christ, which has been removed) by Gaudenzio Ferrari. It is to be wished that some one of these chapels—both chapel and sculptures—were reproduced at South Kensington.

Varallo, which is undoubtedly the most interesting sanctuary in North Italy, has forty-four of these illustrative chapels ; Varese, fifteen ; Orta, eighteen ; and Oropa, seventeen. No one is allowed to enter them, except when repairs are needed ; but when these are

going on, as is constantly the case, it is curious to look
through the grating into the somewhat darkened interior,
and to see a living figure or two among the statues ; a
little motion on the part of a single figure seems to
communicate itself to the rest and make them all more
animated. If the living figure does not move much,
it is easy at first to mistake it for a terra-cotta one. At
Orta, some years since, looking one evening into a chapel
when the light was fading, I was surprised to see a saint
whom I had not seen before ; he had no glory except
what shone from a very red nose ; he was smoking a
short pipe, and was painting the Virgin Mary's face.
The touch was a finishing one, put on with deliberation,
slowly, so that it was two or three seconds before I
discovered that the interloper was no saint.

The figures in the chapels at Oropa are not as good
as the best of those at Varallo, but some of them are
very nice notwithstanding. We liked the seventh
chapel the best—the one which illustrates the sojourn of
the Virgin Mary in the temple. It contains forty-four
figures, and represents the Virgin on the point of com-
pleting her education as head girl at a high-toned academy
for young gentlewomen. All the young ladies are at
work making mitres for the bishop, or working slippers
in Berlin wool for the new curate, but the Virgin sits on
a dais above the others on the same platform with the
venerable lady-principal, who is having passages read
out to her from some standard Hebrew writer. The
statues are the work of a local sculptor, named Aureggio,
who lived at the end of the seventeenth and beginning
of the eighteenth century.

The highest chapel must be a couple of hundred feet
above the main buildings, and from near it there is an
excellent bird's-eye view of the sanctuary and the small

plain behind ; descending on to this last, we entered the
quadrangle from the north-west side and visited the
chapel in which the sacred image of the Madonna is contained. We did not see the image itself, which is only
exposed to public view on great occasions. It is believed
to have been carved by St. Luke the Evangelist. I
must ask the reader to content himself with the following
account of it which I take from Marocco's work upon
Oropa :—

"That this statue of the Virgin is indeed by St. Luke
is attested by St. Eusebius, a man of eminent piety and
no less enlightened than truthful. St. Eusebius discovered its origin by revelation ; and the store which he
set by it is proved by his shrinking from no discomforts
in his carriage of it from a distant country, and by his
anxiety to put it in a place of great security. His desire,
indeed, was to keep it in the spot which was most near
and dear to him, so that he might extract from it the
higher incitement to devotion, and more sensible comfort
in the midst of his austerities and apostolic labours.

"This truth is further confirmed by the quality of the
wood from which the statue is carved, which is commonly
believed to be cedar ; by the Eastern character of the
work ; by the resemblance both of the lineaments and
the colour to those of other statues by St. Luke ; by the
tradition of the neighbourhood, which extends in an un-
broken and well-assured line to the time of St. Eusebius
himself ; by the miracles that have been worked here
by its presence, and elsewhere by its invocation, or even
by indirect contact with it ; by the miracles, lastly,
which are inherent in the image itself,* and which endure

* " Dalle meraviglie finalmente che sono inerenti al simulacro
stesso."—Cenni storico-artistici intorno al santuario di Oropa. (Prof
Maurizio Marocco, Turin, Milan, 1866, p. 329.)

to this day, such as is its immunity from all worm and from the decay which would naturally have occurred in it through time and damp—more especially in the feet, through the rubbing of religious objects against them.

.   .   .   .   .   .

" The authenticity of this image is so certainly and clearly established, that all supposition to the contrary becomes inexplicable and absurd: Such, for example, is a hypothesis that it should not be attributed to the Evangelist, but to another Luke, also called ' Saint,' and a Florentine by birth. This painter lived in the eleventh century—that is to say, about seven centuries after the image of Oropa had been known and venerated ! This is indeed an anachronism.

" Other difficulties drawn either from the ancient discipline of the Church, or from St. Luke the Evangelist's profession, which was that of a physician, vanish at once when it is borne in mind—firstly, that the cult of holy images, and especially of that of the most blessed Virgin, is of extreme antiquity in the Church, and of apostolic origin as is proved by ecclesiastical writers and monuments found in the catacombs which date as far back as the first century (see among other authorities, Nicolas, " La Vergine vivente nella Chiesa," lib. iii. cap. iii. § 2) ; secondly, that as the medical profession does not exclude that of artist, St. Luke may have been both artist and physician ; that he did actually handle both the brush and the scalpel is established by respectable and very old traditions, to say nothing of other arguments which can be found in impartial and learned writers upon such matters.''

I will only give one more extract. It runs :—

" In 1855 a celebrated Roman portrait-painter, after having carefully inspected the image of the Virgin Mary at Oropa, declared it to be certainly a work of the first century of our era."*

I once saw a common cheap china copy of this Madonna announced as to be given away with two pounds of tea, in a shop near Hatton Garden.

The church in which the sacred image is kept is interesting from the pilgrims who at all times frequent it, and from the collection of votive pictures which adorn its walls. Except the votive pictures and the pilgrims the church contains little of interest, and I will pass on to the constitution and objects of the establishment.

The objects are—1. Gratuitous lodging to all comers for a space of from three to nine days as the rector may think fit. 2. A school. 3. Help to the sick and poor. It is governed by a president and six members, who form a committee. Four members are chosen by the communal council, and two by the cathedral chapter of Biella. At the hospice itself there reside a director, with his assistant, a surveyor to keep the fabric in repair, a rector or dean with six priests, called *cappellani*, and a medical man. " The government of the laundry," so runs the statute on this head, " and analogous domestic services are entrusted to a competent number of ladies of sound constitution and good conduct, who live together in the hospice under the direction of an inspectress, and are called daughters of Oropa."

The bye-laws of the establishment are conceived in a kindly genial spirit, which in great measure accounts for its unmistakeable popularity. We understood that the poorer visitors, as a general rule, avail themselves of the

* Marocco, p. 331.

gratuitous lodging, without making any present when
they leave, but in spite of this it is quite clear that they
are wanted to come, and come they accordingly do.
It is sometimes difficult to lay one's hands upon the
exact passages which convey an impression, but as we
read the bye-laws which are posted up in the cloisters,
we found ourselves continually smiling at the manner
in which almost anything that looked like a prohibition
could be removed with the consent of the director. There
is no rule whatever about visitors attending the church ;
all that is required of them is that they do not interfere
with those who do. They must not play games of chance,
or noisy games ; they must not make much noise of
any sort after ten o'clock at night (which corresponds
about with midnight in England). They should not draw
upon the walls of their rooms, nor cut the furniture.
They should also keep their rooms clean, and not cook in
those that are more expensively furnished. This is about
all that they must not do, except fee the servants, which
is most especially and particularly forbidden. If any one
infringes these rules, he is to be admonished, and in case
of grave infraction or continued misdemeanour he may
be expelled and not readmitted.

Visitors who are lodged in the better-furnished apartments can be waited upon if they apply at the office ;
the charge is twopence for cleaning a room, making the
bed, bringing water, &c. If there is more than one bed
in a room, a penny must be paid for every bed over the
first. Boots can be cleaned for a penny, shoes for a halfpenny. For carrying wood, &c., either a halfpenny or a
penny will be exacted according to the time taken.
Payment for these services must not be made to the
servant, but at the office.

The gates close at ten o'clock at night, and open at

sunrise, " but if any visitor wishes to make Alpine excursions, or has any other sufficient reason, he should let the director know." Families occupying many rooms must—when the hospice is very crowded, and when they have had due notice—manage to pack themselves into a smaller compass. No one can have rooms kept for him. It is to be strictly " first come, first served." No one must sublet his room. Visitors must not go away without giving up the key of their room. Candles and wood may be bought at a fixed price.

Any one wishing to give anything to the support of the hospice must do so only to the director, the official who appoints the apartments, the dean or the *cappellani*, or to the inspectress of the daughters of Oropa, but they must have a receipt for even the smallest sum ; alms-boxes, however, are placed here and there, into which the smaller offerings may be dropped (we imagine this means anything under a franc).

The poor will be fed as well as housed for three days gratuitously—provided their health does not require a longer stay ; but they must not beg on the premises of the hospice ; professional beggars will be at once handed over to the mendicity society in Biella, or even perhaps to prison. The poor for whom a hydropathic course is recommended, can have it under the regulations made by the committee—that is to say, if there is a vacant place.

There are *trattorie* and cafés at the hospice, where refreshments may be obtained both good and cheap. Meat is to be sold there at the prices current in Biella ; bread at two centimes the chilogramma more, to pay for the cost of carriage.

Such are the bye-laws of this remarkable institution. Few except the very rich are so under-worked that

two or three days of change and rest are not at times
a boon to them, while the mere knowledge that there is a
place where repose can be had cheaply and pleasantly
is itself a source of strength. Here, so long as the visitor
wishes to be merely housed, no questions are asked ;
no one is refused admittance, except for some obviously
sufficient reason ; it is like getting a reading ticket for the
British Museum, there is practically but one test—that
is to say, desire on the part of the visitor—the coming
proves the desire, and this suffices. A family, we will
say, has just gathered its first harvest ; the heat on the
plains is intense, and the malaria from the rice grounds
little less than pestilential ; what, then, can be nicer
than to lock up the house and go for three days to the
bracing mountain air of Oropa ? So at daybreak off they
all start, trudging, it may be, their thirty or forty miles,
and reaching Oropa by nightfall. If there is a weakly one
among them, some arrangement is sure to be practicable
whereby he or she can be helped to follow more leisurely,
and can remain longer at the hospice. Once arrived, they
generally, it is true, go the round of the chapels, and make
some slight show of pilgrimage, but the main part of their
time is spent in doing absolutely nothing. It is sufficient
amusement to them to sit on the steps, or lie about under
the shadow of the trees, and neither say anything nor do
anything, but simply breathe, and look at the sky and at
each other. We saw scores of such people just resting
instinctively in a kind of blissful waking dream. Others
saunter along the walks which have been cut in the woods
that surround the hospice, or if they have been pent up in
a town and have a fancy for climbing, there are mountain
excursions, for the making of which the hospice affords
excellent headquarters, and which are looked upon with
every favour by the authorities.

It must be remembered also that the accommodation provided at Oropa is much better than what the people are, for the most part, accustomed to in their own homes, and the beds are softer, more often beaten up, and cleaner than those they have left behind them. Besides, they have sheets—and beautifully clean sheets. Those who know the sort of place in which an Italian peasant is commonly content to sleep, will understand how much he must enjoy a really clean and comfortable bed, especially when he has not got to pay for it. Sleep, in the circumstances of comfort which most readers will be accustomed to, is a more expensive thing than is commonly supposed. If we sleep eight hours in a London hotel we shall have to pay from 4d. to 6d. an hour, or from 1d. to 1½d. for every fifteen minutes we lie in bed ; nor is it reasonable to believe that the charge is excessive, when we consider the vast amount of competition which exists. There is many a man the expenses of whose daily meat, drink, and clothing are less than what an accountant would show us we, many of us, lay out nightly upon our sleep. The cost of really comfortable sleep-necessaries cannot, of course, be nearly so great at Oropa as in a London hotel, but they are enough to put them beyond the reach of the peasant under ordinary circumstances, and he relishes them all the more when he can get them.

But why, it may be asked, should the peasant have these things if he cannot afford to pay for them ; and why should he not pay for them if he can afford to do so ? If such places as Oropa were common, would not lazy vagabonds spend their lives in going the rounds of them, &c., &c. ? Doubtless if there were many Oropas, they would do more harm than good, but there are some things which answer perfectly well as rarities or on a small scale, out of which all the virtue would depart if they were common or on a larger one ; and certainly the impression left upon our minds by Oropa was that its effects were excellent.

Granted the sound rule to be that a man should pay for what he has, or go without it ; in practice, however, it is found impossible to carry this rule out strictly. Why does the nation give A. B., for instance, and all comers a large, comfortable, well-ventilated, warm room to sit in, with chair, table, reading-desk, &c., all more commodious than what he may have at home, without making him pay a sixpence for it directly from year's end to year's end ? The three or nine days' visit to Oropa is a trifle in comparison with what we can all of us obtain in London if we care about it enough to take a very small amount of trouble. True, one cannot sleep in the reading-room of the British Museum—not all night, at least—but by day one can make a home of it for years together except during cleaning times, and then it is hard if one cannot get into the National Gallery or South Kensington, and be warm, quiet, and entertained without paying for it.

It will be said that it is for the national interest that people should have access to treasuries of art or knowledge, and therefore it is worth the nation's while to pay for placing the means of doing so at their disposal ; granted, but is not a good bed one of the great ends of knowledge, whereto it must work, if it is to be accounted knowledge at all ? and is it not worth a nation's while that her children should now and again have practical experience of a higher state of things than the one they are accustomed to, and a few days' rest and change of scene and air, even though she may from time to time have to pay something in order to enable them to do so ? There

can be few books which do an averagely-educated Englishman so much good, as the glimpse of comfort which he
gets by sleeping in a good bed in a well-appointed room
does to an Italian peasant ; such a glimpse gives him
an idea of higher potentialities in connection with himself, and nerves him to exertions which he would not
otherwise make. On the whole, therefore, we concluded that if the British Museum reading-room was in
good economy, Oropa was so also ; at any rate, it seemed
to be making a large number of very nice people quietly
happy—and it is hard to say more than this in favour of
any place or institution.

The idea of any sudden change is as repulsive to us as
it will be to the greater number of my readers ; but if
asked whether we thought our English universities would
do most good in their present condition as places of so-
called education, or if they were turned into Oropas,
and all the educational part of the story totally sup-
pressed, we inclined to think they would be more popular
and more useful in this latter capacity. We thought
also that Oxford and Cambridge were just the places,
and contained all the appliances and endowments almost
ready made for constituting two splendid and truly
imperial cities of recreation—universities in deed as
well as in name. Nevertheless, we should not venture
to propose any further actual reform during the present
generation than to carry the principle which is already
admitted as regards the M.A. degree a trifle further, and
to make the B.A. degree a mere matter of lapse of time
and fees—leaving the Little Go, and whatever corresponds
to it at Oxford, as the final examination. This would be
enough for the present.

There is another sanctuary about three hours' walk
over the mountain behind Oropa, at Andorno, and

dedicated to St. John. We were prevented by the weather from visiting it, but understand that its objects are much the same as those of the institution I have just described. I will now proceed to the third sanctuary for which the neighbourhood of Biella is renowned.

Chapter XVI

Graglia

THE sanctuary of Graglia is reached in about two hours from Biella. There are daily diligences. It is not so celebrated as that of Oropa, nor does it stand so high above the level of the sea, but it is a remarkable place and well deserves a visit. The restaurant is perfect —the best, indeed, that I ever saw in North Italy, or, I think, anywhere else. I had occasion to go into the kitchen, and could not see how anything could beat it for the most absolute cleanliness and order. Certainly I never dined better than at the sanctuary of Graglia ; and one dines all the more pleasantly for doing so on a lovely terrace shaded by trellised creepers, and overlooking Lombardy.

I find from a small handbook by Signor Giuseppe Muratori, that the present institution, like that of S. Michele, and almost all things else that achieve success, was founded upon the work of a predecessor, and became great not in one, but in several generations. The site was already venerated on account of a chapel in honour of the *Vergine addolorata* which had existed here from very early times. A certain Nicolao Velotti, about the year 1616, formed the design of reproducing Mount Calvary on this spot, and of erecting perhaps a hundred chapels with terra-cotta figures in them. The famous

Valsesian sculptor, Tabachetti, and his pupils, the brothers Giovanni and Antonio (commonly called " Tanzio "), D'Enrico of Riva in the Val Sesia, all of whom had recently been working at the sanctuary of Varallo, were invited to Graglia, and later on, another eminent native of the Val Sesia, Pietro Giuseppe Martello. These artists appear to have done a good deal of work here, of which nothing now remains visible to the public, though it is possible that in the chapel of S. Carlo and the closed chapels on the way to it, there may be some statues lying neglected which I know nothing about. I was told of no such work, but when I was at Graglia I did not know that the above-named great men had ever worked there, and made no inquiries. It is quite possible that all the work they did here has not perished.

CHAPEL OF S. CARLO AT GRAGLIA

The means at the disposal of the people of Graglia were insufficient for the end they had in view, but subscriptions came in freely from other quarters. Among the valuable rights, liberties, privileges, and immunities that were conferred upon the institution, was one which in itself was a source of unfailing and considerable revenue, namely, the right of setting a robber free once in every year ; also, the authorities there were allowed to sell all kinds of wine and eatables (*robe mangiative*) without paying duty upon them. As far as I can understand, the main work of Velotti's is the chapel of S. Carlo, on the top of a hill some few hundred feet above the present establishment. I give a sketch of this chapel here, but was not able to include the smaller chapels which lead up to it.

A few years later, one Nicolao Garono built a small
oratory at Campra, which is nearer to Biella than Graglia
is. He dedicated it to S. Maria della Neve—to St. Mary
of the Snow. This became more frequented than Graglia
itself, and the feast of the Virgin on the 5th August
was exceedingly popular. Signor Muratori says of
it :—

"This is the popular feast of Graglia, and I can remember how but a few years since it retained on a small
scale all the features of the *sacre campestri* of the Middle
Ages. For some time past, however, the stricter customs
which have been introduced here no less than in other
Piedmontese villages have robbed this feast (as how
many more popular feasts has it not also robbed?) of
that original and spontaneous character in which a
jovial heartiness and a diffusive interchange of the
affections came welling forth from all abundantly. In
spite of all, however, and notwithstanding its decline,
the feast of the Madonna is even now one of those rare
gatherings—the only one, perhaps, in the neighbourhood
of Biella—to which the pious Christian and the curious
idler are alike attracted, and where they will alike find
appropriate amusement."*

How Miltonic, not to say Handelian, is this attitude
towards the Pagan tendencies which, it is clear, pre-

* "Questa è la festa popolare di Graglia, e pochi anni addietro
ancora ricordava in miniatura le feste popolari delle sacre campestri del
medio evo. Da qualche anno in qua, il costume più severo che s'
introdusse in questi paesi non meno che in tutti gli altri del Piemonte,
tolse non poco del carattere originale di questa come di tante altre
festività popolesche, nelle quali erompeva spontanea da tutti i cuori la
diffusiva vicendevolezza degli affetti, e la sincera giovalità dei senti-
menti. Ciò non pertanto, malgrado sì fatta decadenza la festa della
Madonna di Campra è ancor al presente una di quelle rare adunanze
sentimentali, unica forse nel Biellese, alle quali accorre volentieri e
ritrova pascolo appropriato il cristiano divoto non meno che il curioso
viaggiatore." (Del Santuario di Graglia notizie istoriche di Giuseppe
Muratori. Torino, Stamperia reale, 1848, p. 18.)

dominated at the *festa* of St. Mary of the Snow. In
old days a feast was meant to be a time of actual merri-
ment—a praising " with mirth, high cheer, and wine."*
Milton felt this a little, and Handel much. To them an
opportunity for a little paganism is like the scratching
of a mouse to the princess who had been born a cat.
Off they go after it—more especially Handel—under
some decent pretext no doubt, but as fast, nevertheless,
as their art can carry them. As for Handel, he had not
only a sympathy for paganism, but for the shades and
gradations of paganism. What, for example, can be a
completer contrast than between the polished and
refined Roman paganism in Theodora,† the rustic
paganism of " Bid the maids the youths provoke " in
Hercules, the magician's or sorcerer's paganism of the
blue furnace in " Chemosh no more,"‡ or the Dagon
choruses in Samson—to say nothing of a score of other
examples that might be easily adduced ? Yet who can
doubt the sincerity and even fervour of either Milton's
or Handel's religious convictions ? The attitude assumed
by these men, and by the better class of Romanists,
seems to have become impossible to Protestants since
the time of Dr. Arnold.

I once saw a church dedicated to St. Francis. Outside
it, over the main door, there was a fresco of the saint
receiving the stigmata ; his eyes were upturned in a
fine ecstasy to the illuminated spot in the heavens whence
the causes of the stigmata were coming. The church was
insured, and the man who had affixed the plate of the
insurance office had put it at the precise spot in the sky
to which St. Francis's eyes were turned, so that the plate

* Samson Agonistes.
† " Venus laughing from the skies."
‡ Jephthah.

appeared to be the main cause of his ecstasy. Who cared ? No one ; until a carping Englishman came to the place, and thought it incumbent upon him to be scandalised, or to pretend to be so ; on this the authorities were made very uncomfortable, and changed the position of the plate. Granted that the Englishman was right ; granted, in fact, that we are more logical ; this amounts to saying that we are more rickety, and must walk more supported by cramp-irons. All the " earnestness," and " intenseness," and " æstheticism," and " culture " (for they are in the end one) of the present day, are just so many attempts to conceal weakness.

But to return. The church of St. Mary of the Snow at Campra was incorporated into the Graglia institution in 1628. There was originally no connection between the two, and it was not long before the later church became more popular than the earlier, insomuch that the work at Graglia was allowed to fall out of repair. On the death of Velotti the scheme languished, and by and by, instead of building more chapels, it was decided that it would be enough to keep in repair those that were already built. These, as I have said, are the chapels of S. Carlo, and the small ones which are now seen upon the way up to it, but they are all in a semi-ruinous state.

Besides the church of St. Mary of the Snow at Campra, there was another which was an exact copy of the *Santa Casa di Loreto,* and where there was a remarkable echo which would repeat a word of ten syllables when the wind was quiet. This was exactly on the site of the present sanctuary. It seemed a better place for the continuation of Velotti's work than the one he had himself chosen for it, inasmuch as it was where Signor Muratori so well implies a centre of devotion ought to be, namely, in " a milder climate, and in a spot which offers more resistance to the inclemency of the weather, and is better adapted to attract and retain the concourse of the faithful."

The design of the present church was made by an architect of the name of Arduzzi, in the year 1654, and the first stone was laid in 1659. In 1687 the right of liberating a bandit every year had been found to be productive of so much mischief that it was discontinued, and a yearly contribution of two hundred *lire* was substituted. The church was not completed until the second half of the last century, when the cupola was finished mainly through the energy of a priest, Carlo Giuseppe Gastaldi of Netro. This poor man came to his end in a rather singular way. He was dozing for a few minutes upon a scaffolding, and being awakened by a sudden noise, he started up, lost his balance, and fell over on to the pavement below. He died a few days later, on the 17th of October, either 1787 or 1778, I cannot determine which, through a misprint in Muratori's account.

The work was now virtually finished, and the buildings were much as they are seen now, except that a third storey was added to the hospice about the year 1840. It is in the hospice that the apartments are in which visitors are lodged. I was shown all over them, and found them not only comfortable but luxurious—decidedly more so than those of Oropa ; there was the same cleanliness everywhere which I had noticed in the restaurant. As one stands at the windows or on the balconies and looks down on to the tops of the chestnuts, and over these to the plains, one feels almost as if one could fly out of the window like a bird ; for the slope of the hills is so rapid that one has a sense of being already suspended in mid-air.

I thought I observed a desire to attract English visitors in the pictures which I saw in the bedrooms. Thus there was "A view of the black lead mine in Cumberland," a coloured English print of the end of the last century or the beginning of this, after, I think, Loutherbourg, and in several rooms there were English engravings after Martin. The English will not, I think,

SANCTUARY OF GRAGLIA

regret if they yield to these attractions. They will find the air cool, shady walks, good food, and reasonable prices. Their rooms will not be charged for, but they will do well to give the same as they would have paid at an hotel. I saw in one room one of those flippant, frivolous, Lorenzo de' Medici match-boxes on which there was a gaudily-coloured nymph in high-heeled boots and tights, smoking a cigarette. Feeling that I was in a sanctuary, I was a little surprised

that such a matchbox should have been tolerated. I
suppose it had been left behind by some guest. I should
myself select a matchbox with the Nativity, or the
Flight into Egypt upon it, if I were going to stay a week
or so at Graglia. I do not think I can have looked surprised or scandalised, but the worthy official who was
with me could just see that there was something on my
mind. " Do you want a match ? " said he, immediately
reaching me the box. I helped myself, and the matter
dropped.

There were many fewer people at Graglia than at
Oropa, and they were richer. I did not see any poor
about, but I may have been there during a slack time.
An impression was left upon me, though I cannot say
whether it was well or ill founded, as though there were a
tacit understanding between the establishments at Oropa
and Graglia that the one was to adapt itself to the poorer,
and the other to the richer classes of society ; and this
not from any sordid motive, but from a recognition of the
fact that any great amount of intermixture between the
poor and the rich is not found satisfactory to either one
or the other. Any wide difference in fortune does practically amount to a specific difference, which renders the
members of either species more or less suspicious of those
of the other, and seldom fertile *inter se*. The well-to-do
working-man can help his poorer friends better than we
can. If an educated man has money to spare, he will
apply it better in helping poor educated people than those
who are more strictly called the poor. As long as the
world is progressing, wide class distinctions are inevitable ;
their discontinuance will be a sign that equilibrium has
been reached. Then human civilisation will become as
stationary as that of ants and bees. Some may say it
will be very sad when this is so ; others, that it will be

a good thing ; in truth, it is good either way, for progress and equilibrium have each of them advantages and dis- advantages which make it impossible to assign superiority to either ; but in both cases the good greatly overbalances the evil ; for in both the great majority will be fairly well contented, and would hate to live under any other system.

Equilibrium, if it is ever reached, will be attained very slowly, and the importance of any change in a system depends entirely upon the rate at which it is made. No amount of change shocks—or, in other words, is important —if it is made sufficiently slowly, while hardly any change is too small to shock if it is made suddenly. We may go down a ladder of ten thousand feet in height if we do so step by step, while a sudden fall of six or seven feet may kill us. The importance, therefore, does not lie in the change, but in the abruptness of its introduction. Nothing is absolutely important or absolutely unimportant, absolutely good or absolutely bad.

This is not what we like to contemplate. The instinct of those whose religion and culture are on the surface only is to conceive that they have found, or can find, an absolute and eternal standard, about which they can be as earnest as they choose. They would have even the pains of hell eternal if they could. If there had been any means discoverable by which they could torment themselves beyond endurance, we may be sure they would long since have found it out ; but fortunately there is a stronger power which bars them inexorably from their desire, and which has ensured that intolerable pain shall last only for a very little while. For either the circumstances or the sufferer will change after no long time. If the circumstances are intolerable, the sufferer dies : if they are not intolerable, he becomes accustomed to them, and will cease to feel them grievously. No matter what the burden, there always has been, and always must be, a way for us also to escape.

Chapter XVII

Soazza and the Valley of Mesocco

I REGRET that I have not space for any of the sketches I took at Bellinzona, than which few towns are more full of admirable subjects. The Hotel de la Ville is an excellent house, and the town is well adapted for an artist's headquarters. Turner's two water-colour drawings of Bellinzona in the National Gallery are doubtless very fine as works of art, but they are not like Bellinzona, the spirit of which place (though not the letter) is better represented by the background to Basaiti's Madonna and child, also in our gallery, supposing the castle on the hill to have gone to ruin.

At Bellinzona a man told me that one of the two towers was built by the Visconti and the other by Julius Cæsar, a hundred years earlier. So, poor old Mrs. Barratt at Langar could conceive no longer time than a hundred years. The Trojan war did not last ten years, but ten years was as big a lie as Homer knew.

Almost all days in the subalpine valleys of North Italy have a beauty with them of some kind or another, but none are more lovely than a quiet gray day just at the beginning of autumn, when the clouds are drawing lazily and in the softest fleeces over the pine forests high up on the mountain sides. On such days the mountains are very dark till close up to the level of the clouds ; here, if there is dewy or rain-besprinkled pasture, it tells of a luminous silvery colour by reason of the light which the clouds reflect upon it ; the bottom edges of the clouds are also light through the reflection upward from the grass, but I do not know which begins this battledore and shuttlecock arrangement. These things are like quarrels between two old and intimate friends ; one can never say who begins them. Sometimes on a dull gray day like this, I have seen the shadow parts of clouds take a greenish-ashen-coloured tinge from the grass below them.

On one of these most enjoyable days we left Bellinzona for Mesocco on the S. Bernardino road. The air was warm, there was not so much as a breath of wind, but it was not sultry : there had been rain, and the grass, though no longer decked with the glory of its spring flowers, was of the most brilliant emerald, save where flecked with delicate purple by myriads of autumnal crocuses. The level ground at the bottom of the valley where the Moesa runs is cultivated with great care. Here the people have gathered the stones in heaps round any great rock which is too difficult to move, and the whole mass has in time taken a mulberry hue, varied with gray and russet lichens, or blobs of velvety green moss. These heaps of stone crop up from the smooth shaven grass, and are overhung with barberries, mountain ash, and mountain elder with their brilliant scarlet berries— sometimes, again, with dwarf oaks, or alder, or nut, whose leaves have just so far begun to be tinged as to increase the variety of the colouring. The first sparks of autumn's yearly conflagration have been kindled, but the fire is not yet raging as in October ; soon after which, indeed, it will have burnt itself out, leaving the trees as it were charred, with here and there a live coal of a red leaf or two still smouldering upon them.

As yet lingering mulleins throw up their golden spikes amid a profusion of blue chicory, and the gourds run along upon the ground like the fire mingled with the hail in "Israel in Egypt." Overhead are the umbrageous chestnuts loaded with their prickly harvest. Now and again there is a manure heap upon the grass itself, and lusty wanton gourds grow out from it along the ground like vegetable octopi. If there is a stream it will run with water limpid as air, and as full of dimples as "While Kedron's brook" in "Joshua" :—

While Kedron's brook to Jor-dan's stream its sil - ver tri - bute

pays ; Or while the glo-rious sun shall beam on Canaan golden

How quiet and full of rest does everything appear
to be. There is no dust nor glare, and hardly a sound
save that of the unfailing waterfalls, or the falling cry
with which the peasants call to one another from afar.*

So much depends upon the aspect in which one sees
a place for the first time. What scenery can stand, for
example, a noontide glare? Take the valley from Lanzo
to Viù. It is of incredible beauty in the mornings and
afternoons of brilliant days, and all day long upon a gray
day; but in the middle hours of a bright summer's day
it is hardly beautiful at all, except locally in the shade
under chestnuts. Buildings and towns are the only things
that show well in a glare. We perhaps, therefore, thought
the valley of the Moesa to be of such singular beauty on
account of the day on which we saw it, but doubt whether
it must not be absolutely among the most beautiful of
the subalpine valleys upon the Italian side.

The least interesting part is that between Bellinzona
and Roveredo, but soon after leaving Roveredo the

* I cannot give this cry in musical notation more nearly than as
follows :—

Accelerando.

valley begins to get narrower and to assume a more mountain character. Ere long the eye catches sight of a white church tower and a massive keep, near to one another and some two thousand feet above the road. This is Santa Maria in Calanca. One can see at once that it must be an important place for such a district, but it is strange why it should be placed so high. I will say more about it later on.

Presently we passed Cama, where there is an inn, and where the road branches off into the Val Calanca. Alighting here for a few minutes we saw a *cane lupino*— that is to say, a dun mouse-coloured dog about as large as a mastiff, and with a very large infusion of wolf blood in him. It was like finding one's self alone with a wolf— but he looked even more uncanny and ferocious than a wolf. I once saw a man walking down Fleet Street accompanied by one of these *cani lupini*, and noted the general attention and alarm which the dog caused. En-couraged by the landlord, we introduced ourselves to the dog at Cama, and found him to be a most sweet person, with no sense whatever of self-respect, and shrinking from no ignominy in his importunity for bits of bread. When we put the bread into his mouth and felt his teeth, he would not take it till he had looked in our eyes and said as plainly as though in words, " Are you quite sure that my teeth are not painful to you ? Do you really think I may now close my teeth upon the bread without causing you any inconvenience ? " We assured him that we were quite comfortable, so he swallowed it down, and presently began to pat us softly with his foot to remind us that it was our turn now.

Before we left, a wandering organ-grinder began to play outside the inn. Our friend the dog lifted up his voice and howled. I am sure it was with pleasure. If he had disliked the music he would have gone away. He was not at all the kind of person who would stay a concert out if he did not like it. He howled because he was stirred to the innermost depths of his nature. On this he became intense, and as a matter of course made a fool of himself ; but he was in no way more ridiculous than an Art Professor whom I once observed as he was holding forth to a number of working men, whilst escorting them round the Italian pictures in the National Gallery. When the organ left off he cast an appealing look at Jones, and we could

SOAZZA CHURCH

almost hear the words, " What *is* it out of ? " coming from his eyes. We did not happen to know, so we told him that it was " Ah che la morte " from " Il Trovatore," and he was quite contented. Jones even thought he looked as much as to say, " Oh yes, of course, how stupid of me ; I thought I knew it." He very well may have done so, but I am bound to say that I did not see this.

Near to Cama is Grono, where Baedeker says there is a chapel containing some ancient frescoes. I searched Grono in vain for any such chapel. A few miles higher up, the church of Soazza makes its appearance perched upon the top of its hill, and soon afterwards the splendid ruin of Mesocco on another rock or hill which rises in the middle of the valley.

The mortuary chapel of Soazza church is the subject my friend Mr. Gogin has selected for the etching at the beginning of this volume. There was a man mowing another part of the churchyard when I was there. He was so old and lean that his flesh seemed little more than parchment stretched over his bones, and he might have been almost taken for Death mowing his own acre. When he was gone some children came to play, but he had left his scythe behind him. These children were beyond my strength to draw, so I turned the subject over to Mr. Gogin's stronger hands. Children are dynamical; churches and frescoes are statical. I can get on with statical subjects, but can do nothing with dynamical ones. Over the door and windows are two frescoes of skeletons holding mirrors in their hands, with a death's head in the mirror. This reflected head is supposed to be that of the spectator to whom death is holding up the image of what he will one day become. I do not remember the inscription at Soazza; the one in the Campo Santo at Mesocco is, " Sicut vos estis nos fuimus, et sicut nos sumus vos eritis."*

On my return to England I mentioned this inscription to a friend who, as a young man, had been an excellent Latin scholar; he took a panic into his head that " eritis " was not right for the second person plural of the future tense of the verb " esse." Whatever it was, it was not " eritis." This panic was speedily communicated to myself, and we both puzzled for some time to think what the future of " esse " really was. At last we turned to a grammar and found that " eritis " was right after all. How skin-deep that classical training penetrates

---

* " Such as ye are, we once were, and such as we are, ye shall be."

on which we waste so many years, and how completely we drop it as soon as we are left to ourselves.

On the right-hand side of the door of the mortuary chapel there hangs a wooden tablet inscribed with a poem to the memory of Maria Zara. It is a pleasing poem, and begins :—

> "Appena al trapassar il terzo lustro
> Maria Zara la sua vita finì.
> Se a Soazza ebbe la sua colma
> A Roveredo la sua tomba . . .

she found," or words to that effect, but I forget the Italian. This poem is the nearest thing to an Italian rendering of "Affliction sore long time I bore" that I remember to have met with, but it is longer and more grandiose generally.

Soazza is full of beautiful subjects, and indeed is the first place in the valley of the Moesa which I thought good sketching ground, in spite of the general beauty of the valley. There is an inn there quite sufficient for a bachelor artist. The clergyman of the place is a monk, and he will not let one paint on a feast-day. I was told that if I wanted to paint on a certain feast-day I had better consult him ; I did so, but was flatly refused permission, and that too as it appeared to me with more peremptoriness than a priest would have shown towards me.

It is at Soazza that the ascent of the San Bernardino becomes perceptible ; hitherto the road has seemed to be level all the way, but henceforth the ascent though gradual is steady. Mesocco Castle looks very fine as soon as Soazza is passed, and gets finer and finer until it is actually reached. Here is the upper limit of the chestnuts, which leave off upon the lower side of Mesocco Castle. A few yards off the castle on the upper side is the ancient church of S. Cristoforo, with its huge St. Christopher on the right-hand side of the door. St. Christopher is a very favourite saint in these parts; people call him S. Cristofano, and even S. Carpofano. I think it must be in the church of S. Cristoforo at Mesocco that the frescoes are which Baedeker writes of as being near Grono. Of these I will speak at length in the next chapter. About half or three-quarters of a mile higher up the road than the castle is Mesocco itself.

Chapter XVIII

Mesocco, S. Bernardino, and S. Maria in Calanca

AT the time of my first visit there was an inn kept by one Desteffanis and his wife, where I stayed nearly a month, and was made very comfortable. Last year, however, Jones and I found it closed, but did very well at the Hotel Toscani. At the Hotel Desteffanis there used to be a parrot which lived about loose and had no cage, but did exactly what it liked. Its name was Lorrito. It was a very human bird ; I saw it eat some bread and milk from its tin one day and then sidle along a pole to a place where there was a towel hanging. It took a corner of the towel in its claw, wiped its beak with it, and then sidled back again. It would sometimes come and see me at breakfast ; it got from a chair-back on to the table by dropping its head and putting its round beak on to the table first, making a third leg as it were of its head ; it would then waddle to the butter and begin helping itself. It was a great respecter of persons and knew the landlord and landlady perfectly well. It yawned just like a dog or a human being, and this not from love of imitation but from being sleepy. I do not remember to have seen any other bird yawn. It hated boys because the boys plagued it sometimes. The boys generally go barefoot in summer, and if ever a boy came near the door of the hotel this parrot would go straight for his toes.

The most striking feature of Mesocco is the castle, which, as I have said, occupies a rock in the middle of the valley, and is one of the finest ruins in Switzerland. More interesting than the castle, however, is the church

CASTLE OF MESOCCO

of S. Cristoforo. Before I entered it I was struck with the fresco on the *facciata* of the church, which, though the *facciata* bears the date 1720, was painted in a style so much earlier than that of 1720 that I at first imagined I had found here another old master born out of due time ; for the fresco was in such a good state of preservation that it did not look more than 150 years old, and it was hardly likely to have been preserved when the *facciata* was renovated in 1720. When, however, my friend Jones joined me, he blew that little romance away by discovering a series of names with dates scrawled upon it from " 1481. viii. Febraio " to the present century. The lowest part of the fresco must be six feet from the ground, and it must rise at least ten or a dozen feet more, so the writings upon it are not immediately obvious, but they will be found on looking at all closely.

It is plain, therefore, that when the *facciata* was repaired the original fresco was preserved; it cannot be, as I had supposed, the work of a local painter who had taken his ideas of rocks and trees from the frescoes inside the church. That I am right in supposing the curious blanc-mange-mould-looking objects on either side St. Christopher's legs to be intended for rocks will be clear to any one who has seen the frescoes inside the church, where mountains with trees and towns upon them are treated on exactly the same principle. I cannot think the artist can have been quite easy in his mind about them.

S. CRISTOFORO

On entering the church the left-hand wall is found to be covered with the most remarkable series of frescoes in the Italian Grisons. They are disposed in three rows, one above the other, occupying the whole wall of the church as far as the chancel. The top row depicts a series of incidents prior

to the Crucifixion, and is cut up by the pulpit at the
chancel end. These events are treated so as to form a
single picture.

The second row is in several compartments. There is a
saint in armour on horseback, life-size, killing a dragon,
and a queen who seems to have been leading the dragon
by a piece of red tape buckled round its neck—unless,
indeed, the dragon is supposed to have been leading the
queen. The queen still holds the tape and points heaven-
ward. Next to this there is a very nice saint on horseback, who is giving a cloak to a man who is nearly naked.
Then comes St• Michael trampling on the dragon, and
holding a pair of scales in his hand, in which are two little
souls of a man and of a woman. The dragon has a hook
in his hand, and thrusting this up from under St. Michael,
he hooks it on to the edge of the scale with the woman in
it, and drags her down. The man, it seems, will escape.
Next to this there is a compartment in which a monk is
offering a round thing to St. Michael, who does not seem
to care much about it ; there are other saints and martyrs
in this compartment, and St. Anthony with his pig, and
Sta. Lucia holding a box with two eyes in it, she being
patroness of the eyesight as well as of mariners. Lastly,
there is the Adoration, ruined by the pulpit.

Below this second compartment are twelve frescoes,
each about three and a half feet square, representing
the twelve months—from a purely secular point of view.
January is a man making and hanging up sausages ;
February, a man chopping wood ; March, a•youth pro-
claiming spring with two horns to his mouth, and his hair
flying all abroad ; April is a young man on horseback
carrying a flower in his hand ; May, a knight, not in
armour, going out hawking with his hawk on one finger,
his bride on a pillion behind him, and a dog beside the

horse; June is a mower; July, another man reaping

FRESCO AT MESOCCO—MARCH

twenty-seven ears of corn; August, an invalid going to

FRESCO AT MESOCCO—APRIL

see his doctor ; October, a man knocking down chestnuts

FRESCO AT MESOCCO—MAY

from a tree and a woman catching them ; November is

FRESCO AT MESOCCO—AUGUST

hidden and destroyed by the pulpit ; December is a
butcher felling an ox with a hatchet.

We could find no signature of the artist, nor any
date on the frescoes to show when they were painted ;
but while looking for a signature we found a name
scratched with a knife or stone, and rubbed the tracing
which I reproduce, greatly reduced, here ; Jones thinks
the last line was not written by Lazarus Bovollinus, but
by another who signs A. T.

The Boelini were one of the principal families in
Mesocco. Gaspare Boelini, the head of the house, had
been treacherously thrown over the castle walls and
killed by order of Giovanni Giacomo Triulci in the year
1525, because as chancellor of the valley he declined to
annul the purchase of the castle of Mesocco, which Triulci
had already sold to the people of Mesocco, and for which
he had been in great part paid. His death is recorded on
a stone placed by the roadside under the castle.

Examining the wall further, we found a little to the
right that the same Lazzaro Bovollino (I need hardly
say that " Bovollino " is another way of spelling " Boe-

lini ") scratched his name again some sixteen years later,
as follows :—

1550   adj (?)

26 Decemb.   morijm (?)

Lazzaro Bovollino

*

15 L ———— B 50

The handwriting is not so good as it was when he
wrote his name before ; but we observed, with sympathy, that the writer had dropped his Latin. Close by is
scratched " Gullielmo B°."

The mark between the two letters L and B was the
family mark of the Boelini, each family having its mark,
a practice of which further examples will be given
presently.

We looked still more, and on the border of one of the
frescoes we discovered—

Veneris

" 1481 die ~~Jovis~~ vii j Februarij hoines di Misochi et Soazza fecerunt
fidelitatem in manibus di Johani Jacobi Triulzio,"

—" The men of Mesocco and Soazza did fealty to John
Jacob Triulci on Friday the 8th of February 1481."
The day originally written was Thursday the 7th of
February, but " Jovis " was scratched out and " Veneris "
written above, while another " i " was intercalated among
the i's of the viij of February. We could not determine
whether some hitch arose so as to cause a change of day,
or whether " Thursday " and " viij " were written by a
mistake for " Friday " and " viiij," but we imagined both
inscription and correction to have been contemporaneous
with the event itself. It will be remembered that on the
St. Christopher outside the church there is scratched
" 1481. 8 Febraio " and nothing more. The mistake of

the day, therefore, if it was a mistake, was made twice, and was corrected inside the church but not upon the fresco outside—perhaps because a ladder would have had to be fetched to reach it. Possibly the day had been originally fixed for Thursday the 8th, and a heavy snow-storm prevented people from coming till next day.

I could not find that any one in Mesocco, not even my excellent friend Signor à Marca, the *curato* himself, knew anything about either the inscriptions or the cause of their being written. No one was aware even of their existence; on borrowing, however, the history of the Valle Mesolcina by Signor Giovanni Antonio à Marca,[*] I found what I think will throw light upon the matter. The family of De Sax had held the valley of Mesocco for over four hundred years, and sold it in 1480 to John Jacob Triulci, who it seems tried to cheat him out of a large part of the purchase money later on; probably this John Jacob Triulci had the frescoes painted to con-ciliate the clergy and inaugurate his entry into possession. Early in 1481 he made the inhabitants of the valley do fealty to him. I may say that as soon as he had entered upon possession, he began to oppress the people by de-manding tolls on all produce that passed the castle. This the people resisted. They were also harassed by Peter De Sax, who made incursions into the valley and seized property, being unable to get his money out of John Jacob Triulci.

Other reasons that make me think the frescoes were painted in 1480 are as follows. The spurs worn by the young men in the April and May frescoes (pp. 211, 212) are about the date 1460. Their facsimiles can be seen in the Tower of London with this date assigned to them. The frescoes, therefore, can hardly have been painted

* Lugano, 1838.

before this time ; but they were probably painted later, for in the St. Christopher there is a distinct hint at anatomy ; enough to show that the study of anatomy introduced by Leonardo da Vinci was beginning to be talked about as more or less the correct thing. This would hardly be the case before 1480, as Leonardo was not born till 1452. By February 1481 the frescoes were already painted ; this is plain because the inscription—which, I think, may be taken as a record made at the time that fealty was done—is scratched over them. Peter De Sax, if he was selling his property, is not likely to have had the frescoes painted just before he was going away ; I think it most likely, therefore, that they were painted in 1480, when the valley of Mesocco passed from the hands of the De Sax family to those of the Triulci.

Underneath the inscription about the doing fealty there is scratched in another hand, and very likely years after the event it commemorates—" 1548 fu liberata la Vallata." This date is contradicted (and, I believe, corrected) by another inscription hard by, also in another hand, which says—

" 1549.   La valle di Misocho comprò la libertà da casa Triulcia
per 2400 scuti."

This inscription is signed thus :—

Carlo à Marca had written his name along with three others in 1606 on another part of the frescoes. Here are the signatures :—

CARLO A.M.,
1623.

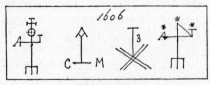

SIGNATURES

Two of these signatures belong to members of the Triulci family, as appears by the trident, which translates the name. The T in each case is doubtless for " Triulci." Four years earlier still, Carlo à Marca had written his name, with that of his wife or fiancée, on the fresco of St. Christopher on the *facciata* of the church, for we found there—

1602 { Carlo à Marca.
       Margherita dei Paglioni.

There is one other place where his name appears, or rather a part of it, for the inscription is half hidden by a gallery, erected probably in the last century.

The à Marca family still flourish in Mesocco. The *curato* is an à Marca, so is the postmaster. On the walls of a house near the convent there is an inscription to the effect that it was given by his fellow-townsmen to a member of the à Marca family, and the best work on the history of the valley is the work of Giovanni Antonio à Marca from which I have already quoted.

Returning to the frescoes, we found that the men of Soazza and Mesocco did fealty again to John Jacob Triulci on the feast of St. Bartholomew, the 24th day of August 1503 ; this I believe to have been the son of the original purchaser, but am not certain ; if so, he is the Triulci who had Gaspare Boelini thrown down from the castle walls. The people seem by another inscription to have done fealty again upon the same day of the following year.

On the St. Christopher we found one date, 1530, scratched on the right ankle, and several of 1607, apparently done at one time. One date was scratched in the left-hand corner—

1498 .   .   .
il Conte di (Misocho ?)

There are also other dates—1627, 1633, 1635, 1626; and right across the fresco there is written in red chalk, in a bold sixteenth or seventeenth century handwriting—

"Il parlar di li homini da bene deve valer più che quello degli altri."

—"The word of a man of substance ought to carry more weight than that of other people ; " and again—

"Non ha la fede ognun come tu chredi ;
Non chreder almen [quello?] che non vedi"

—"People are not so worthy of being believed as you think they are ; do not believe anything that you do not see yourself."

Big with our discoveries, we returned towards our inn, Jones leaving me sketching by the roadside. Presently an elderly English gentleman of some importance, judging from his manner, came up to me and entered into conversation. Englishmen do not often visit Mesocco, and I was rather surprised. "Have you seen that horrid fresco of St. Christopher down at that church there ? " said he, pointing towards it. I said I had. "It's very bad," said he decidedly ; "it was painted in the year 1725." I had been through all that myself, and I was a little cross into the bargain, so I said, "No ; the fresco is very good. It is of the fifteenth century, and the *facciata* was restored in 1720, not in 1725. The old fresco was preserved." The old gentleman looked a little scared. "Oh," said he, "I know nothing about art—but I will see you again at the hotel ; " and left me at once. I never saw him again. Who he was, where he came from, how he departed, I do not know. He was the only Englishman I saw during my stay of some four weeks at Mesocco.

On the first day of my first visit to Mesocco in 1879, I had gone on to S. Bernardino, and just before getting there, looking down over the great stretches of pasture land above S. Giacomo, could see that there was a storm raging lower down in the valley about where Mesocco should be ; I never saw such inky blackness in clouds before, and the conductor of the diligence said that he had seen nothing like it. Next morning we learnt that a water-spout had burst on the mountain above Anzone, a hamlet of Mesocco, and that the water had done a great deal of damage to the convent at Mesocco. Returning a few days later, I saw where the torrent had flowed by the mud upon the grass, but could not have believed such a stream of water (running with the velocity with which it must have run) to have been possible under any circumstances in that place unless I had actually seen its traces. It carried great rocks of several cubic yards as though they had been small stones, and among other mischief it had knocked down the garden wall of the convent of S. Rocco and covered the garden with débris. As I looked at it I remembered what Signor Bullo had told me at Faido about the inundations of 1868, " It was not the great rivers," he said, " which did the damage : it was the *ruscelli* " or small streams. So in revolutions it is not the heretofore great people, but small ones swollen under unusual circumstances who are most conspicuous and do most damage. Padre Bernardino, of the convent of S. Rocco, asked me to make him a sketch of the effect of the inundation, which I was delighted to do. It was not, however, exactly what he wanted, and, moreover, it got spoiled in the mounting, so I did another and he returned me the first with an inscription upon it which I reproduce below.

First came the words—

Ricordo al Mesocco

Then came my sketch ; and then—

Veduta della Chiesa, Giardino, ed Ospizio di S. Rocco,
dopo la visita fatta del triste Torrente di Anzone,
l'infausta sera del giorno quattro Agosto 1879

P. Berndo.

The English of which is as follows :—" View of the
church, garden, and hospice of S. Rocco, after the visita-
tion inflicted upon them by the sad torrent of Anzone,
on the unhallowed evening of the 4th of August 1879."
I regret that the " no " of Padre Bernardino's name,
through being written in faint ink, was not reproduced
in my facsimile. I doubt whether Padre Bernardino
would have got the second sketch out of me, if I had not
liked the inscription he had written on the first so much
that I wanted to be possessed of it. Besides, he wrote
me a note addressed " all' egregio pittore S. Butler."
To be called an egregious painter was too much for me,
so I did the sketch. I was once addressed as " L'esimio
pittore." I think this is one degree better even than
" egregio."

The damage which torrents can do must be seen to
be believed. There is not a streamlet, however innocent
looking, which is not liable occasionally to be turned into
a furious destructive agent, carrying ruin over the pastures
which at ordinary times it irrigates. Perhaps in old
times people deified and worshipped streams because
they were afraid of them. Every year each one of the great
Alpine roads will be interrupted at some point or another
by the tons of stones and gravel that are swept over it
perhaps for a hundred yards together. I have seen the
St. Gothard road more than once soon after these inter-
ruptions and could not have believed such damage possible ;

in 1869 people would still shudder when they spoke of the inundations of 1868. It is curious to note how they will now say that rocks which have evidently been in their present place for hundreds of years, were brought there in 1868 ; as for the torrent that damaged S. Rocco when I was in the valley of Mesocco, it shaved off the strong parapet of the bridge on either side clean and sharp, but the arch was left standing, the flood going right over the top. Many scars are visible on the mountain tops which are clearly the work of similar water-spouts, and altogether the amount of solid matter which gets taken down each year into the valleys is much greater than we generally think. Let any one watch the Ticino flowing into the Lago Maggiore after a few days' heavy rain, and consider how many tons of mud per day it must carry into and leave in the lake, and he will wonder that the gradual filling-up process is not more noticeable from age to age than it is.

Anzone, whence the sad torrent derives its name, is an exquisitely lovely little hamlet close to Mesocco. Another no less beautiful village is Doera, on the other side of the Moesa, and half a mile lower down than Mesocco. Doera overlooks the castle, the original hexagonal form of which can be made out from this point. It must have been much of the same plan as the castle at Eynsford in Kent—of which, by the way, I was once assured that the oldest inhabitant could not say " what it come from." While I was copying the fresco outside the chapel at Doera, some charming people came round me. I said the fresco was very beautiful. " Son persuaso," said the spokesman solemnly. Then he said there were some more pictures inside and we had better see them ; so the keys were brought. We said that they too were very beautiful. " Siam persuasi," was the reply in chorus.

Then they said that perhaps we should like to buy them
and take them away with us. This was a more serious
matter, so we explained that they were very beautiful,
but that these things had a charm upon the spot which
they would lose if removed elsewhere. The nice people
at once replied, " Siam persuasi," and so they left us.
It was like a fragment from one of Messrs. Gilbert and
Sullivan's comic operas.

For the rest, Mesocco is beautifully situated and surrounded by waterfalls. There is a man there who takes
the cows and goats out in the morning for their several
owners in the village, and brings them home in the evening.
He announces his departure and his return by blowing
a twisted shell, like those that Tritons blow on fountains
or in pictures ; it yields a softer sound than a horn ;
when his shell is heard people go to the cow-house and
let the cows out ; they need not drive them to join the
others, they need only open the door ; and so in the
evening, they only want the sound of the shell to tell
them that they must open the stable-door, for the cows
or goats when turned from the rest of the mob make
straight to their own abode.

There are two great avalanches which descend every
spring ; one of them when I was there last was not quite
gone until September ; these avalanches push the air
before them and compress it, so that a terrific wind
descends to the bottom of the valley and mounts up on to
the village of Mesocco. One year this wind snapped a
whole grove of full-grown walnuts across the middle of
their trunks, and carried stones and bits of wood up
against the houses at some distance off ; it tore off part
of the covering from the cupola of the church, and twisted
the weathercock awry in the fashion in which it may still
be seen, unless it has been mended since I left.

The judges at Mesocco get four francs a day when they are wanted, but unless actually sitting they get nothing. No wonder the people are so nice to one another and quarrel so seldom.

The walk from Mesocco to S. Bernardino is delightful ; it should take about three hours. For grassy slopes and flowers I do not know a better, more especially from S. Giacomo onward. In the woods above S. Giacomo there are some bears, or were last year. Five were known— a father, mother, and three young ones—but two were killed. They do a good deal of damage, and the Canton offers a reward for their destruction. The Grisons is the only Swiss Canton in which there are bears still remaining.

San Bernardino, 5500 feet above the sea, pleased me less than Mesocco, but there are some nice bits in it. The Hotel Brocco is the best to go to. The village is about two hours below the top of the pass ; the walk to this is a pleasant one. The old Roman road can still be seen in many places, and is in parts in an excellent state even now. San Bernardino is a fashionable watering-place and has a chalybeate spring. In the summer it often has as many as two or three thousand visitors, chiefly from the neighbourhood of the Lago Maggiore and even from Milan. It is not so good a sketching ground —at least so I thought—as some others of a similar character that I have seen. It is not comparable, for example, to Fusio. It is little visited by the English.

On our way down to Bellinzona again we determined to take S. Maria in Calanca, and accordingly were dropped by the diligence near Gabbiolo, whence there is a path across the meadows and under the chestnuts which leads to Verdabbio. There are some good bits near the church of this village, and some quaint modern frescoes on a

public-house a little off the main footpath, but there is
no accommodation. From this village the path ascends
rapidly for an hour or more, till just as one has made
almost sure that one must have gone wrong and have got
too high, or be on the track to an *alpe* only, one finds
one's self on a wide beaten path with walls on either side.
We are now on a level with S. Maria itself, and turning
sharply to the left come in a few minutes right upon the
massive keep and the *campanile,* which are so striking
when seen from down below. They are much more striking

APPROACH TO STA. MARIA

when seen from close at hand. The sketch I give does
not convey the notion—as what sketch can convey it?
—that one is at a great elevation, and it is this which
gives its especial charm to S. Maria in Calanca.

The approach to the church is beautiful, and the
church itself full of interest. The village was evidently
at one time a place of some importance, though it is not
easy to understand how it came to be built in such a
situation. Even now it is unaccountably large. There
is no accommodation for sleeping, but an artist who could
rough it would, I think, find a good deal that he would
like. On p. 226 is a sketch of the church and tower as seen

from the opposite side to that from which the sketch on p. 224 was taken.

The church seems to have been very much altered, if indeed the body of it was not entirely rebuilt, in 1618 —a date which is found on a pillar inside the church. On going up into the gallery at the west end of the church, there is found a Nativity painted in fresco by a local artist, one Agostino Duso of Roveredo, in the

STA. MARIA, APPROACH TO CHURCH

year 1727, and better by a good deal than one would anticipate from the epoch and habitat of the painter. On the other side of the same gallery there is a Death of the Virgin, also by the same painter, but not so good. On the left-hand side of the nave going towards the altar there is a remarkable picture of the battle of Lepanto, signed " Georgius Wilhelmus Grœsner Constantiensis fecit A.D. 1649," and with an inscription to the effect that it was painted for the confraternity of the most holy

Rosary, and by them set up " in this church of St. Mary commonly called of Calancha." The picture displays very little respect for academic principles, but is full of spirit and sensible painting.

Above this picture there hang two others—also very interesting, from being examples of, as it were, the last groans of true art while being stifled by academicism

FRONT VIEW OF STA. MARIA

—or it may be the attempt at a new birth, which was nevertheless doomed to extinction by academicians while yet in its infancy. Such pictures are to be found all over Italy. Sometimes, as in the case of the work of Dedomenici, they have absolute merit—more commonly they have the relative merit of showing that the painter was trying to look and feel for himself, and a picture does much when it conveys this impression. It is a small still voice, which, however small, can be heard through and above the roar of cant which tries to drown it. We want a book about the unknown Italian painters in out-of-the-way Italian valleys during the times of the decadence of art. There is ample material for one who has the time at his command.

We lunched at the house of the incumbent, a monk, who was very kind to us. We found him drying French marigold blossoms to colour his *risotto* with during the winter. He gave us some excellent wine, and took us over the tower near the church. Nothing can be more lovely than the monk's garden. If æsthetic people are ever going to get tired of sun-flowers and lilies, let me suggest to them that they will find a weary utterness in chicory and seed onions which they should not overlook ; I never felt chicory and seed onions till I was in the monk's garden at S. Maria in Calanca. All about the terrace or artificial level ground on which the church is placed, there are admirable bits for painting, and if there was only accommodation so that one could get up as high as the *alpi*, I can fancy few better places to stay at than S. Maria in Calanca.

Chapter XIX

The Mendrisiotto

WE stayed a day or two at Bellinzona, and then went on over the Monte Cenere to Lugano. My first acquaintance with the Monte Cenere was made some seven-and-thirty years ago when I was a small boy. I remember with what delight I found wild narcissuses growing in a meadow upon the top of it, and was allowed to gather as many as I liked. It was not till some thirty years afterwards that I again passed over the Monte Cenere in summer time, but I well remembered the narcissus place, and wondered whether there would still be any of them growing there. Sure enough when we got to the top, there they were as thick as cowslips in an English meadow. At Lugano, having half-an-hour to spare, we paid our respects to the glorious frescoes by Bernardino Luini, and to the façade of the duomo, and then went on to Mendrisio.

The neighbourhood of Mendrisio, or, as it is called, the "Mendrisiotto," is a rich one. Mendrisio itself should be the headquarters; there is an excellent hotel there, the Hotel Mendrisio, kept by Signora Pasta, which cannot be surpassed for comfort and all that makes a hotel pleasant to stay at. I never saw a house where the arrangements were more perfect; even in the hottest weather I found the rooms always cool and airy, and the nights never oppressive. Part of the secret of this may be that Mendrisio lies higher than it appears to do, and the hotel, which is situated on the slope of the hill, takes all the breeze there is. The lake of Lugano is about 950 feet above the sea. The river falls rapidly between Mendrisio and the lake, while the hotel is high above the river. I do not see, therefore, how the hotel can be less than 1200 feet above the sea-line ; but whatever height it is, I never felt the heat oppressive, though on more than one occasion I have stayed there for weeks together in July and August.

Mendrisio being situated on the railway between Lugano and Como, both these places are within easy reach. Milan is only a couple of hours off, and Varese a three or four hours' carriage drive. It lies on the very last slopes of the Alps, so that whether the visitor has a fancy for mountains or for the smiling beauty of the *colline*, he may be equally gratified. There are excellent roads in every direction, and none of them can be taken without its leading to some new feature of interest ; I do not think any English family will regret spending a fortnight at this charming place.

Most visitors to Mendrisio, however, make it a place of passage only, *en route* for the celebrated hotel on the Monte Generoso, kept by Dr. Pasta, Signora Pasta's brother-in-law. The Monte Generoso is very fine ; I know few places of which I am fonder ; whether one looks down at evening upon the lake of Lugano thousands of feet below, and then lets the eye wander upward again and rest upon the ghastly pallor of Monte Rosa, or whether one takes the path to the Colma and saunters over green slopes carpeted with wild-flowers, and studded with the gentlest cattle, all is equally delightful. What a sense of vastness and freedom is there on the broad heaving slopes of these subalpine spurs. They are just

high enough without being too high. The South Downs
are very good, and by making believe very much I have
sometimes been half able to fancy when upon them that
I might be on the Monte Generoso, but they are
only good as a quartet is good if one cannot get a
symphony.

I think there are more wild-flowers upon the Monte
Generoso than upon any other that I know, and among
them numbers of beautiful wild narcissuses, as on the
Monte Cenere. At the top of the Monte Generoso, among
the rocks that jut out from the herbage, there grows—
unless it has been all uprooted—the large yellow auricula,
and this I own to being my favourite mountain wild-
flower. It is the only flower which, I think, fairly beats
cowslips. Here too I heard, or thought I heard, the song
of that most beautiful of all bird songsters, the *passero
solitario*, or solitary sparrow—if it is a sparrow, which I
should doubt.

Nobody knows what a bird can do in the way of
song until he has heard a *passero solitario*. I think
they still have one at the Hotel Mendrisio, but am not
sure. I heard one there once, and can only say that I
shall ever remember it as the most beautiful warbling
that I ever heard come out of the throat of bird. All
other bird singing is loud, vulgar, and unsympathetic
in comparison. The bird itself is about as big as a starling,
and is of a dull blue colour. It is easily tamed, and becomes
very much attached to its master and mistress, but it is
apt to die in confinement before very long. It fights all
others of its own species ; it is now a rare bird, and is
doomed, I fear, ere long to extinction, to the regret of all
who have had the pleasure of its acquaintance. The
Italians are very fond of them, and Professor Vela told me
they will even act like a house dog and set up a cry if any

strangers come. The one I saw flew instantly at my finger when I put it near its cage, but I was not sure whether it did so in anger or play. I thought it liked being listened to, and as long as it chose to sing I was delighted to stay, whereas as a general rule I want singing birds to leave off.*

People say the nightingale's song is so beautiful; I am ashamed to own it, but I do not like it. It does not use the diatonic scale. A bird should either make no attempt to sing in tune, or it should succeed in doing so. Larks are Wordsworth, and as for canaries, I would almost sooner hear a pig having its nose ringed, or the grinding of an axe. Cuckoos are all right; they sing in tune. Rooks are lovely; they do not pretend to tune. Seagulls again, and the plaintive creatures that pity themselves on moorlands, as the plover and the curlew, or the birds that lift up their voices and cry at eventide when there is an eager air blowing upon the mountains and the last yellow in the sky is fading—I have no words with which to praise the music of these people. Or listen to the chuckling of a string of soft young ducks, as they glide single-file beside a ditch under a hedgerow, so close together that they look like some long brown serpent, and say what sound can be more seductive.

* Butler always regretted that he did not find out about Medea Colleone's *passero solitario* in time to introduce it into *Alps and Sanctuaries*. Medea was the daughter of Bartolomeo Colleone, the famous *condottiere*, whose statue adorns the Campo SS. Giovanni e Paolo at Venice. Like Catullus's Lesbia, whose immortal *passer* Butler felt sure was also a *passero solitario*, she had the misfortune to lose her pet. Its little body can still be seen in the Capella Colleone, up in the old town at Bergamo, lying on a little cushion on the top of a little column, and behind it there stands a little weeping willow tree whose leaves, cut out in green paper, droop over the corpse. In front of the column is the inscription, " Passer Medeæ Colleonis," and the whole is covered by a glass shade about eight inches high. Mr. Festing Jones has kindly allowed me to borrow this note from his " Diary of a Tour through North Italy to Sicily."—R. A. S.

Many years ago I remember thinking that the birds in New Zealand approached the diatonic scale more nearly than European birds do. There was one bird, I think it was the New Zealand thrush, but am not sure, which used to sing thus :—

I was always wanting it to go on :—

But it never got beyond the first four bars. Then there was another which I noticed the first day I landed, more than twenty years since, and whose song descended by very nearly perfect semitones as follows :—

but the semitones are here and there in this bird's song a trifle out of tune, whereas in that of the other there was no departure from the diatonic scale. Be this, however, as it may, none of these please me so much as the *passero solitario*.

The only mammals that I can call to mind at this moment as showing any even apparent approach to an appreciation of the diatonic scale are the elephant and the rhinoceros. The braying (or whatever is the technical term for it) of an elephant comprises a pretty accurate third, and is of a rich mellow tone with a good deal of brass in it. The rhinoceros grunts a good fourth, beginning, we will say, on C, and dropping correctly on to the G below.

The Monte Generoso, then, is a good place to stay a few days at, but one soon comes to an end of it. The top of a mountain is like an island in the air, one is cooped up upon it unless one descends; in the case of the Monte Generoso there is the view of the lake of Lugano, the walk to the Colma, the walk along the crest of the hill by the farm, and the view over Lombardy, and that is all. If one goes far down one is haunted by the recollection that when one is tired in the evening one will have all one's climbing to do, and, beautiful as the upper parts of the Monte Generoso are, there is little for a painter there except to study cattle, goats, and clouds. I recommend a traveller, therefore, by all means to spend a day or two at the hotel on the Monte Generoso, but to make his longer sojourn down below at Mendrisio, the walks and excursions from which are endless, and all of them beautiful.

Among the best of these is the ascent of the Monte Bisbino, which can be easily made in a day from Mendrisio; I found no difficulty in doing it on foot all the way there and back a few years ago, but I now prefer to take a trap as far as Sagno, and do the rest of the journey on foot, returning to the trap in the evening. Every one who knows North Italy knows the Monte Bisbino. It is a high pyramidal mountain with what seems a little white chapel on the top that glistens like a star when the sun is full upon it. From Como it is seen most plainly, but it is distinguishable over a very large part of Lombardy when the sun is right ; it is frequently ascended from Como and Cernobbio, but I believe the easiest way of getting up it is to start from Mendrisio with a trap as far as Sagno.

A mile and a half or so after leaving Mendrisio there is a village called Castello on the left. Here, a little off the road on the right hand, there is the small church of S. Cristoforo, of great antiquity, containing the remains of some early frescoes, I should think of the thirteenth or early part of the fourteenth century.

As usual, people have scratched their names on the frescoes. We found one name " Battista," with the date " 1485 " against it. It is a mistake to hold that the English scribble their names about more than other people. The Italians like doing this just as well as we do. Let the reader go to Varallo, for example, and note the names scratched up from the beginning of the sixteenth century to the present day, on the walls of the chapel containing the Crucifixion. Indeed, the Italians seem to have begun the habit long before we did, for we very rarely find names scratched on English buildings so long ago as the fifteenth century, whereas in Italy they are common. The earliest I can call to mind in England at this moment (of course, excepting the names written in the Beauchamp Tower) is on the church porch at Harlington, where there is a name cut and dated in one of the early years of the seventeenth century. I never even in Italy saw a name scratched on a wall with an earlier date than 1480.

Why is it, I wonder, that these little bits of soul-fossil, as it were, touch us so much when we come across them ? A fossil does not touch us—while a fly in amber does. Why should a fly in amber interest us and give us a slightly solemn feeling for a moment, when the fossil of a megatherium bores us ? I give it up ; but few of us can see the lightest trifle scratched off casually and idly long ago, without liking it better than almost any great thing of the same, or ever so much earlier date, done with purpose and intention that it should remain. So when we left S. Cristoforo it was not the old church, nor the frescoes, but the name of the idle fellow who had scratched his name " Battista . . . 1485," that we carried away with us. A little bit of old world life and entire want of earnestness, preserved as though it were a smile in amber.

In the Val Sesia, several years ago, I bought some tobacco that was wrapped up for me in a yellow old MS. which I in due course examined. It was dated 1797, and was a leaf from the book in which a tanner used to enter the skins which his customers brought him to be tanned.

" October 24," he writes, " I received from Signora Silvestre, called the widow, the skin of a goat branded in the neck.—(I am not to give it up unless they give me proof that she is the rightful owner.) Mem. I delivered it to Mr. Peter Job (Signor Pietro Giobbe).

" October 27.—I receive two small skins of a goat, very thin and branded in the neck, from Giuseppe Gianote of Campertogno.

" October 29.—I receive three skins of a chamois from Signor Antonio Cinere of Alagna, branded in the neck." Then there is a subsequent entry written small. " I receive also a little gray marmot's skin weighing thirty ounces."

I am sorry I did not get a sheet with the tanner's name. I am sure he was an excellent person, and might have been trusted with any number of skins, branded

or unbranded. It is nearly a hundred years ago since
that little gray marmot's skin was tanned in the Val
Sesia; but the wretch will not lie quiet in his grave;
he walks, and has haunted me once a month or so any
time this ten years past. I will see if I cannot lay him
by prevailing on him to haunt some one or other of my
readers.

Chapter XX

Sanctuary on Monte Bisbino

BUT to return to S. Cristoforo. In the Middle Ages there was a certain duke who held this part of the country and was notorious for his exactions. One Christmas eve when he and his whole household had assembled to their devotions, the people rose up against them and murdered them inside the church. After this tragedy the church was desecrated, though monuments have been put up on the outside walls even in recent years. There is a fine bit of early religious sculpture over the door, and the traces of a fresco of Christ walking upon the water, also very early.

Returning to the road by a path of a couple of hundred yards, we descended to cross the river, and then ascended again to Morbio Superiore. The view from the piazza in front of the church is very fine, extending over the whole Mendrisiotto, and reaching as far as Varese and the Lago Maggiore. Below is Morbio Inferiore, a place of singular beauty. A couple of Italian friends were with us, one of them Signor Spartaco Vela, son of Professor Vela. He called us into the church and showed us a beautiful altar-piece—a Madonna with saints on either side, apparently moved from some earlier church, and, as we all agreed, a very fine work, though we could form no idea who the artist was.

From Morbio Superiore the ascent is steep, and it

will take half-an-hour or more to reach the level bit
of road close to Sagno. This, again, commands the
most exquisite views, especially over Como, through
the trunks of the trees. Then comes Sagno itself, the
last village of the Canton Ticino and close to the Italian
frontier. There is no inn with sleeping accommodation
here, but if there was, Sagno would be a very good place
to stay at. They say that some of its inhabitants sometimes smuggle a pound or two of tobacco across the Italian
frontier, hiding it in the fern close to the boundary, and

TOP OF MONTE BISBINO

whisking it over the line on a dark night, but I know not
what truth there is in the allegation ; the people struck
me as being above the average in respect of good looks
and good breeding—and the average in those parts is a
very high one.

Immediately behind Sagno the old paved pilgrim's
road begins to ascend rapidly. We followed it, and in
half-an-hour reached the stone marking the Italian
boundary ; then comes some level walking, and then
on turning a corner the monastery at the top of the
Monte Bisbino is caught sight of. It still looks small,
but one can now see what an important building it

really is, and how different from the mere chapel which it appears to be when seen from a distance. The sketch which I give is taken from about a mile further on than the place where the summit is first seen.

Here some men joined us who lived in a hut a few hundred feet from the top of the mountain and looked after the cattle there during the summer. It is at their *alpe* that the last water can be obtained, so we resolved to stay there and eat the provisions we had brought with us. For the benefit of travellers, I should say they will find the water by opening the door of a kind of outhouse ; this covers the water and prevents the cows from dirtying it. There will be a wooden bowl floating on the top. The water outside is not drinkable, but that in the outhouse is excellent.

The men were very good to us ; they knew me, having seen me pass and watched me sketching in other years. It had unfortunately now begun to rain, so we were glad of shelter : they threw faggots on the fire and soon kindled a blaze ; when these died down and it was seen that the sparks clung to the kettle and smouldered on it, they said that it would rain much, and they were right. It poured during the hour we spent in dining, after which it only got a little better ; we thanked them, and went up five or six hundred feet till the monastery at length loomed out suddenly upon us from the mist, when we were close to it but not before.

There is a restaurant at the top which is open for a few days before and after a *festa*, but generally closed ; it was open now, so we went in to dry ourselves. We found rather a roughish lot assembled, and imagined the smuggling element to preponderate over the religious, but nothing could be better than the way in which they treated us. There was one gentleman, however, who was no smuggler, but who had lived many years in London and had now settled down at Rovenna, just below on the lake of Como. He had taken a room here and furnished it for the sake of the shooting. He spoke perfect English, and would have none but English things about

Veduta della chiesa sul Monte Bisbino Comune di Rovenna coll' Effigie della miracolosa B.V. MARIA che si venera in detto Santuario.

him. He had Cockle's antibilious pills, and the last numbers of the " Illustrated London News " and " Morning Chronicle ; " his bath and bath-towels were English, and there was a box of Huntley & Palmer's biscuits on his dressing - table. He was delighted to see some Englishmen, and showed us everything that was to be seen—among the rest the birds he kept in cages to lure those that he intended to shoot. He also took us behind the church, and there we found a very beautiful marble statue of the Madonna and child, an admirable work, with painted eyes and the dress gilded and figured. What an extraordinary number of fine or, at the least, interesting things one finds in Italy which no one knows anything about. In one day, poking about at random, we had seen some early frescoes at S. Cristoforo, an

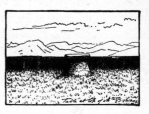

TABLE ON MONTE BISBINO

excellent work at Morbio, and here was another fine thing sprung upon us. It is not safe ever to pass a church in Italy without exploring it carefully. The church may be new and for the most part full of nothing but what is odious, but there is no knowing what fragment of earlier work one may not find preserved.

Signor Barelli, for this was our friend's name, now gave us some prints of the sanctuary, one of which I reproduce on p. 240. Behind the church there is a level piece of ground with a table and stone seats round it. The view from here in fine weather is very striking. As it was, however, it was perhaps hardly

CHAPEL OF S. NICOLAO

less fine than in clear weather, for the clouds had now raised themselves a little; though very little, above the sanctuary, but here and there lay all ragged down below us, and cast beautiful reflected lights upon the lake and town of Como. Above, the heavens were still black and lowering.   Over against us was the Monte Generoso, very sombre, and scarred with snow-white torrents ; below, the dull, sullen slopes of the Monte Bisbino, and the lake of Como ; further on, the Mendrisiotto and the blue-black plains of Lombardy. I have been at the top of the Monte Bisbino several times, but never was more impressed with it. At all times, however, it is a marvellous place.

Coming down we kept the ridge of the hill instead of taking the path by which we ascended. Beautiful views of the monastery are thus obtained. The flowers in spring must be very varied ; and we still found two or three large kinds of gentians and any number of cyclamens. Presently Vela dug up a fern root of the common *Polypodium vulgare ;* he scraped it with his knife and gave us some to eat. It is not at all bad, and tastes very much like liquorice. Then we came upon the little chapel of S. Nicolao. I do not know whether there is anything good inside or no. Then we reached Sagno and returned to Mendrisio ; as we re-crossed the stream between Morbio Superiore and Castello we found it had become a raging torrent, capable of any villainy.

Chapter XXI

A Day at the *Cantine*

NEXT day we went to breakfast with Professor Vela, the father of my friend Spartaco, at Ligornetto. After we had admired the many fine works which Professor Vela's studio contains, it was agreed that we should take a walk by S. Agata, and spend the afternoon at the *cantine*, or cellars where the wine is kept. Spartaco had two painter friends staying with him whom I already knew, and a young lady, his cousin ; so we all went together across the meadows. I think we started about one o'clock, and it was some three or four by the time we got to the *cantine*, for we kept stopping continually to drink wine. The two painter visitors had a fine comic vein, and enlivened us continually with bits of stage business which were sometimes uncommonly droll. We were laughing incessantly, but carried very little away with us except that the drier one of the two, who was also unfortunately deaf, threw himself into a rhapsodical attitude with his middle finger against his cheek, and his eyes upturned to heaven, but to make sure that his finger should stick to his cheek he just wetted the end of it against his tongue first. He did this with unruffled gravity, and as if it were the only thing to do under the circumstances.

The young lady who was with us all the time enjoyed everything just as much as we did ; once, indeed, she thought they were going a little too far—not as among themselves—but considering that there were a couple of earnest-minded Englishmen with them : the pair had begun a short performance which certainly did look as if it might develop into something a little hazardous. " Minga far tutto," she exclaimed rather promptly— " Don't do all." So what the rest would have been we shall never know.

Then we came to some precipices, whereon it at once occurred to the two comedians that they would commit suicide. The pathetic way in which they shared the contents of their pockets among us, and came back more than once to give little additional parting messages which occurred to them just as they were about to take the fatal plunge, was irresistibly comic, and was the more remarkable for the spontaneousness of the whole thing and the admirable way in which the pair played into one another's hands. The deaf one even played his deafness, making it worse than it was so as to heighten the comedy. By and by we came to a stile which they pretended to have a delicacy in crossing, but the lady helped them over. We concluded that if these young men were average specimens of the Italian student—and I should say they were—the Italian character has an enormous fund of pure love of fun—not of mischievous fun, but of the very best kind of playful humour, such as I have never seen elsewhere except among Englishmen.

Several times we stopped and had a bottle of wine at one place or another, till at last we came to a beautiful shady place looking down towards the lake of Lugano where we were to rest for half-an-hour or so. There was a *cantina* here, so of course we had more wine. In that air, and with the walk and incessant state of laughter in which we were being kept, we might drink *ad libitum,*

and the lady did not refuse a second small *bicchiere*.
On this our deaf friend assumed an anxious, fatherly air.
He said nothing, but put his eyeglass in his eye, and looked
first at the lady's glass and then at the lady with an
expression at once kind, pitying, and pained ; he looked
backwards and forwards from the glass to the lady
more than once, and then made as though he were going
to quit a scene in which it was plain he could be of no
further use, throwing up his hands and eyes like the old
steward in Hogarth's " Marriage à la mode." They never
seemed to tire, and every fresh incident at once suggested its appropriate treatment. Jones asked them
whether they thought they could mimic me. " Oh dear,
yes," was the answer ; " we have mimicked him hundreds
of times," and they at once began.

At last we reached Professor Vela's own *cantina*,
and here we were to have our final bottle. There were
several other *cantine* hard by, and other parties that had
come like ourselves to take a walk and get some wine.
The people bring their evening meal with them up to the
cantina and then sit on the wall outside, or go to a rough
table and eat it. Instead, in fact, of bringing their wine
to their dinner, they take their dinner to their wine.
There was one very fat old gentleman who had got the
corner of the wall to sit on, and was smoking a cigar with
his coat off. He comes, I am told, every day at about
three during the summer months, and sits on the wall
till seven, when he goes home to bed, rising at about four
o'clock next morning. He seemed exceedingly good-
tempered and happy. Another family who owned
a *cantina* adjoining Professor Vela's, had brought their
evening meal with them, and insisted on giving us a
quantity of excellent river cray-fish which looked like
little lobsters. I may be wrong, but I thought this

family looked at us once or twice as though they thought we were seeing a little more of the Italians absolutely *chez eux* than strangers ought to be allowed to see. We can only say we liked all we saw so much that we would fain see it again, and were left with the impression that we were among the nicest and most loveable people in the world.

I have said that the *cantine* are the cellars where the people keep their wine. They are caves hollowed out into the side of the mountain, and it is only certain localities that are suitable for the purpose. The *cantine*, therefore, of any village will be all together. The *cantine* of Mendrisio, for example, can be seen from the railroad, all in a row, a little before one gets into the town ; they form a place of *réunion* where the village or town unites to unbend itself on *feste* or after business hours. I do not know exactly how they manage it, but from the innermost chamber of each *cantina* they run a small gallery as far as they can into the mountain, and from this gallery, which may be a foot square, there issues a strong current of what, in summer, is icy cold air, while in winter it feels quite warm. I could understand the equableness of the temperature of the mountain at some yards from the surface of the ground, causing the *cantina* to feel cool in summer and warm in winter, but I was not prepared for the strength and iciness of the cold current that came from the gallery. I had not been in the innermost *cantina* two minutes before I felt thoroughly chilled and in want of a greatcoat.

Having been shown the *cantine*, we took some of the little cups which are kept inside and began to drink. These little cups are common crockery, but at the bottom there is written, Viva Bacco, Viva l'Italia, Viva la Gioia, Viva Venere, or other such matter ; they are to be had in every crockery shop throughout the Mendrisiotto, and are very pretty. We drank out of them, and ate the cray-fish which had been given us. Then seeing that it was getting late, we returned together to Besazio, and there parted, they descending to Ligornetto and we to Mendrisio, after a day which I should be glad to think would be as long and pleasantly remembered by our Italian friends as it will assuredly be by ourselves.

SOMMAZZO

The excursions in the neighbourhood of Mendrisio are endless. The walk, for example, to S. Agata and thence to Meride is exquisite. S. Agata itself is perfect, and commands a splendid view. Then there is the little chapel of S. Nicolao on a ledge of the red precipice. The walk to this by the village of Sommazzo is as good as anything can be, and the quiet terrace leading to the church door will not be forgotten by those who have seen it.

Sommazzo itself from the other side of the valley comes as on p. 247. There is Cragno, again, on the Monte Generoso, or Riva with its series of pictures *in tempera* by the brothers Giulio Cesare and Camillo Procaccini, men who, had they lived before the days of academies, might have done as well as any, except the few whom no academy can mould, but who, as it was, were carried away by fluency and facility. It is useless, however, to specify. There is not one of the many villages which can be seen from any rising ground in the neighbourhood, but what contains something that is picturesque and interesting, while the *coup d'œil*, as a whole, is always equally striking, whether one is on the plain and looks towards the mountains, or looks from the mountains to the plains.

Chapter XXII

Sacro Monte, Varese

FROM Mendrisio we took a trap across the country to Varese, passing through Stabbio, where there are some baths that are much frequented by Italians in the summer. The road is a pleasant one, but does not go through any specially remarkable places. Travellers taking this road had better leave every cigarette behind them on which they do not want to pay duty, as the custom-house official at the frontier takes a strict view of what is due to his employers. I had, perhaps, a couple of ounces of tobacco in my pouch, but was made to pay duty on it, and the searching of our small amount of luggage was little less than inquisitorial.

From Varese we went without stopping to the Sacro Monte, four or five miles beyond, and several hundred feet higher than the town itself. Close to the first chapel, and just below the arch through which the more sacred part of the mountain is entered upon, there is an excellent hotel called the Hotel Riposo, kept by Signor Piotti ; it is very comfortable, and not at all too hot even in the dog-days ; it commands magnificent views, and makes very good headquarters.

Here we rested and watched the pilgrims going up and down. They seemed very good-humoured and merry. Then we looked through the grating of the first chapel

inside the arch, and found it to contain a representation of the Annunciation. The Virgin had a real washing-
stand, with a basin and jug, and a piece of real soap.
Her slippers were disposed neatly under the bed, so also
were her shoes, and, if I remember rightly, there was
everything else that Messrs. Heal & Co. would send for
the furnishing of a lady's bedroom.

I have already said perhaps too much about the
realism of these groups of painted statuary, but will
venture a word or two more which may help the reader
to understand the matter better as it appears to Catholics
themselves. The object is to bring the scene as vividly
as possible before people who have not had the opportunity of being able to realise it to themselves through
travel or general cultivation of the imaginative faculties.
How can an Italian peasant realise to himself the notion
of the Annunciation so well as by seeing such a chapel as
that at Varese? Common sense says, either tell the
peasant nothing about the Annunciation, or put every
facility in his way by the help of which he will be able to
conceive the idea with some definiteness.

We stuff the dead bodies of birds and animals which
we think it worth while to put into our museums. We
put them in the most life-like attitudes we can, with bits
of grass and bush, and painted landscape behind them :
by doing this we give people who have never seen the
actual animals, a more vivid idea concerning them than
we know how to give by any other means. We have not
room in the British Museum to give a loose rein to realism
in the matter of accessories, but each bird or animal in the
collection is so stuffed as to make it look as much alive
as the stuffer can make it—even to the insertion of glass
eyes. We think it well that our people should have an
opportunity of realising these birds and beasts to them-

selves, but we are shocked at the notion of giving them a similar aid to the realisation of events which, as we say, concern them more nearly than any others in the history of the world. A stuffed rabbit or blackbird is a good thing. A stuffed Charge of Balaclava again is quite legitimate ; but a stuffed Nativity is, according to Protestant notions, offensive.

Over and above the desire to help the masses to realise the events in Christ's life more vividly, something is doubtless due to the wish to attract people by giving them what they like. This is both natural and legitimate. Our own rectors find the prettiest psalm and hymn tunes they can for the use of their congregations, and take much pains generally to beautify their churches. Why should not the Church of Rome make herself attractive also ? If she knows better how to do this than Protestant churches do, small blame to her for that. For the people delight in these graven images. Listen to the hushed " oh bel ! " which falls from them as they peep through grating after grating ; and the more tawdry a chapel is, the better, as a general rule, they are contented. They like them as our own people like Madame Tussaud's. Granted that they come to worship the images ; they do ; they hardly attempt to conceal it. The writer of the authorised handbook to the Sacro Monte at Locarno, for example, speaks of " the solemn coronation of the image that is there revered "—" la solenne coronazione del simulacro ivi venerato " (p. 7). But how, pray, can we avoid worshipping images ? or loving images ? The actual living form of Christ on earth was still not Christ, it was but the image under which His disciples saw Him ; nor can we see more of any of those we love than a certain more versatile and warmer presentment of them than an artist can counterfeit. The ultimate " them " we see not.

How far these chapels have done all that their founders expected of them is another matter. They have undoubtedly strengthened the hands of the Church in their immediate neighbourhood, and they have given an incalculable amount of pleasure, but I think that in the Middle Ages people expected of art more than art can do. They hoped a fine work of art would exercise a deep and permanent effect upon the lives of those who lived near it. Doubtless it does have some effect—enough to make it worth while to encourage such works, but nevertheless the effect is, I imagine, very transient. The only thing that can produce a deep and permanently good influence upon a man's character is to have been begotten of good ancestors for many generations—or at any rate to have reverted to a good ancestor—and to live among nice people.

The chapels themselves at Varese, apart from their contents, are very beautiful. They come as fresh one after the other as a set of variations by Handel. Each one of them is a little architectural gem, while the figures they contain are sometimes very good, though on the whole not equal to those at Varallo. The subjects are the mysteries of joy, namely, the Annunciation (immediately after the first great arch is passed), the Salutation of Mary by Elizabeth, the Nativity, the Presentation, and the Disputing with the Doctors. Then there is a second arch, after which come the mysteries of grief—the Agony in the Garden, the Flagellation, the Crowning with Thorns, the Ascent to Calvary, and the Crucifixion. Passing through a third arch, we come to the mysteries of glory—the Resurrection, the Ascension, the Descent of the Holy Ghost, and the Assumption of the Virgin Mary. The Dispute in the Temple is the chapel which left the deepest impression upon us. Here the various

attitudes and expressions of the doctors are admirably
rendered. There is one man, I think he must have been a
broad churchman and have taken in the "Spectator"; his
arms are folded, and he is smiling a little, with his head
on one side. He is not prepared, he seems to say, to deny
that there is a certain element of truth in what this
young person has been saying, but it is very shallow, and

SACRO MONTE OF VARESE

in all essential points has been refuted over and over again ;
he has seen these things come and go so often, &c. But
all the doctors are good. The Christ is weak, and so
are the Joseph and Mary in the background ; in fact,
throughout the whole series of chapels the wicked or
worldly and indifferent people are well done, while the
saints are a feeble folk : the sculptor evidently neither
understood them nor liked them, and could never get
beyond silliness ; but the artist who has lately done

them up has made them still weaker and sillier by giving them all pink noses.

Shortly after the sixth chapel has been passed the road turns a corner, and the town on the hill (see preceding page) comes into full view. This is a singularly beautiful spot. The chapels are worth coming a long way to see, but this view of the town is better still : we generally

SACRO MONTE OF VARESE, NEARER VIEW

like any building that is on the top of a hill ; it is an instinct in our nature to do so ; it is a remnant of the same instinct which makes sheep like to camp at the top of a hill ; it gives a remote sense of security and vantage-ground against an enemy. The Italians seem hardly able to look at a high place without longing to put something on the top of it, and they have seldom done so with better effect than in the case of the Sacro

Monte at Varese. From the moment of its bursting upon
one on turning the corner near the seventh, or Flagellation
chapel, one cannot keep one's eyes off it, and one fancies,
as with S. Michele, that it comes better and better with
every step one takes ; near the top it composes, as on
p. 254, but without colour nothing can give an adequate
notion of its extreme beauty. Once at the top the interest
centres in the higgledy-pigglediness of the houses, the

TERRACE AT THE SACRO MONTE, VARÈSE

gay colours of the booths where strings of beads and other
religious knick-knacks are sold, the glorious panorama,
and in the inn where one can dine very well, and I should
imagine find good sleeping accommodation. The view
from the balcony outside the dining-room is wonderful,
and above is a sketch from the terrace just in front of
the church.

There is here no single building comparable to the
sanctuary of Sammichele, nor is there any trace of

that beautiful Lombard work which makes so much impression upon one in the church on the Monte Pirchiriano; the architecture is late, and *barocco*, not to say *rococo*, reigns everywhere; nevertheless the effect of the church is good. The visitor should get the sacristan to show him a very fine *pagliotto* or altar cloth of raised embroidery, worked in the thirteenth century. He will also do well to walk some little distance behind the town

SACRO MONTE FROM ABOVE

on the way to S. Maria dei fiori (St. Mary of the flowers) and look down upon the town and Lombardy. I do not think he need go much higher than this, unless he has a fancy for climbing.

The Sacro Monte is a kind of ecclesiastical Rosherville Gardens, eminently the place to spend a happy day. We happened by good luck to be there during one of the great *feste* of the year, and saw I am afraid to say how many thousands of pilgrims go up and down. They were admirably behaved, and not one of them tipsy. There was an old English gentleman at the Hotel Riposo who told us that there had been another such *festa* not many weeks previously, and that he had seen one drunken man there—an Englishman—who kept abusing all he saw and crying out, " Manchester's the place for me."

The processions were best at the last part of the ascent ; there were pilgrims, all decked out with coloured feathers, and priests and banners and music and crimson and gold and white and glittering brass against the cloudless blue sky. The old priest sat at his open window to receive the offerings of the devout as they passed ; but he did not seem to get more than a few *bambini* modelled in wax. Perhaps he was used to it. And the band played the *barocco* music on the *barocco* little piazza and we were all *barocco* together. It was as though the clergyman at Ladywell had given out that, instead of having service as usual, the congregation would go in procession to the Crystal Palace with all their traps, and that the band had been practising " Wait till the clouds roll by " for some time, and on Sunday as a great treat they should have it.

The Pope has issued an order saying he will not have masses written like operas. It is no use. The Pope can do much, but he will not be able to get contrapuntal music into Varese. He will not be able to get anything more solemn than " La Fille de Madame Angot " into Varese. As for fugues——! I would as soon take an English bishop to the Surrey pantomime as to the Sacro Monte on a *festa*.

Then the pilgrims went into the shadow of a great rock behind the sanctuary, spread themselves out over the grass and dined.

Chapter XXIII

Angera and Arona

FROM the Hotel Riposo we drove to Angera, on the Lago Maggiore. There are many interesting things to see on the way. Close to Velate, for example, there is the magnificent bit of ruin which is so striking a feature as seen from the Sacro Monte. A little further on, at Luinate, there is a fine old Lombard *campanile* and some conventual buildings which are worth sparing five minutes or so to see. The views hereabouts over the lake of Varese and towards Monte Rosa are exceedingly fine. The driver should be told to go a mile or so out of his direct route in order to pass Oltrona, near Voltrone. Here there was a monastery which must once have been an important one. Little of old work remains, except a very beautiful cloister of the thirteenth or fourteenth century, which should not be missed. It measures about twenty-one paces each way : the north side has round arches made of brick; the arches are supported by small columns about six inches through, each of which has a different capital ; the middle is now garden ground. A few miles nearer Angera there is Brebbia, the church of which is an excellent specimen of early Lombard work. We thought we saw the traditions of Cyclopean masonry in the occasional irregularity of the string-courses. The stones near the bottom of the wall are very massive, and the west wall is not, if I remember rightly, bonded into

the north and south walls, but these walls are only built
up against it as at Giornico. The door on the south side
is simple, but remarkably beautiful. It looks almost
as if it might belong to some early Norman church in
England, and the stones have acquired a most exquisite
warm colour with age. At Ispra there is a *campanile*
which Mr. Ruskin would probably disapprove of, but

CASTLE OF ANGERA

which we thought lovely. A few kilometres further on a
corner is turned, and the splendid castle of Angera is
caught sight of.

Before going up to the castle we stayed at the inn on
the left immediately on entering the town, to dine.
They gave us a very good dinner, and the garden was
a delightful place to dine in. There is a kind of red
champagne made hereabouts which is very good; the
figs were ripe, and we could gather them for ourselves and

eat *ad libitum*. There were two tame sparrows hopping
continually about us ; they pretended to make a little
fuss about allowing themselves to be caught, but they
evidently did not mind it. I dropped a bit of bread and
was stooping to pick it up ; one of them on seeing me
move made for it and carried it off at once ; the action was
exactly that of one who was saying, " I don't particularly
want it myself, but I'm not going to let you have it."

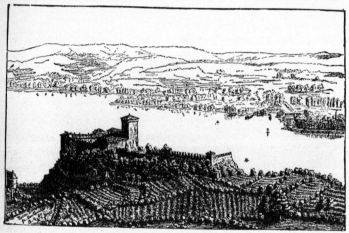

CASTLE OF ANGERA, FROM S. QUIRICO

Presently some *cacciatori* came with a poodle-dog.
They explained to us that though the poodle was " a
truly hunting dog," he would not touch the sparrows,
which to do him justice he did not. There was a tame
jay also, like the sparrows going about loose, but, like
them, aware when he was well off.

After dinner we went up to the castle, which I have
now visited off and on for many years, and like always
better and better each time I go there. I know no place
comparable to it in its own way. I know no place so

pathetic, and yet so impressive, in its decay. It is not a
ruin—all ruins are frauds—it is only decayed. It is
a kind of Stokesay or Ightham Mote, better preserved
than the first, and less furnished than the second, but on
a grander scale than either, and set in incomparably
finer surroundings. The path towards it passes the
church, which has been spoiled. Outside this there are

TERRACE AT CASTLE OF ANGERA, NO. 1

parts of old Roman columns on some temple, stuck
in the ground; inside are two statues called St. Peter
and St. Paul, but evidently effigies of some magistrates
in the Roman times. If the traveller likes to continue the
road past the church for three-quarters of a mile or so,
he will get a fine view of the castle, and if he goes up to
the little chapel of S. Quirico on the top of the hill on his
right hand, he will look down upon it and upon Arona.
We will suppose, however, that he goes straight for the

castle itself ; every moment as he approaches it, it will
seem finer and finer ; presently he will turn into a vineyard
on his left, and at once begin to climb.

Passing under the old gateway—with its portcullis
still ready to be dropped, if need be, and with the iron
plates that sheathe it pierced with bullets—as at S.
Michele, the visitor enters at once upon a terrace from

TERRACE AT CASTLE OF ANGERA, NO. II

which the two foregoing illustrations were taken.   I
know nothing like this terrace.   On a summer's afternoon
and evening it is fully shaded, the sun being behind the
castle.   The lake and town below are still in sunlight.
This, I think, is about the best time to see the castle—say
from six to eight on a July evening, or at any hour on a
gray day.

Count Borromeo, to whom the castle belongs, allows
it to be shown, and visitors are numerous.   There is

very little furniture inside the rooms, and the little
there is is decaying ; the walls are covered with pictures,
mostly copies, and none of them of any great merit, but
the rooms themselves are lovely. Here is a sketch of the
one in which San Carlo Borromeo was born, but the one
on the floor beneath is better still. The whole of this part
was built about the year 1350, and inside, where the

ROOM IN WHICH S. CARLO BORROMEO WAS BORN

weather has not reached, the stones are as sharp as if
they had been cut yesterday. It was in the great *Sala* of
this castle that the rising against the Austrians in 1848
was planned ; then there is the *Sala di Giustizia*, a fine
room, with the remains of frescoes ; the roof and the
tower should also certainly be visited. All is solid
and real, yet it is like an Italian opera in actual life.
Lastly, there is the kitchen, where the wheel still remains
in which a turnspit dog used to be put to turn it

and roast the meat ; but this room is not shown to strangers.

The inner court of the castle is as beautiful as the outer one. Through the open door one catches glimpses of the terrace, and of the lake beyond it. I know Ightham, Hever, and Stokesay, both inside and out, and I know the outside of Leeds ; these are all of them exquisitely beautiful, but neither they nor any other such place that I have ever seen please me as much as the castle of Angera.

We stayed talking to my old friend Signor Signorelli, the *custode* of the castle, and his family, and sketching upon the terrace until Tonio came to tell us that his boat was at the quay waiting for us. Tonio is now about fourteen years old, but was only four when I first had the pleasure of making his acquaintance. He is son to Giovanni, or as he is more commonly called, Giovannino, a boatman of Arona. The boy is deservedly a great favourite, and is now a *padrone* with a boat of his own, from which he can get a good living.

He pulled us across the warm and sleepy lake, so far the most beautiful of all even the Italian lakes ; as we neared Arona, and the wall that runs along the lake became more plain, I could not help thinking of what Giovanni had told me about it some years before, when Tonio was lying curled up, a little mite of an object, in the bottom of the boat. He was extolling a certain family of peasants who live near the castle of Angera, as being models of everything a family ought to be. " There," he said, " the children do not speak at meal-times ; the *polenta* is put upon the table, and each takes exactly what is given him ; even though one of the children thinks another has got a larger helping than he has, he will eat his piece in silence. My children are

not like that ; if Marietta thinks Irene has a bigger
piece than she has, she will leave the room and go to the
wall."

" What," I asked, " does she go to the wall for ? "

" Oh ! to cry ; all the children go to the wall to
cry."

I thought of Hezekiah. The wall is the crying place,
playing, lounging place, and a great deal more, of all
the houses in its vicinity. It is the common drawing-
room during the summer months ; if the weather is too
sultry, a boatman will leave his bed and finish the night
on his back upon its broad coping ; we who live in a
colder climate can hardly understand how great a blank
in the existence of these people the destruction of the
wall would be.

We soon reached Arona, and in a few minutes were
in that kind and hospitable house the Hotel d'Italia,
than which no better hotel is to be found in Italy.

Arona is cooler than Angera. The proverb says,
" He who would know the pains of the infernal regions,
should go to Angera in the summer and to Arona in the
winter." The neighbourhood is exquisite. Unless
during the extreme heat of summer, it is the best place
to stay at on the Lago Maggiore. The Monte Motterone
is within the compass of a single day's excursion ; there
is Orta, also, and Varallo easily accessible, and any
number of drives and nearer excursions whether by
boat or carriage.

One day we made Tonio take us to Castelletto near
Sesto Calende, to hear the bells. They ring the bells
very beautifully at Vogogna, but, unless my recollection of
a good many years ago fails me, at Castelletto they ring
them better still.

At Vogogna, while we were getting our breakfast,

we heard the bells strike up as follows, from a *campanile* on the side of the hill :—

They did this because a baby had just died, but we were told it was nothing to what they would have done if it had been a grown-up person.

At Castelletto we were disappointed; the bells did not ring that morning; we hinted at the possibility of paying a small fee to the ringer and getting him to ring them, but were told that "la gente" would not at all approve of this, and so I was unable to take down the chimes at Castelletto as I had intended to do. I may say that I had a visit from some Italian friends a few years ago, and found them hardly less delighted with our English mode of ringing than I had been with theirs. It would be very nice if we could ring our bells sometimes in the English and sometimes in the Italian way. When I say the Italian way—I should say that the custom of ringing, as above described, is not a common one—I have only heard it at Vogogna and Castelletto, though doubtless it prevails elsewhere.

We were told that the people take a good deal of pride in their bells, and that one village will be jealous of another, and consider itself more or less insulted if the bells of that other can be heard more plainly than its own can be heard back again. There are two villages in the Brianza called Balzano and Cremella ; the dispute between these grew so hot that each of them changed their bells three times, so as to try and be heard the loudest. I believe an honourable compromise was in the end arrived at.

In other respects Castelletto is a quiet, sleepy little place. The Ticino flows through it just after leaving the lake. It is very wide here, and when flooded must carry down an enormous quantity of water. Barges go down it at all times, but the river is difficult of navigation and requires skilful pilots. These pilots are well paid, and Tonio seemed to have a great respect for them. The views of Monte Rosa are superb.

One of the great advantages of Arona, as of Mendrisio, is that it commands such a number of other places. There is rail to Milan, and again to Novara, and each station on the way is a sub-centre ; there are also the steamers on the lake, and there is not a village at which they stop which will not repay examination, and which is not in its turn a sub-centre. In England I have found by experience that there is nothing for it but to examine every village and town within easy railway distance ; no books are of much use : one never knows that something good is not going to be sprung upon one, and few indeed are the places where there is no old public-house, or overhanging cottage, or farmhouse and barn, or bit of De Hooghe-like entry which, if one had two or three lives, one would not willingly leave unpainted. It is just the same in North Italy ; there is not a village which can be passed over with a light heart.

Chapter XXIV

Locarno

WE were attracted to Locarno by the approaching fêtes in honour of the fourth centenary of the apparition of the Virgin Mary to Fra Bartolomeo da Ivrea, who founded the sanctuary in consequence.

The programme announced that the festivities would begin on Saturday, at 3.30 P.M., with the carrying of the sacred image (*sacro simulacro*) of the Virgin from the Madonna del Sasso to the collegiate church of S. Antonio. There would then be a benediction and celebration of the holy communion. At eight o'clock there were to be illuminations, fireworks, balloons, &c., at the sanctuary and the adjacent premises.

On Sunday at half-past nine there was to be mass at the church of S. Antonio, with a homily by Monsignor Paolo Angelo Ballerini, Patriarch of Alexandria *in partibus*, and blessing of the crown sent by Pope Leo XIII for the occasion. S. Antonio is the church the roof of which fell in during service one Sunday in 1865, through the weight of the snow, killing sixty people. At half-past three a grand procession would convey the Holy Image to a pretty temple which had been erected in the market-place. The image was then to be crowned by the Patriarch, carried round the town in procession, and returned to the church of S. Antonio. At eight o'clock

there were to be fireworks near the port; a grand
illumination of a triumphal arch, an illumination of
the sanctuary and chapels with Bengal lights, and
an artificial apparition of the Madonna (*Apparizione
artificiale della Beata Vergine col Bambino*) above the
church upon the Sàcro Monte. Next day the Holy Image
was to be carried back from the church of S. Antonio

SACRO MONTE, LOCARNO, NO. I

to its normal resting-place at the sanctuary. We wanted
to see all this, but it was the artificial apparition of the
Madonna that most attracted us.

Locarno is, as every one knows, a beautiful town.
Both the Hotel Locarno and the Hotel della Corona are
good, but the latter is, I believe, the cheaper. At the
castello there is a fresco of the Madonna, ascribed, I
should think rightly, to Bernardino Luini, and at the

cemetery outside the town there are some old frescoes
of the second half of the fifteenth century, in a ruinous
state, but interesting. If I remember rightly there are
several dates on them, averaging 1475–80. They might
easily have been done by the same man who did the
frescoes at Mesocco, but I prefer these last. The great
feature, however, of Locarno is the Sacro Monte which
rises above it. From the wooden bridge which crosses

SACRO MONTE, LOCARNO, NO. II

the stream just before entering upon the sacred precincts,
the church and chapels and road arrange themselves
as on p. 269.

On the way up, keeping to the steeper and abrupter
route, one catches sight of the monks' garden—a little
paradise with vines, beehives, onions, lettuces, cabbages,
marigolds to colour the *risotto* with, and a little plot of
great luxuriant tobacco plants. Amongst the foliage
may be now and again seen the burly figure of a monk

with a straw hat on. The best view of the sanctuary
from above is the one which I give on p. 270.

The church itself is not remarkable, but it contains
the best collection of votive pictures that I know in any
church, unless the one at Oropa be excepted ; there is
also a modern Italian " Return from the Cross " by Ciseri,

CLOISTER AT SACRO MONTE, LOCARNO

which is very much admired, but with which I have
myself no sympathy whatever. It is an Academy picture.

The cloister looking over the lake is very beautiful.
In the little court down below—which also is of great
beauty—there is a chapel containing a representation of
the Last Supper in life-sized coloured statues as at Varallo,
which has a good deal of feeling, and a fresco (?) behind

it which ought to be examined, but the chapel is so dark
that this is easier said than done.   There is also a fresco
down below in the chapel where the founder of the
sanctuary is buried which should not be passed over.
It is dated 1522, and is Luinesque in character.   When
I was last there, however, it was hardly possible to see
anything, for everything was being turned topsy-turvy by
the arrangements which were being made for the approaching fêtes.   These were very gay and pretty ; they must
have cost a great deal of money, and I was told that the
municipality in its collective capacity was thought
mean, because it had refused to contribute more than
100 francs, or £4 sterling.   It does seem rather a small
sum certainly.

On the afternoon of Friday the 13th of August the
Patriarch Monsignor Ballerini was to arrive by the
three o'clock boat, and there was a crowd to welcome
him.   The music of Locarno was on the quay playing
a selection, not from " Madame Angot " itself, but from
something very like it—light, gay, sparkling opera
bouffe—to welcome him.   I felt as I had done when I
found the matchbox in the sanctuary bedroom at Graglia :
not that I minded it myself, but as being a little unhappy
lest the Bishop might not quite like it.

I do not see how we could welcome a bishop—we
will say to a confirmation—with a band of music at all.
Fancy a brass band of some twenty or thirty ranged
round the landing stage at Gravesend to welcome the
Bishop of London, and fancy their playing we will say
" The two Obadiahs," or that horrid song about the
swing going a little bit higher !   The Bishop would be
very much offended.   He would not go a musical inch
beyond the march in " Le Prophète," nor, willingly,
beyond the march in " Athalie."   Monsignor Ballerini,

however, never turned a hair ; he bowed repeatedly to
all round him, and drove off in a carriage and pair,
apparently much pleased with his reception. We Protestants do not understand, nor take any very great pains
to understand, the Church of Rome. If we did, we should
find it to be in many respects as much in advance of us
as it is behind us in others.

One thing made an impression upon me which haunted
me all the time. On every important space there were
advertisements of the programme, the substance of which
I have already given. But hardly, if at all less noticeable,
were two others which rose up irrepressible upon every
prominent space, searching all places with a subtle
penetrative power against which precautions were
powerless. These advertisements were not in Italian but
in English, nevertheless they were neither of them
English—but both, I believe, American. The one was
that of the Richmond Gem cigarette, with the large
illustration representing a man in a hat smoking, so
familiar to us here in London. The other was that of
Wheeler & Wilson's sewing machines.

As the Patriarch drove off in the carriage the man
in the hat smoking the Richmond Gem cigarette leered
at him, and the woman working Wheeler & Wilson's
sewing machine sewed at him. During the illuminations the unwonted light threw its glare upon the effigies
of saints and angels, but it illumined also the man in
the black felt hat and the woman with the sewing machine ;
even during the artificial apparition of the Virgin Mary
herself upon the hill behind the town, the more they let
off fireworks the more clearly the man in the hat came
out upon the walls round the market-place, and the bland
imperturbable woman working at her sewing machine.
I thought to myself that when the man with the hat

appeared in the piazza the Madonna would ere long cease to appear on the hill.

Later on, passing through the town alone, when the people had gone to rest, I saw many of them lying on the pavement under the arches fast asleep. A brilliant moon illuminated the market-place ; there was a pleasant sound of falling water from the fountain ; the lake was bathed in splendour, save where it took the reflection of the mountains—so peaceful and quiet was the night that there was hardly a rustle in the leaves of the aspens. But whether in moonlight or in shadow, the busy persistent vibrations that rise in Anglo-Saxon brains were radiating from every wall, and the man in the black felt hat and the bland lady with the sewing machine were there— lying in wait, as a cat over a mouse's hole, to insinuate themselves into the hearts of the people so soon as they should wake.

Great numbers came to the festivities. There were special trains from Biasca and all intermediate stations, and special boats. And the ugly flat-nosed people came from the Val Verzasca, and the beautiful people came from the Val Onsernone and the Val Maggia, and I saw Anna, the curate's housekeeper, from Mesocco, and the old fresco painter who told me he should like to pay me a visit, and suggested five o'clock in the morning as the most appropriate and convenient time. The great procession contained seven or eight hundred people. From the balcony of the Hotel della Corona I counted as well as I could and obtained the following result :—

Women	120
Men with white shirts and red capes . . .	85
Men with white shirts and no capes . . .	(?)
The music from Intra	30
Men with white shirts and blue capes . .	25

Men with white shirts and no capes . . .	25
Men with white shirts and green capes . .	12
Men with white shirts and no capes . . .	36
The music of Locarno	30
Girls in blue, pink, white and yellow, red, white	50
Choristers	3
Monks	6
Priests	66
Canons	12
His Excellency Paolo Angelo Ballerini, Patriarch of Alexandria in Egypt, escorted by the firemen, and his private cortège of about 20 .	25
Government ushers	(?)
The Grand Council, escorted by 22 soldiers and 6 policemen	28
The clergy without orders	30
	583

In the evening, there, sure enough, the apparition of the Blessed Virgin was. The church of the Madonna was unilluminated and all in darkness, when on a sudden it sprang out into a blaze, and a great transparency of the Virgin and child was lit up from behind. Then the people said, " Oh bel ! "

I was myself a little disappointed. It was not a good apparition, and I think the effect would have been better if it had been carried up by a small balloon into the sky. It might easily have been arranged so that the light behind the transparency should die out before the apparition must fall again, and also that the light inside the transparency should not be reflected upon the balloon that lifted it ; the whole, therefore, would appear to rise from its own inherent buoyancy. I am confident it would have been arranged in this way if the thing had been in the hands of the Crystal Palace people.

There is a fine old basilicate church dedicated to S.

Vittore at the north end of Locarno. It is the mother church of these parts and dates from the eighth or ninth century. The frescoes inside the apse were once fine, but have been repainted and spoiled. The tower is much later, but is impressive. It was begun in 1524 and left incomplete in 1527, probably owing to the high price of provisions which is commemorated in the following words written on a stone at the top of the tower inside :—

1527

Furm. [fromento—corn] cost lib. 6.
Segale [barley]   lib. 5.
Milio   [millet]   lib 4.

I suppose these were something like famine prices ; at any rate, a workman wrote this upon the tower and the tower stopped.

Chapter XXV

Fusio

WE left Locarno by the conveyance which leaves every day at four o'clock for Bignasco, a ride of about four hours. The Ponte Brolla, a couple of miles out of Locarno, is remarkable, and the road is throughout (as a matter of course) good. I sat next an old priest, an excellent kindly man, who talked freely with me, and scolded me roundly for being a Protestant more than once.

He seemed much surprised when I discarded reason as the foundation of our belief. He had made up his mind that all Protestants based their convictions upon reason, and was not prepared to hear me go heartily with him in declaring the foundation of any durable system to lie in faith. When, however, it came to requiring me to have faith in what seemed good to him and his friends, rather than to me and mine, we did not agree so well. He then began to shake death at me ; I met him with a reflection that I have never seen in print, though it is so obvious that it must have occurred to each one of my readers. I said that every man is an immortal to himself : he only dies as far as others are concerned ; to himself he cannot, by any conceivable possibility, do so. For how can he know that he is dead until he *is* dead ? And when he *is* dead, how can he know that he is dead? If he does, it is an abuse of terms to say that he is dead. A man can know no more about the end of his life than he did about the beginning. The most horrible and loathed death still resolves itself into being badly frightened, and not a little hurt towards the end of one's life, but it can never come to being unbearably hurt for long together. Besides, we are at all times, even during life, dead and dying to by far the greater part of our past selves. What we call dying is only dying to the balance, or residuum. This made the priest angry. He folded his arms and said, " Basta, basta," nor did he speak to me again. It is because I noticed the effect it produced upon my fellow-passenger that I introduce it here.

Bignasco is at the confluence of the two main branches of the Maggia. The greater part of the river comes down from the glacier of Basodino, which cannot be seen from Bignasco; I know nothing of this valley beyond having seen the glacier from the top of the pass between Fusio and Dalpe. The smaller half of the river comes down from Fusio, the valley of Sambucco, and the lake of Naret. The accommodation at Bignasco is quite enough for a bachelor; the people are good, but the inn is homely. From Bignasco the road ascends rapidly to Peccia, a village which has suffered terribly from inundations, and from Peccia it ascends more rapidly still—Fusio being reached in about three hours from Bignasco. There is an excellent inn at Fusio kept by Signor Dazio, to whose energy the admirable mountain road from Peccia is mainly due. On the right just before he crosses the bridge, the traveller will note the fresco of the Crucifixion, which I have mentioned at page 140.

Fusio is over 4200 feet above the level of the sea. I

do not know wherein its peculiar charm lies, but it is the best of all the villages of a kindred character that I know. Below is a sketch of it as it appears from the cemetery.

There is another good view from behind the village; at sunset this second view becomes remarkably fine.

FUSIO FROM THE CEMETERY

The houses are in deep cool shadow, but the mountains behind take the evening sun, and are sometimes of an incredible splendour. It is fine to watch the shadows creeping up them, and the colour that remains growing richer and richer until the whole is extinguished; this view, however, I am unable to give.

I hold Signor Dazio of Fusio so much as one of my most particular and valued friends, and I have such a special affection for Fusio itself, that the reader must bear in mind that he is reading an account given by a partial witness.   Nevertheless, all private preferences

STREET VIEW IN FUSIO

apart, I think he will find Fusio a hard place to beat. At the end of June and in July the flowers are at their best, and they are more varied and beautiful than any-where else I know.   At the very end of July and the

beginning of August the people cut their hay, and then
for a while the glory of the place is gone, but by the end
of August or the beginning of September the grass has
grown long enough to re-cover the slopes with a velvety
verdure, and though the flowers are shorn, yet so they
are from other places also.

There are many walks in the neighbourhood for those
who do not mind mountain paths. The most beautiful
of them all is to the valley of Sambucco, the upper end
of which is not more than half-an-hour from Signor
Dazio's hotel. For some time one keeps to the path
through the wooded gorge, and with the river foaming
far below ; in early morning while this path is in shade,
or, again, after sunset, it is one of the most beautiful of
its kind that I know. After a while a gate is reached, and
an open upland valley is entered upon—evidently an old
lake filled up, and neither very broad nor very long, but
grassed all over, and with the river winding through it
like an English brook. This is the valley of Sambucco.
There are two collections of *stalle* for the cattle, or *monti*
—one at the nearer end and the other at the farther.

The floor of the valley can hardly be less than 5000
feet above the sea. I shall never forget the pleasure
with which I first came upon it. I had long wanted
an ideal upland valley ; as a general rule high valleys
are too narrow, and have little or no level ground. If
they have any at all there often is too much as with the
one where Andermatt and Hospenthal are—which would
in some respects do very well—and too much cultivated,
and do not show their height. An upland valley should
first of all be in an Italian-speaking country ; then it
should have a smooth, grassy, perfectly level floor of
say neither much more nor less than a hundred and fifty
yards in breadth and half-a-mile in length. A small river

should go babbling through it with occasional smooth
parts, so as to take the reflections of the surrounding
mountains. It should have three or four fine larches or
pines scattered about it here and there, but not more.
It should be completely land-locked, and there should
be nothing in the way of human handiwork save a few
chalets, or a small chapel and a bridge, but no tilled land
whatever. Here even in summer the evening air will be
crisp, and the dew will form as soon as the sun goes off ;
but the mountains at one end of it will keep the last rays
of the sun. It is then the valley is at its best, especially
if the goats and cattle are coming together to be milked.

The valley of Sambucco has all this and a great deal
more, to say nothing of the fact that there are excellent
trout in it. I have shown it to friends at different times,
and they have all agreed with me that for a valley neither
too high nor too low, nor too big nor too little, the valley
of Sambucco is one of the best that any of us know of—
I mean to look at and enjoy, for I suppose as regards
painting it is hopeless. I think it can be well rendered by
the following piece of music as by anything else* :—

* Handel's third set of organ Concertos, No. 3.

One day Signor Dazio brought us in a chamois foot. He explained to us that chamois were now in season, but that even when they were not, they were sometimes to be had, inasmuch as they occasionally fell from the rocks and got killed. As we looked at it we could not help reflecting that, wonderful as the provisions of animal and vegetable organisms often are, the marvels of adaptation are sometimes almost exceeded by the feats which an animal will perform with a very simple and even clumsy instrument if it knows how to use it. A chamois foot is a smooth and slippery thing, such as no respectable bootmaker would dream of offering to a mountaineer : there is not a nail in it, nor even an apology for a nail ; the surefootedness of its owner is an assumption only— a piece of faith or impudence which fulfils itself. If some other animal were to induce the chamois to believe that it should at the least have feet with suckers to them, like a fly, before venturing in such breakneck places, or if by any means it could get to know how bad a foot it really has, there would soon be no more chamois. The chamois continues to exist through its absolute refusal to hear reason upon the matter. But the whole question is one of extreme intricacy ; all we know is that some animals and plants, like some men, devote great pains to the perfection of the mechanism with which they wish to work, while others rather scorn appliances, and concentrate their attention upon the skilful use of whatever they happen to have. I think, however, that in the clumsiness of the chamois foot must lie the explanation of the fact that sometimes when chamois are out of season, they do nevertheless actually tumble off the rocks and get killed ; being killed, of course it is only natural that they should sometimes be found, and if found, be eaten ; but they are not good for much.

After a day or two's stay in this delightful place, we left at six o'clock one brilliant morning in September for Dalpe and Faido, accompanied by the excellent Signor Guglielmoni as guide. There are two main passes from Fusio into the Val Leventina—the one by the Sassello Grande to Nante and Airolo, and the other by the Alpe di Campolungo to Dalpe. Neither should be attempted by strangers without a guide, though neither of them presents the smallest difficulty. There is a third and

longer pass by the Lago di Naret to Bedretto, but I
have never been over this. The other two are both good ;
on the whole, however, I think I prefer the second.
Signor Guglielmoni led us over the freshest grassy slopes
conceivable—slopes that four or five weeks earlier had
been gay with tiger and Turk's-cap lilies, and the
flaunting arnica, and every flower that likes mountain
company. After a three hours' walk we reached the
top of the pass, from whence on the one hand one can
see the Basodino glacier, and on the other the great
Rheinwald glaciers above Olivone. Other small glaciers
show in valleys near Biasca which I know nothing about,
and which I imagine to be almost a *terra incognita*, except
to the inhabitants of such villages as Malvaglia in the
Val Blenio.

When near the top of the pass we heard the whistle
of a marmot. Guglielmoni told us he had a tame one
once which was very fond of him. It slept all the winter,
but turned round once a fortnight to avoid lying too
long upon one side. When it woke up from its winter
sleep it no longer recognised him, but bit him savagely
right through the finger ; by and by its recollection returned to it, and it apologised.

From the summit, which is about 7600 feet above the
sea, the path descends over the roughest ground that
is to be found on the whole route. Here there are good
specimens of asbestos to be picked up abundantly, and
the rocks are full of garnets ; after about six or seven
hundred feet the Alpe di Campolungo is reached, and this
again is an especially favourite place with me. It is an
old lake filled up, surrounded by peaks and precipices
where some snow rests all the year round, and traversed
by a stream. Here, just as we had done lunching, we
were joined by a family of knife-grinders, who were also

crossing from the Val Maggia to the Val Leventina. We
had eaten all we had with us except our bread; this
Guglielmoni gave to one of the boys, who seemed as much
pleased with it as if it had been cake. Then after taking
a look at the Lago di Tremorgio, a beautiful lake some
hundreds of feet below, we went on to the Alpe di Cadoni-
ghino where our guide left us.

At this point pines begin, and soon the path enters
them; after a while we catch sight of Prato, and eventu-
ally come down upon Dalpe. In another hour and a
quarter Faido is reached. The descent to Faido from
the summit of the pass is much greater than the ascent
from Fusio, for Faido is not more than 2300 feet above
the sea, whereas, as I have said, Fusio is over 4200 feet.
The descent from the top of the pass to Faido is about
5300 feet, while to Fusio it is only 3400. The reader,
therefore, will see that he had better go from Fusio to
Faido, and not *vice versa*, unless he is a good walker.

Chapter XXVI

Fusio Revisited

THIS last year Jones and I sent for Guglielmoni to take us over the Sassello Grande from Airolo to Fusio. Soon after starting we were joined by a peasant woman and her daughter who were returning to their home at Mugno in the Val Maggia some twenty minutes' walk below Fusio. They had come the day before over the Sassello Pass through Fusio carrying two hundred eggs and several fowls to Airolo. They had had to climb a full four thousand feet ; the path is rugged in the extreme ; neither of them had any shoes or stockings ; the weather was very wet ; the clouds hung low ; the wind on the Colma blew so hard that, though the rain was coming down in torrents, it was impossible to hold up an umbrella, and they did not know the little road there is. Happily, before they got above the Valle di Sambucco they had fallen in with Guglielmoni, on his way to meet us ; otherwise one does not see how they could have got over. As it was, they did not break a single egg, but they were a good deal scared and asked us to let them go back in our company. We found them delightful people ; the girl was very pretty and the mother still comely, with a singularly pleasing expression. We found out what they had done with their eggs and fowls. They sold the eggs for nine centimes apiece, whereas at Fusio they would have got but five. The fowls fetched three francs apiece as against two they would have got at Fusio. Altogether they had made the best part of twenty francs by their journey, over and above what they would have made if they had stayed at home, and thought they had done good business.

The weather was perfect for the return journey. After passing Nante we noticed by the side of the path several round burnt patches some four feet in diameter which struck us as rather strange, so we asked Guglielmoni about them. He said there had been ants' nests there, and the people burnt them because the ants did so much damage. He showed us one that was in process of reconstruction, the ants building upon the remains of their ruined home, and pointed out the deep channel which the ants had worn in the ground through their habit of entering and quitting their old-established nest by one main road. We had thought the channel was a rill artificially cut for irrigation, and it was not till Guglielmoni showed us how impossible this was that we came to see he was right. He showed us a disused road that had led to a nest now destroyed, and on two or three other occasions showed us roads leading from one nest to another.

He told us several more things about marmots which I may mention as opinions held by the Fusians, but upon which I should be sorry to base a theory. He said their fat was so subtle that it would go through glass and could not therefore be kept in a bottle. He said it would go through a man's hand. I said : "Let us try," but it appeared that it might take three or four hours in getting through, so we delayed the experiment for a more convenient season. I asked how the marmots held their own fat if it would go through skin. I was answered that at the end of summer, when the marmots are very fat, they no longer hold it and their fur is greasy. I could not contradict this from personal knowledge and was obliged to let it pass. He said marmots' fat was good for rheumatism and sprains, but that it must never be used for a broken bone, as the ends of the bone would not grow together again if the fat reached them. Badgers' fat, he said, was very good, but it was not so sovereign a remedy as marmots'. There are badgers about Fusio, though not so many as lower down the valley in the chestnut country. We saw some badgers' fat later on at Tesserete ; it was kept in a tin which was certainly very greasy, but we did not think that the fat had gone through the tin.

Then we met an old gentleman with a Rembrandt-Rabbi far-away look in his eyes. He wore a coarse but clean linen shirt, and was otherwise neat in his attire. He looked as if he had suffered much and had been chastened rather than soured by it. We talked a little and the conversation turned upon deceit. I said that deceit was a necessary alloy for truth which, without this hardening addition, like gold without an alloy of copper, would be unworkable.

" Chi non sa ingannare," I said in conclusion, " non sa parlare il vero."

The old gentleman seemed to like this, and so we parted. Guglielmoni told us he was a painter and liable to temporary fits of insanity. During these fits he would go up by himself into the mountains, like some old prophet going out into the wilderness, and stay there till the fit was over, living no one knew where or how.

Cheese is the principal product of these valleys. I asked Guglielmoni whether there was any sign of the upper pastures becoming impoverished by the annual removal of so much cheese. He said the soil about Fusio did not yield as much by a third as it had yielded when he was a boy, but I hardly think it likely that there is much difference. He did not see why taking away so many hundredweight, or rather tons, of cheese yearly should impoverish the land, for, he said, the cows manured it. He did not see that the cheeses should be taken into account. At one time he said that two hundred years hence the Alpe di Campo la Turba would not be worth feeding ; at another that the cows left what they ate behind them. Our own impression was that, what with insect and bird life and the fertilising power of snow and the frequent addition of new soil by avalanches, there was probably no harm done, and that the grass was there or thereabouts much what it always had been since people had first begun to feed it. I have myself known these *alpi* off and on ever since 1843, and can perceive no difference, except that the glaciers, especially at Grindelwald, have receded very considerably, and even this may be only fancy.

I asked Guglielmoni whether the *Alpigiani*—the people who spend the summer in the *alpi*—ever get pulmonary complaints. " Oh si," was his answer, and he nodded as though it were common, which I can well believe ; but it is more difficult to understand how the few robust *Alpigiani* escape. The majority seemed to us to be prematurely worn and to live in a state almost of squalor. What would a doctor say to the damp floor covered with mildew growing on spilt milk and fragments of half-made cheese ? What about men sleeping night after night in a room built in the middle of a dung-heap, with never a ray of sunshine save a little near the door and an occasional beam through crannies in the walls ? What *nidus* can be conceived more favourable for the development of organic germs ? How can any one escape who spends a summer in one of these huts ? I should say the worst and most insanitary cellar into which human beings are huddled in London is not more un-wholesome than these *alpi* in the middle of the finest air in Europe.

Guglielmoni had some edelweiss in his hat, and we asked him the Italian name for it. He replied that it had no other name. The passion for this flower has evidently spread from the north. The Italians are great at suppressing unnecessary details. I was going up once in the *posta* from Varallo to Fobello and had an American-ised Italian cook for my only fellow-traveller. I asked him the name of a bird I happened to see, and he said :

" Oh, he not got no name. There is two birds got names. There is the *gazza ;* he spik very nice. I have one ; he spik beautiful. And there is the *merlo ;* he sing very pretty. The other, they not got no names ; they not want no names ; every one call them what he choose."

And so it is with the flowers. There is the rose and perhaps half-a-dozen more plants, but as for the others " they not got no names ; they not want no names."

My fellow-traveller, speaking of the villagers in the villages we passed through, said :

" They all right as long as they stop here, but when they go away and travel, then they not never happy no more."

When we reached the floor of the Valle di Sambucco, the people were milking the few cattle that remained there, and the milk purred into the pails as with a deep hum of satisfaction. The sun was setting red upon the Piz Campo Tencia ; the water was as clear as the air, and the air in the deep shadow of the bottom of the valley had something of the deep blue as well as of the trans-

parency of the water. We passed the gorge in twilight
and presently were again at Fusio. We ordered some
wine for the women who had accompanied us, and as
they sat waiting for it with their hands folded before them
they looked so good and holy and quiet that one would
have thought they were returning from a pilgrimage.

I have nothing to retract from what I have said in
praise of Fusio. It is the most old-world subalpine
village that I know. It was probably burnt down some
time in the Middle Ages and perhaps the scare thus caused
led to its being rebuilt not in wood but in stone. The
houses are much built into one another as at S. Remo;
the roofs are all of them made of large stones; there are
a good many wooden balconies, but it is probably because
it has been chiefly built of stone that we now see it much
as it must have looked two or even three centuries ago.
If any one wants to know what kind of village the people
of three hundred years ago beheld, at Fusio he will find
an almost untouched specimen of what he wants. For
picturesqueness I know no subalpine village so good.
Sit down wherever one will there is a subject ready
made. The back of the village is perhaps more mediæval
in appearance than the front. Its quaint picturesqueness,
the beauty of its flowers, the brilliancy of its meadows,
and the genial presence of Signor Dazio prevent me from
allowing any great length of time to pass without a visit
to Fusio.

I said to Jones once: "It is worth while going to
Fusio if only to please Signor Dazio."

"Yes," said Jones, "and he is so very easily pleased."

It is just this that makes it so pleasant to try to please
him. I believe all the people in Fusio are good. I asked
Guglielmoni once what happened when any one did
something wrong. He seemed bewildered. The case

had not arisen within his recollection. I pressed him and said that it might arise even at Fusio, and what would happen then ? Had they a prison or a lock-up of any kind ? He said they had none, and he supposed the offender would have to be taken down the valley to Cevio, about fourteen or fifteen miles off—but the case had not arisen.

At Fusio, in spite of all its flowers, there are no bees ; the summer is too short and they would have to be fed too long. Nevertheless, we got the best honey at Fusio that we got anywhere. Signor Dazio said it was from his own hives at Locarno and had not been " elongated " in any way. What was bought at the shops, he said, was almost invariably " elongated " with flour, sugar and a variety of other things.

The hotel has been much improved during these last two years ; the kitchen has been taken downstairs and the old one thrown into the dining-room, which has been newly decorated after a happily-conceived and tastefully-executed scheme. The visitor is to suppose himself seated in a large open belvedere upon the roof of the house, over which a light iron trellis-work has been thrown and gracefully festooned with a profusion of brilliant flowers. In the sky, which is of unclouded blue, birds of lustrous plumage are engaged in carrying a wreath, presumably for the brow of one of the visitors. The lower part of the heavens is studded with commodious hat pegs, two or three doors, the windows, and a substantial fire-place. The gorgeous parrot of the establishment has chosen the point where the sky unites with the right-hand corner of the chimney-piece as the most convenient spot to perch on, and his presence there gives life and nature to the scene. We were struck with the wise reticence of the painter in not putting another parrot at the opposite corner ; there is a verisimilitude about one bird which would have been lost with two, for few houses have more than one parrot. The effect of the whole is singularly gay and pleasing. For an English household I admit that there is nothing to compare with Mr. Morris's wall-papers—except, of course, his poetry—but there is an over-the-garden-walliness, if the expression may be pardoned, about these Italian decorations, a frank meretriciousness, both of design and colour, which will be found infinitely refreshing and may be looked for in vain in the works of our English masters of decoration.

The day after our arrival was the feast of the Assumption of the Madonna, and the next day was the feast of S. Rocco, the patron saint of Fusio, so the bells were ringing continually. There are only three bells, but they are good ones ; they were brought up from Peccia some forty years ago, long before Signor Dazio had the present road made ; he was then a boy and assisted at the very arduous task of bringing them up. Like bells generally in North Italy they hang half-way out of the windows of the *campanile*, instead of being wholly within the belfry as our English bells are. This is why an Italian *campanile* is such a much more slender object than an English belfry ; it has less to cover. When the bells are rung by being raised and swung in and out of the window, there is one ringer to each bell, and the following is all that is attempted :

This, however, is varied with another and very different effect to which I have alluded in Chapter XXIII, but of which I can now speak at greater length inasmuch as we went up among the bells and saw how it was done.

The ringer has a light cord for each bell ; he fastens one end of the cord by an iron hook to a hole in the clapper and the other to a beam of the belfry. The cords are just long enough to hold the clapper an inch or so off the side of the bell, the weight of the clapper keeping the cord tight. The ringer has thus three tight cords before him, on which he plays by hitting the middle of which-ever one he wants with his hand ; this depresses it and brings the clapper suddenly against the bell. He sits so that he can easily reach all the strings, and sets to work playing on the cords as though on a clumsy three-stringed harp. He plays out of his head without any music, and it is wonderful what variety he makes this rude instrument produce and how responsive it is to moods requiring different shades of expression. Of course, when the player's resources are enlarged by the addition of two more bells, as at Castelletto and Vogogna, he can produce an infinitely more varied effect.

The notes, according to the pitch of Signor Dazio's piano, were G, A, and B, and when we watched the ringer we saw that he frequently played the B with the G ; some-times he struck the B with the A, no doubt intending it as an *appoggiatura*, and, at a distance, this was the effect produced. But when he struck the two notes together and made the B louder than the A it had the effect of varying the tune. He never played his tunes in precisely the same way twice running, and this makes it difficult to say with certainty what they were, but, omitting variations, the two favourite tunes went like this :

This last he treated almost like a patter song, making it go as fast as ever he could. Give the Italian three bells, a belfry, and some bits of string and he will play with them and with you by the hour together with infinite variety. Give the German five bells and he will know a single figure, which he will probably have got an Italian to make for him, and will repeat it till you have to close the windows to keep the sound out, and the bottom bell will make a noise like the smell of a crushed cockroach. This is what happened to us in the valley of Gressoney at Issime, where German influences and the German language prevail.

It was at Issime, by the by, that we saw the most beautiful woman that either of us ever saw. She was gathering French beans in the little garden in front of the hotel and had her apron full of leeks and celery. No words can give an idea of the dignity and grace with which she moved, and as for her head, it was what Leonardo da Vinci, Gaudenzio Ferrari, and Bernardino Luini all tried to get without ever getting it. As long as she was in sight it was impossible to look at anything else, and at the same time there was a something about her which forbade staring.

S. Rocco is the saint who is always pointing to the dreadful wound in his poor leg ; accordingly he is invoked by people who are out of health and thanked by those who have recovered. Near the first *stalle* in one of the neighbouring valleys there is a chapel where we saw three women praying. It had been prettily decorated with edelweiss, mountain-elder berries, thistle flowers, and everything gay that could be got. There was nothing of interest inside it, except a votive picture of a little man in a tailed coat who had got a bad leg like S. Rocco and was expostulating about it to the Virgin Mary. I

have seldom seen any even tolerably serious frescoes in
any of these small wayside oratories ; they are usually
done by some local man who has cultivated the Madonna
touch, as it may be called, much as some English amateurs
cultivate the tree touch, and with about as happy a
result. The three women had crossed by the Sassello
Grande from Nante, starting with earliest daybreak.
It seems that one of them had for a time been deprived
of her reason, but her sister had prayed at this chapel that
it might be restored and her prayer had been granted ;
so the two sisters and another woman come over every
year as near the feast of S. Rocco as they can, and repeat
their thanks at this spot.

The feast of S. Rocco is kept at Fusio with considerable
solemnity. Jones happened to be outside the church and
kissed a relic of the saint which was handed round after
service. I was sorry not to have been there at the
moment, but I joined in the procession and helped to
carry S. Rocco out of the church and down the valley
to Peccia. There a table covered with a handsome
cloth had been placed in the middle of the road, and on
this the bearers rested the silvered statue. The officiating
priest approached it, said some appropriate words before
it, I believe in Latin, at any rate I could not catch them,
and then we all turned home again. When the procession
doubled round we could see the faces of the people as
they met us in pairs. First came the women, one of them
bearing a crucifix turned so that the people following
might see the figure on the cross. Then came the men
in white shirts, some carrying candles, among whom we
saw Guglielmoni, and some bearing the image of the saint.
Then came the men of the place in their ordinary dress,
and we followed last of all. The older women wore the
Fusio costume, which is now fast disappearing ; many

of them wore white linen drapery over their heads, but
we did not understand why some did and some did not.
Immediately before the statue of S. Rocco came two nuns
from Italy who were seeking alms for some purpose in
connection with the Church.

We thought the people did not as a general rule look
in robust health ; some few, both men and women, seemed
to have little or nothing the matter with them, but most
of them looked as though they were suffering from the
unwholesome conditions under which they live, for the
conditions in the villages are not much healthier than in
the *alpi*. The houses in such a village as Fusio are few
of them even tolerably wholesome. Signor Dazio's houses
are all that can be wished for in this respect, but in
too many of the others the rooms are low, without
sufficient sunlight, and too many of them are far from
inodorous.

We see a place like Fusio in summer, but what must
it be after, say, the middle of October ? How chill and
damp, with reeking clouds that search into every corner.
What, again, must it be a little later, when snow has
fallen that lies till the middle of May ? The men go
about all day in great boots, working in the snow at
whatever they can find to do ; they come in at night
tired and with their legs and feet half frozen. The
main room of the house may have a *stufa* in it, but how
about the bedrooms ? With single windows and the
thermometer outside down to zero, if the room is warm
enough to thaw and keep things damp it is as much as
can be expected. Fancy an elderly man after a day's
work in snow climbing up, like David, step by step to a
bed in such a room as this. How chill it must strike him
as he goes into it, and how cold must be the bed itself
till he has been in it an hour or two. We asked Guglielmoni

how he warmed his house in winter and what he did about his bedroom. He said he put his wife and children into the warm room and slept himself in one that on inquiry proved to have only single windows and no stove. It then turned out that he had been at death's door this last spring and the one before, and that the doctors at Locarno said he had serious chest mischief. The wonder is that he is alive at all. I advised him to get a half-crown petroleum burner and, if he felt he had caught cold, to keep it in his room burning all night. He asked how much it would cost and, when told from twenty to twenty-five centimes a night, said this was prohibitive, and I have no doubt to him with his wife and family it was.

One cause of the mischief doubtless lies in the fact that the high-altitude houses have descended with insufficient modification from ancestors adapted to a warmer climate. Their forefathers were built for the plains. These houses should have been begotten of Russian or Canadian dwellings, not of Piedmontese or Lombard. At any rate, if a reform is to be initiated it should begin by a study of the Canadian or Russian house.

But it is not only the hard, long cold winters, with rough living of every kind, that weigh the people down ; the monotony of the snow, seven months upon the ground, is enough to bow even the strongest spirit. It is not as if one could get the " Times " every morning at break-fast and theatres, concerts, exhibitions of pictures, social gatherings of every kind. Day after day not a blade of grass can be seen, not a little bit of green any-where, save the mockery of the pine-trees. I once spent a remarkably severe winter at Montreal and saw the thermometer for a month at 22° below zero in the main street of the city. True, it was warm enough indoors, and grass does not usually grow in houses, so that one ought not to have missed it ; nevertheless one did miss it, as one misses a dead friend whom one may have been seeing but seldom. There is a depressing effect about long cold and snow which one feels whether one is cold or not. I suspect it is the monotony of the snow-surface that is so fatiguing. I used to trudge up to the far end of Montreal Mountain every day because there was a space of a few yards there on which the snow positively would not lie by reason of the wind. Here I could see a few roots of brown dried grass and moss with a tinge of yellow in it, having looked at which for a little while I would return comparatively contented. If the monotony of surface was found so depressing even in a city like Montreal, where so many interests and amusements were open, what must it be in a place like Fusio, where there are none ?

The two great foes of life are the two extremes of change. Too much, that is to say too sudden change and too little change are alike fatal. That is why there is so little organic life a few feet below the surface of the earth. It gets too slow altogether and things won't stand it. Cut away for months together the incessant changes involved in the changed vibrations consequent upon looking at a surface whose colour is varied, and a monotony is induced which should be relieved by the entry of as much other change as possible to supply the place of what is lost.

What a vineyard for the Church is there not in these subalpine valleys, if she would only work in it ! The beauty and sweetness of the children show what the people are by nature and prove that the raw material is splendid. Their flowers are not gayer and lovelier than their children ; but they do not get a fair chance.

If the Church would only use her means and leisure to teach people how to make themselves as healthy and happy in this life as their case admits ! If she would do this with a single eye to facts and to the happiness of the people, cutting caste, dogma, prescription, and self-aggrandisement direct or indirect, what a hold would she not soon have upon a grateful people. Nay, if the priests would only set the example of washing, of keeping their houses clean and their bedrooms warm and light and dry, and of being at some pains with their cookery, their example would be enough without their preaching. I grant honourable exceptions, but the upland clergy are as a rule little above their flocks in regard to cleanliness of house and person ; instead of facing the many problems that surround them, they rather, I am afraid, have every desire to avoid them. They do not want their people to learn continually better and better in health and wealth how to live ; they want things to go on indefinitely as hitherto, only they hold that the people should be even more docile and obedient than they are. I may be wrong, but this is certainly the impression that remains with me.

The priest himself must have a hard time of it in winter. We see the church steps basking in the morning sun of August. It is an easy matter then to dawdle into church and sit quiet for a while amid a droning old-world smell of cheese, ancestor, dry-rot, *Alpigiano*, and stale incense, and to read the plaintive epitaphing about the dear, good people " whose souls we pray thee visit with the everlasting peace that waits on saints and angels."

As the clouds come and go the gray-green cobweb-chastened light ebbs and flows over the ceiling. If a hen has laid an egg outside and has begun to cackle, it is an event of magnitude. A peasant hammering his scythe, the clack of a wooden shoe upon the pavement, the dripping of the fountain, all these things, with such concert as they keep, invite the dewy-feathered sleep till the old woman comes and rings the bell for *mezzo giorno*.

This is the sunny side of subalpine church-going, but how is it when these steps are hidden under a metre of frozen snow? How about five o'clock on a Christmas morning, when the priest can hardly get down the steps leading from his house into the church from the fury of the wind and the driving of the fine midge-like snow? Even when the horrors of the middle passage have been overcome and the church has been reached, surely it is a nice, cosy place for an infirm old gentleman or lady with bronchitic tendencies! How is it conceivable that any one should keep even decently well who has to go to church in a high subalpine village at five, six, seven, eight, or in fact at any hour before about noon upon a winter morning? And yet they go, and some of them reach good old ages. Still one would think that, if a little pains were taken, the thing might be managed so that more of them could reach better old ages. As for the priest, he will carry the last sacraments of the Church any distance, in any weather, at any hour of the night, in summer or winter, but he must have an awful time of it every now and then. So, for the matter of that, has an English country parson or doctor. Still, the Alpine roads are rougher and the snow deeper, and the pay, poor as it often is in England, is here still poorer.

After a few days at Fusio, Guglielmoni took us over to Faido in the Val Leventina by the pass that we had not yet crossed—the one that goes by the Lago di Naret and Bedretto. From Faido we returned home. We looked at nothing between the top of the St. Gothard Pass and Boulogne, nor did we again begin to take any interest in life till we saw the science-ridden, art-ridden, culture-ridden, afternoon-tea-ridden cliffs of old England rise upon the horizon.

Appendix A

Wednesbury Cocking

(See p. 55)

I KNOW nothing of the date of this remarkable ballad, or the source from which it comes. I have heard one who should know say, that when he was a boy at Shrewsbury school it was done into Greek hexameters, the lines (with a various reading in them) :

" The colliers and nailers left work,
   And all to old Scroggins' went jogging ; "

being translated :

"Ἔργον χαλκότυποι καὶ τέκτονες ἄνδρες ἔλειπον
Σκρωγινιοῦ μεγάλου ζητοῦντες εὐκτίμενον δῶ.

I have been at some pains to find out more about this translation, but have failed to do so. The ballad itself is as follows :

At Wednesbury there was a cocking,
   A match between Newton and Scroggins ;
The colliers and nailers left work,
   And all to old Spittle's went jogging.
To see this noble sport,
   Many noblemen resorted ;
And though they'd but little money,
   Yet that little they freely sported.

There was Jeffery and Colborn from Hampton,
   And Dusty from Bilston was there ;
Flummery he came from Darlaston,
   And he was as rude as a bear.
There was old Will from Walsall,
   And Smacker from Westbromwich come ;
Blind Robin he came from Rowley,
   And staggering he went home.

Ralph Moody came hobbling along,
   As though he some cripple was mocking,
To join in the blackguard throng,
   That met at Wednesbury cocking.
He borrowed a trifle of Doll,
   To back old Taverner's grey ;
He laid fourpence-halfpenny to fourpence,
   He lost and went broken away.

But soon he returned to the pit,
   For he'd borrowed a trifle more money,
And ventured another large bet,
   Along with blobbermouth Coney.
When Coney demanded his money,
   As is usual on all such occasions,
He cried, —— thee, if thee don't hold thy rattle,
   I'll pay thee as Paul paid the Ephasians.

The morning's sport being over,
   Old Spittle a dinner proclaimed,
Each man he should dine for a groat,
   If he grumbled he ought to be ——,
For there was plenty of beef,
   But Spittle he swore by his troth,
That never a man should dine
   Till he ate his noggin of broth.

The beef it was old and tough,
   Off a bull that was baited to death,
Barney Hyde got a lump in his throat,
   That had like to have stopped his breath,
The company all fell into confusion,
   At seeing poor Barney Hyde choke;
So they took him into the kitchen,
   And held him over the smoke.

They held him so close to the fire,
   He frizzled just like a beef-steak,
They then threw him down on the floor,
   Which had like to have broken his neck.
One gave him a kick on the stomach,
   Another a kick on the brow,
His wife said, Throw him into the stable,
   And he'll be better just now.

Then they all returned to the pit,
   And the fighting went forward again;
Six battles were fought on each side,
   And the next was to decide the main.
For they were two famous cocks
   As ever this country bred,
Scroggins's a dark-winged black,
   And Newton's a shift-winged red.

The conflict was hard on both sides,
   Till Brassy's black-winged was choked;
The colliers were tarnationly vexed,
   And the nailers were sorely provoked.
Peter Stevens he swore a great oath,
   That Scroggins had played his cock foul;
Scroggins gave him a kick on the head,
   And cried, Yea, —— —— thy soul.

The company then fell in discord,
   A bold, bold fight did ensue ;
——, ——, and bite was the word,
   Till the Walsall men all were subdued.
Ralph Moody bit off a man's nose,
   And wished that he could have him slain,
So they trampled both cocks to death,
   And they made a draw of the main.

The cock-pit was near to the church,
   An ornament unto the town ;
On one side an old coal pit,
   The other well gorsed around.
Peter Hadley peeped through the gorse,
   In order to see them fight ;
Spittle jobbed out his eye with a fork,
   And said, —— thee, it served thee right.

Some people may think this strange,
   Who Wednesbury never knew ;
But those who have ever been there,
   Will not have the least doubt it's true ;
For they are as savage by nature,
   And guilty of deeds the most shocking ;
Jack Baker whacked his own father,
   And thus ended Wednesbury cocking.

Appendix B

Reforms Instituted at S. Michele in the year 1478

(See p. 105)

THE palmiest days of the sanctuary were during the time that Rodolfo di Montebello or Mombello was abbot—that is to say, roughly, between the years 1325–60. " His rectorate," says Claretta, " was the golden age of the Abbey of La Chiusa, which reaped the glory acquired by its head in the difficult negotiations entrusted to him by his princes. But after his death, either lot or intrigue caused the election to fall upon those who prepared the ruin of one of the most ancient and illustrious monasteries in Piedmont."*

By the last quarter of the fifteenth century things got so bad that a commission of inquiry was held under one Giovanni di Varax in the year 1478. The following extracts from the ordinances then made may not be unwelcome to the reader. The document from which they are taken is to be found, pp. 322–336 of Claretta's work. The text is evidently in many places corrupt or misprinted, and there are several words which I have looked for in vain in all the dictionaries—Latin, Italian, and French—in the reading-room of the British Museum

* " Storia diplomatica dell' antica abbazia di S. Michele della Chiusa," by Gaudenzio Claretta. Turin, Civelli & Co. 1870. P. 116.

which seemed in the least likely to contain them. I
should say that for this translation, I have availed myself,
in part, of the assistance of a well-known mediæval
scholar, the Rev. Ponsonby A. Lyons, but he is in no way
responsible for the translation as a whole.

After a preamble, stating the names of the commissioners, with the objects of the commission and the
circumstances under which it had been called together,
the following orders were unanimously agreed upon, to
wit :—

" Firstly, That repairs urgently required to prevent
the building from falling into a ruinous state (as shown
by the ocular testimony of the commissioners, assisted
by competent advisers whom they instructed to survey
the fabric), be paid for by a true tithe, to be rendered
by all priors, provosts, and agents directly subject to
the monastery. This tithe is to be placed in the hands
of two merchants to be chosen by the bishop commendatory, and a sum is to be taken from it for the restora-
tion of the fountain which played formerly in the monastery. The proctors who collect the tithes are to be
instructed by the abbot and commendatory not to press
harshly upon the contributories by way of expense and
labour ; and the money when collected is, as already
said, to be placed in the hands of two suitable merchants,
clients of the said monastery, who shall hold it on trust
to pay it for the above-named purposes, as the reverends
the commendatory and chamberlain and treasurer of
the said monastery shall direct. In the absence of one
of these three the order of the other two shall be sufficient.

" Item, it is ordered that the *mandés*,* or customary

---

* " Item, ordinaverunt quod fiant mandata seu ellemosinæ con-
suetæ quæ sint valloris quatuor prebendarum religiosorum omni die ut
moris est." (Claretta, Storia diplomatica, p. 325.) The *mandatum*

alms, be made daily to the value of what would suffice
for the support of four monks.

"Item, that the offices in the gift of the monastery
be conferred by the said reverend the lord commendatory, and that those which have been hitherto at the
personal disposition of the abbot be reserved for the
pleasure of the Apostolic See. Item, that no one do
beg a benefice without reasonable cause and consonancy
of justice. Item, that those who have had books, privileges, or other documents belonging to the monastery
do restore them to the treasury within three months
from the publication of these presents, under pain of
excommunication. Item, that no one henceforth take
privileges or other documents from the monastery without
a deposit of caution money, or taking oath to return the
same within three months, under like pain of excommunication. Item, that no laymen do enter the treasury
of the monastery without the consent of the prior of
cloister,* nor without the presence of those who hold
the keys of the treasury, or of three monks, and that
those who hold the keys do not deliver them to laymen.
Item, it is ordered that the places subject to the said
monastery be visited every five years by persons in holy
orders, and by seculars ; and that, in like manner, every
five years a general chapter be held, but this period may be
extended or shortened for reasonable cause ; and the

generally refers to " the washing of one another's feet," according to
the mandate of Christ during the last supper. In the Benedictine
order, however, with which we are now concerned, alms, in lieu of the
actual washing of feet, are alone intended by the word.

* The prior-claustralis, as distinguished from the prior-major, was
the working head of a monastery, and was supposed never, or hardly
ever, to leave the precincts. He was the vicar-major of the prior-
major. The prior-major was vice-abbot when the abbot was absent,
but he could not exercise the full functions of an abbot. The abbot,
prior-major, and prior-claustralis may be compared loosely to the
master, vice-master, and senior tutor of a large college.

proctors-general are to be bound in each chapter to bring
their procurations, and at some chapter each monk is to
bring the account of the fines and all other rights appertain-
ing to his benefice, drawn up by a notary in public form,
and undersigned by him, that they may be kept in the
treasury, and this under pain of suspension. Item, that
henceforth neither the office of prior nor any other benefice
be conferred upon laymen. The lord abbot is in future to
be charged with the expense of all new buildings that are
erected within the precincts of the monastery. He is
also to give four pittances or suppers to the convent during
infirmary time, and six pints of wine according to the
custom.* Furthermore, he is to keep beds in the monastery for the use of guests, and other monks shall return
these beds to the chamberlain on the departure of the
guests, and it shall be the chamberlain's business to attend
to this matter. Item, delinquent monks are to be punished
within the monastery and not without it. Item, the
monks shall not presume to give an order for more than
two days' board at the expense of the monastery, in the
inns at S. Ambrogio, during each week, and they shall
not give orders for fifteen days unless they have relations
on a journey staying with them, or nobles, or persons

* " Item, quod dominus abbas teneatur dare quatuor pitancias seu
cenas conventui tempore infirmariæ, et quatuor sextaria vini ut con-
suetum est " (Claretta, Storia diplomatica, p. 326). The " infirmariæ
generales " were stated times during which the monks were to let
blood—" Stata nimirum tempora quibus sanguis monachis minuebatur,
seu vena secabatur." (Ducange.) There were five " minutiones
generales " in each year—namely, in September, Advent, before Lent,
after Easter, and after Pentecost. The letting of blood was to last
three days ; after the third day the patients were to return to matins
again, and on the fourth they were to receive absolution. Bleeding
was strictly forbidden at any other than these stated times, unless for
grave illness. During the time of blood-letting the monks stayed in
the infirmary, and were provided with supper by the abbot. During
the actual operation the brethren sat all together after orderly fashion
in a single room, amid silence and singing of psalms.

above suspicion, and the same be understood as applying to officials and cloistered persons.*

" Item, within twelve months from date the monks are to be at the expense of building an almshouse in S. Ambrogio, where one or two of the oldest and most respected among them are to reside, and have their portions there, and receive those who are in religion. Item, no monk is to wear his hair longer than two fingers broad.† Item, no hounds are to be kept in the monastery for hunting, nor any dogs save watch-dogs. Persons in religion who come to the monastery are to be entertained there for two days, during which time the cellarer is to give them bread and wine, and the pittancer‡ pittance.

" Item, women of bad character, and indeed all women, are forbidden the monk's apartments without the prior's license, except in times of indulgence, or such as are noble or above suspicion. Not even are the women

---

* " Item, quod religiosi non audeant in Sancto Ambrosio videlicet in hospiciis concedere ultra duos pastos videlicet officiariis singulis hebdomadis claustrales non de quindecim diebus nisi forte aliquæ personæ de eorum parentelâ transeuntes aut nobiles aut tales de quibus verisimiliter non habetur suspicio eos secum morari faciant, et sic intelligatur de officiariis et de claustralibus " (Claretta, Storia diplomatica, p. 326).

† The two fingers are the barber's, who lets one finger, or two, or three, intervene between the scissors and the head of the person whose hair he is cutting, according to the length of hair he wishes to remain.

‡ " Cellarius teneatur ministrare panem et vinum et pittanciarius pittanciam " (Claretta, Stor. dip., p. 327). Pittancia is believed to be a corruption of "pietantia." " Pietantiæ modus et ordo sic conscripti . . . observentur. In primis videlicet, quod pietantiarius qui pro tempore fuerit omni anno singulis festivitatibus infra scriptis duo ova in brodio pipere et croco bene condito omnibus et singulis fratribus. . . tenebitur ministrare." (Decretum pro Monasterio Dobirluc., A.D. 1374, apud Ducange.) A " pittance " ordinarily was served to two persons in a single dish, but there need not be a dish necessarily, for a piece of raw cheese or four eggs would be a pittance. The pittancer was the official whose business it was to serve out their pittances to each of the monks. Practically he was the *maître d'hôtel* of the establishment.

from San Pietro, or any suspected women, to be admitted without the prior's permission.

" The monks are to be careful how they hold con-
verse with suspected women, and are not to be found
in the houses of such persons, or they will be punished.
Item, the epistle and gospel at high mass are to be
said by the monks in church, and in Lent the epistle is
to be said by one monk or sub-deacon.

" Item, two candelabra are to be kept above the
altar when mass is being said, and the lord abbot is to
provide the necessary candles.

" Any one absent from morning or evening mass is
to be punished by the prior, if his absence arises from
negligence.

" The choir, and the monks residing in the monastery, are to be provided with books and a convenient
breviary* . . . . according to ancient custom and statute,
nor can those things be sold which are necessary or
useful to the convent.

*   *   *   *   *

" Item, all the religious who are admitted and enter
the monastery and religion, shall bring one alb and
one amice, to be delivered into the hands of the treasurer
and preserved by him for the use of the church.

*   *   *   *   *

" The treasurer is to have the books that are in daily
use in the choir re-bound, and to see that the capes
which are unsewn, and all the ecclesiastical vestments
under his care are kept in proper repair. He is to have
the custody of the plate belonging to the monastery,
and to hold a key of the treasury. He is to furnish in each

* Here the text seems to be corrupt.

year an inventory of the property of which he has charge,
and to hand the same over to the lord abbot. He is to
make one common pittance* of bread and wine on the
day of the feast of St. Nicholas in December, according
to custom ; and if it happens to be found necessary to
make a chest to hold charters, &c., the person whose business it shall be to make this shall be bound to make it.

" As regards the office of almoner, the almoner shall
each day give alms in the monastery to the faithful
poor—to wit, barley bread to the value of twopence
current money, and on Holy Thursday he shall make
an alms of threepence† to all comers, and shall give
them a plate of beans and a drink of wine. Item, he is
to make alms four times a year—that is to say, on Christmas Day, on Quinquagesima Sunday, and at the feasts
of Pentecost and Easter ; and he is to give to every man
a small loaf of barley and a grilled pork chop,‡ the third
of a pound in weight. Item, he shall make a pittance to
the convent on the vigil of St. Martin of bread, wine, and
mincemeat dumplings,§—that is to say, for each person
two loaves and two . . . ‖ of wine and some leeks,—and
he is to lay out sixty shillings (?) in fish and seasoning,
and all the servants are to have a ration of dumplings ;
and in the morning he is to give them a dumpling cooked
in oil, and a quarter of a loaf, and some wine. Item, he

---

* That is to say, he is to serve out rations of bread and wine to
every one.

† " Tres denarios."

‡ " Unam carbonatam porci." I suppose I have translated this
correctly ; I cannot find that there is any substance known as " car-
bonate of pork."

§ " Rapiolla " I presume to be a translation of " raviolo," or
" raviuolo," which, as served at San Pietro at the present day, is a
small dumpling containing minced meat and herbs, and either boiled
or baked according to preference.

‖ " Luiroletos." This word is not to be found in any dictionary :
litre (?).

shall give another pittance on the feast of St. James—to wit, a good sheep and some cabbages* with seasoning.

" Item, during infirmary time he must provide four meat suppers and two pints† (?) of wine, and a pittance of mincemeat dumplings during the rogation days, as do the sacristan and the butler. He is also to give each monk one bundle of straw in every year, and to keep a servant who shall bring water from the spring for the service of the mass and for holy water, and light the fire for the barber, and wait at table, and do all else that is reasonable and usual ; and the said almoner shall also keep a towel in the church for drying the hands, and he shall make preparation for the *mandés* on Holy Thursday, both in the monastery and in the cloister. Futhermore, he must keep beds in the hospital of S. Ambrogio, and keep the said hospital in such condition that Christ's poor may be received there in orderly and godly fashion ; he must also maintain the chapel of St. Nicholas, and keep the chapel of St. James in a state of repair, and another part of the building contiguous to the chapel. Item, it shall devolve upon the chamberlain to pay yearly to each of the monks of the said monastery of St. Martin who say mass, except those of them who hold office, the sum of six florins and six groats,‡ and to the treasurer, precentor, and surveyor,§

---

* " Caulos cabutos cum salsa " (choux cabotés ?).
† " Sextaria."   ‡ " Grossos."
§ " Operarius, i.e. Dignitas in Collegiis Canonicorum et Monasteriis, cui operibus publicis vacare incumbit . . . Latius interdum patebant operarii munera siquidem ad ipsum spectabat librorum et ornamentorum provincia." (Ducange.)   " Let one priest and two laymen be elected in every year, who shall be called *operarii* of the said Church of St. Lawrence, and shall have the care of the whole fabric of the church itself . . . but it shall also pertain to them to receive all the moneys belonging to the said church, and to be at the charge of all necessary repairs, whether of the building itself or of the ornaments." (Statuta Eccl. S. Laur. Rom. apud Ducange.)

to each one of them the same sum for their clothing, and
to each of the young monks who do not say mass four
florins and six groats. And in every year he is to do one
O* for the greater priorate† during Advent. Those who
have benefices and who are resident within the monastery,
but whose benefice does not amount to the value of their
clothes, are to receive their clothes according to the
existing custom.

" Item, the pittancer shall give a pittance of cheese
and eggs to each of the monks on every day from the
feast of Easter to the feast of the Holy Cross in September—to wit, three quarters of a pound of cheese ; but
when there is a principal processional duplex feast,
each monk is to have a pound of cheese *per diem*, except
on fast days, when he is to have half a pound only.
Also on days when there is a principal or processional
feast, each one of them, including the hebdomadary,
is to have five eggs. Also, from the feast of Easter to
the octave of St. John the Baptist the pittancer is to
serve out old cheese, and new cheese from the octave of
St. John the Baptist to the feast of St. Michael. From
the feast of St. Michael to Quinquagesima the cheese
is to be of medium quality. From the feast of the Holy
Cross in September until Lent the pittancer must serve
out to each monk three quarters of a pound of cheese,
if it is a feast of twelve lessons, and if it is a feast of three
lessons, whether a week-day or a vigil, the pittancer
is to give each monk but half a pound of cheese. He
is also to give all the monks during Advent nine pounds
of wax extra allowance, and it is not proper that the
pittancer should weigh out cheese for any one on a Friday

* O. The seven antiphons which were sung in Advent were called
O's. (Ducange.)
† " Pro prioratu majori." I have been unable to understand what
is here intended.

unless it be a principal processional or duplex feast, or a principal octave. It is also proper, seeing there is no fast from the feast of Christmas to the octave of the Epiphany, that every man should have his three quarters of a pound of cheese *per diem*. Also, on Christmas and Easter days the pittancer shall provide five dumplings per monk *per diem*, and one plate of sausage meat,* and he shall also give to each of the servants on the said two days five dumplings for each several day ; and the said pittancer on Christmas Day and on the day of St. John the Baptist shall make a relish,† or seasoning, and give to each monk one good glass thereof, that is to say, the fourth part of one‡ . . for each monk—to wit, on the first, second, and third day of the feast of the Nativity, the Circumcision, the Epiphany, and the Purification of the Blessed Virgin ; and the pittancer is to put spice in the said relish, and the cellarer is to provide wine and honey, and during infirmary time those who are being bled are to receive no pittance from the pittancer. Further, from the feast of Easter to that of the Cross of September, there is no fast except on the prescribed vigils ; each monk, therefore, should always have three quarters of a pound of cheese after celebration on a week-day until the above-named day. Further, the pittancer is to provide for three *mandés* in each week during the whole year, excepting Lent, and for each *mandé* he is to find three pounds of cheese. From the feast of St. Michael to that of St. Andrew he is to provide for an additional *mandé* in each week. Item, he is to pay the prior of

---

    * " Carmingier."
    † " Primmentum vel salsam."
    ‡ " Biroleti." I have not been able to find the words " carmingier," " primmentum," and " biroletus " in any dictionary. " Biroletus " is probably the same as " luiroletus " which we have met with above, and the word is misprinted in one or both cases.

the cloister six florins for his fine* . . . and three florins
to the . . . ,† and he should also give five eggs *per
diem* to the hebdomadary of the high altar, except in
Lent. Further, he is to give to the woodman, the baker,
the keeper of the church, the servants of the Infirmary,
the servant at the Eleemosynary, and the stableman,
to each of them one florin in every year. Item, any
monks who leave the monastery before vespers when it
is not a fast, shall lose one quarter of a pound of cheese,
even though they return to the monastery after vespers ;
but if it is a fast day, they are to lose nothing. Item,
the pittancer is to serve out mashed beans to the servants
of the convent during Lent as well as to those who are
in religion, and at this season he is to provide the prior of
the cloister and the hebdomadary with bruised cicerate ;‡
but if any one of the same is hebdomadary, he is only to
receive one portion. If there are two celebrating high
mass at the high altar, each of them is to receive one plate
of the said bruised cicerate.

" As regards the office of cantor, the cantor is to intone
the antiphon ' *ad benedictus ad magnificat* ' at terce,§
and at all other services, and he is himself to intone the
antiphons or provide a substitute who can intone them ;
and he is to intone the psalms according to custom.
Also if there is any cloistered person who has begun his
week of being hebdomadary, and falls into such sickness

* " Item, priori claustrali pro suâ duplâ sex florinos." " Dupla "
has the meaning " mulcta " assigned to it in Ducange among others,
none of which seem appropriate here. The translation as above,
however, is not satisfactory.

† " Pastamderio." I have been unable to find this word in any
dictionary. The text in this part is evidently full of misprints and
corruptions.

‡ " Ciceratam fractam." This word is not given in any dictionary.
Cicer is a small kind of pea, so cicerata fracta may perhaps mean
something like pease pudding.

§ Terce. A service of the Roman Church,

that he cannot celebrate the same, the cantor is to say or celebrate three masses. The cantor is to lead all the monks of the choir at matins, high mass, vespers, and on all other occasions. On days when there is a processional duplex feast, he is to write down the order of the office ; that is to say, those who are to say the invitatory,* the lessons, the epistle of the gospel† and those who are to wear copes at high mass and at vespers. The cantor must sing the processional hymns which are sung on entering the church, but he is exempt from taking his turn of being hebdomadary by reason of his intoning the offices ; and he is to write down the names of those who celebrate low masses and of those who get them said by proxy ; and he is to report these last to the prior that they may be punished. The cantor or his delegate is to read in the refectory during meal times and during infirmary time, and he who reads in the refectory is to have a quart [?] of bread, as also are the two junior monks who wait at table. The cantor is to instruct the boys in the singing of the office and in morals, and is to receive their portions of bread, wine and pittance, and besides all this he is to receive one florin for each of them, and he is to keep them decently ; and the prior is to certify himself upon this matter, and to see to it that he victuals them properly and gives them their food.

" The sacristan is to provide all the lights of the church whether oil or wax, and he is to give out small candles to the hebdomadary, and to keep the eight lamps that burn both night and day supplied with oil. He is to keep the lamps in repair and to buy new ones

---

* " Invitatorium." Ce nom est donné à un verset qui se chante ou se récite au commencement de l'office de matines. Il varie selon les fêtes et même les féries. Migne. Encyclopédie Théologique.

† " Epistolam Evangelii." There are probably several misprints here.

if the old are broken, and he is to provide the incense.
He is to maintain the covered chapel of St. Nicholas,
and the whole church except the portico of the same ;
and the lord abbot is to provide sound timber for doors
and other necessaries. He is to keep the frames* of
the bells in repair, and also the ropes for the same, and
during Lent he is to provide two pittances of eels to the
value of eighteen groats for each pittance, and one other
pittance of dumplings and seasoning during rogation
time, to wit, five dumplings cooked in oil for each person,
and one quart of bread and wine, and all the house
domestics and serving men of the convent who may be
present are to have the same. At this time all the
monks are to have one quarter of a pound of cheese from
the sacristan. And the said sacristan should find the
convent two pittances during infirmary time and two
pints† of wine, and two suppers, one of chicken and salt
meat, with white chestnuts, inasmuch as there is only
to be just so much chicken as is sufficient. Item, he is to
keep the church clean. Item, he has to pay to the
keeper of the church one measure of barley, and eighteen
groats for his clothes yearly, and every Martinmas he
is to pay to the cantor sixty soldi, and he shall place a‡
. . . or boss § in the choir during Lent. Also he must do
one O in Advent and take charge of all the ornaments of
the altars and all the relics. Also on high days and when
there is a procession he is to keep the paschal candle
before the altar, as is customary, but on other days he
shall keep a burning lamp only, and when the candle is
burning the lamp may be extinguished.

* * * * *

* " Monnas." Word not to be found.
† " Sextaria." ‡ Word missing in the original.
§ " Borchiam." Word not to be found. *Borchia* in Italian is a kind
of ornamental boss.

" As touching the office of infirmarer, the infirmarer
is to keep the whole convent fifteen days during infirmary
time, to wit, the one-half of them for fifteen days and the
other half for another fifteen days, except that on the
first and last days all the monks will be in the infirmary.
Also when he makes a pittance he is to give the monks
beef and mutton,* sufficient in quantity and quality, and
to receive their portions. The prior of the cloister,
cantor, and cellarer may be in the infirmary the whole
month. And the infirmarer is to keep a servant, who
shall go and buy meat three times a week, to wit, on
Saturdays, Mondays, and Wednesdays, but at the
expense of the sender, and the said servant shall on
the days following prepare the meat at the expense
of the infirmarer ; and he shall salt it and make
seasoning as is customary, to wit, on all high days and
days when there is a processional duplex feast, and on
other days. On the feast of St. Michael he shall serve out
a seasoning made of sage and onions ; but the said
servant shall not be bound to go and buy meat during
Advent, and on Septuagesima and Quinquagesima
Sundays he shall serve out seasoning. Also when the
infirmarer serves out fresh meat, he is to provide fine
salt. Also the said servant is to go and fetch medicine
once or oftener when necessary, at the expense of the
sick person, and to visit him. If the sick person requires
it, he can have aid in the payment of his doctor, and the
lord abbot is to pay for the doctor and medicines of all
cloistered persons.

" On the principal octaves the monks are to have
seasoning, but during the main feasts they are to have
seasoning upon the first day only. The infirmarer is
not bound to do anything or serve out anything on

---

* " Teneatur dare religiosis de carnibus bovinis et montonis decenter."

days when no flesh is eaten. The cellarer is to do this, and during the times of the said infirmaries, the servants of the monastery and convent are to be, as above, on the same footing as those who are in religion, that is to say, half of them are to be bled during one fifteen days, and the other half during the other fifteen days, as is customary.

"Item, touching the office of cellarer, it is ordered that the cellarer do serve out to the whole convent bread, wine, oil, and salt ; as much of these two last as any one may require reasonably, and this on all days excepting when the infirmarer serves out kitchen meats, but even then the cellarer is to serve his rations to the hebdomadary. Item, he is to make a pittance of dumplings with seasoning to the convent on the first of the rogation days ; each monk and each servant is to have five dumplings uncooked with his seasoning, and one cooked with [oil ?] and a quart of bread and wine, and each monk is to have one quarter of a pound of cheese. Item, upon Holy Thursday he is to give to the convent a pittance of leeks and fish to the value of sixty soldi, and . . . ,* Item, another pittance upon the first day of August ; and he is to present the convent with a good sheep and cabbages with seasoning. Item, in infirmary time he is to provide two pittances, one of fowls and the other of salt meat and white chestnuts, and he is to give two pints of wine. Item, in each week he is to give one flagon [?].† Item, the cellarer is to provide napkins and plates at meal times in the refectory, and he is to find the bread for making seasoning, and the vinegar for the mustard ; and he is to do an O in Advent, and in Lent he is to provide white chestnuts, and cicerate all the year. From the feast of St. Luke to the octave

* " Foannotos." Word not to be found.   † " Laganum.'

of St. Martin he is to provide fresh chestnuts, to wit, on feasts of twelve lessons ; and on dumpling days he is to find the oil and flour with which to make the dumplings.

"Item, as to the office of surveyor, it is ordered that the surveyor do pay the master builder and also the wages of the day labourers ; the lord abbot is to find all the materials requisite for this purpose. Item, the surveyor is to make good any plank or post or nail, and he is to repair any hole in the roofs which can be repaired easily, and any beam or piece of boarding. Touching the aforesaid materials it is to be understood that the lord abbot furnish beams, boards, rafters, scantling, tiles, and anything of this description ;* the said surveyor is also to renew the roof of the cloister, chapter, refectory, dormitory, and portico ; and the said surveyor is to do an O in Advent.

"Item, concerning the office of porter. The porter is to be in charge of the gate night and day, and if he go outside the convent, he must find a sufficient and trust-worthy substitute ; on every feast day he is† . . . to lose none of his provender ; and to receive his clothing in spring as though he were a junior monk ; and if he is in holy orders, he is to receive clothing money ; and to have his *pro ratâ* portions in all distributions. Item, the said porter shall enjoy the income derived from S. Michael of Canavesio ; and when a monk is received into the monastery, he shall pay to the said porter five good sous ; and the said porter shall shut the gates of the convent at sunset, and open them at sunrise."

The rest of the document is little more than a *resumé*

---

* " Enredullas hujusmodi " [et res ullas hujusmodi ?].
† " In processionibus deferre et de suâ prebendâ nihil perdat vesti-arium vere suum salvatur eidem sicut uni monacullo."

of what has been given, and common form to the effect
that nothing in the foregoing is to override any orders
made by the Holy Apostolic See which may be preserved
in the monastery, and that the rights of the Holy See
are to be preserved in all respects intact. If doubts arise
concerning the interpretation of any clause they are to
be settled by the abbot and two of the senior monks.

Author's Index

Abruptness of introduction the measure of importance, 196

Absolute, we would have an absolute standard if we could, 196

Absolutely, nothing is anything, 196

Academies and their influence, 146–59, 226, 248

Academy picture, the desire to paint an, 142

—— Ciseri's, at Locarno, 271

Accidentals, a maze of metaphysical, 23

Action, foundations of, lie deeper than reason, 107

Adaptation and illusion, 44

Adipose cushion of Italy, 92

Advertisements, American, at Locarno, 273

Æstheticism, culture, earnestness, and intenseness, all methods of trying to conceal weakness, 192

Affection a *sine quâ non* for success, 158

Agape and *gnosis*, 17

Airolo, 25

Alcohol and imagination, 46

Alda, Il Salto della bella, 104

All things to all men, 66

Allen, Grant, 69

Almoner, the, of S. Michele, 315

Alone, should we like to see a picture when we are, 23, 158

Alpi and *monti*, difference between, 35

Alpine roads, the steps by which they have advanced, 59

Alps, narrowness of the, 61

Altar cloth, a fine embroidered, 256

Altar-piece at Morbio Superiore, 237

Amateurs, wanted a periodical written and illustrated by, 156

Amber, a smile in, 235

Ambrogio, S., and neighbourhood, 113

American advertisements at Locarno, 273

Ancestors, to have been begotten of good ones for many generations, 252

Andermatt, 24

Andorno, 186

Angel, drawing an, down, 42

Angera, 258

Animals and plants, cause of their divergence, 153

Ants near Faido, 38

— and bees, stationary civilisation of, 195

— and their nests, 288

Anzone, the sad torrent of, 220

Apparition, artificial, of the B.V.M., 275

Appliances, creatures and their, 283

Apprenticeship *v.* the academic system, 150

Arona, 265

Art for art's sake, 156

— Italian, causes of its decline, 141

— moral effect of, 252

Asbestos on pass between Fusio and Dalpe, 285

Asplenium alternifolium, 37

Ass dressed in sacerdotal robes, 67

326

Index

THE END

The World In Your Pocket

Handy pocket-sized editions of works by classic authors. Many of the titles are not otherwise available in paperback. The series now incorporates Continental and Travel Classics in the same format.

☐ **A PASSION IN THE DESERT**
Honoré de Balzac

The tales in this volume are among Balzac's best. Written before his long novels and stylistically different, they deal with the romantic, the strange, the bizarre and even the fanciful incidents of life.

ISBN 0 86299 249 4 £2.50

☐ **THE JOURNAL OF A DISAPPOINTED MAN**
W.N.P. Barbellion

An inspired and expressive masterpiece 'by a scientist with an artist's sensitivity; a literary man with scientific training', who, knowing he was dying of an incurable disease, crammed a lifetime of intensity into his few short years.

ISBN 0 86299 098 X £2.95

☐ **ELSIE AND THE CHILD AND OTHER STORIES**
Arnold Bennett

A tale of Riceyman Steps, a Five Towns story, and eleven stories set in the London of the 1920s make up this collection.

ISBN 0 86299 210 9 £2.95

☐ **HELEN WITH THE HIGH HAND**
Arnold Bennett

A splendid domestic comedy set in Bennett's beloved Potteries.

ISBN 0 86299 076 9 £1.95

☐ **WHOM GOD HATH JOINED**
Arnold Bennett

Bennett on his home ground of the Five Towns. With great sympathy and realism he tells the story of two domestic tragedies which, in their different ways, lead to the divorce court.

ISBN 0 86299 207 9 £2.95

☐ **MY FATHER'S LIFE**
Rétif De La Bretonne

A brilliant, vivid and noble picture of peasant life in 18th-century France.

ISBN 0 86299 176 5 £2.95

☐ **THE BLACK MONK AND OTHER STORIES**
Anton Chekhov

Twelve stories characteristic of the Russian master at his best.

ISBN 0 86299 230 3 £2.95

☐ **THE BITER BIT AND OTHER STORIES**
Wilkie Collins

Tales of detection, mystery and suspense.

ISBN 0 86299 070 X £2.50

☐ **THE DEAD SECRET**
Wilkie Collins

A story set in a dark mansion in remote Cornwall.

ISBN 0 86299 2524 £3.95

☐ **WITHIN THE TIDES**
Joseph Conrad

Four tales from this modern master; two set in the East, one in Spain during the Peninsular War and one, telling of the effect of greed, set in home waters.

ISBN 0 86299 099 8 £1.95

☐ **CAPTAIN SINGLETON**
Daniel Defoe

The fictionalized journal of a maritime adventurer.

ISBN 0 86299 073 4 £2.95

☐ **THE HAUNTED MAN AND THE HAUNTED HOUSE**
Charles Dickens

Two of the best from the master of the ghost story.

ISBN 0 86299 214 1 £1.95

☐ **THE SIGNALMAN AND OTHER GHOST STORIES**
Charles Dickens

Stories to be read at dusk in front of a blazing fire.

ISBN 0 86299 152 8 £1.95

☐ **THE EXPLOITS OF BRIGADIER GERARD**
Sir Arthur Conan Doyle

In Gerard, Conan Doyle created a really memorable and living character, a vain, brave French brigadier with an amusing touch of stupidity, during the Napoleonic Wars.

ISBN 0 86299 148 X £1.95

☐ **THE LOST WORLD**
Sir Arthur Conan Doyle

The discovery of a nightmare world beyond civilization. A Professor Challenger story.

ISBN 0 86299 072 6 £1.95

☐ **THE LADY OF THE CAMELLIAS**
Alexandre Dumas

The translation by Edmund Gosse of Dumas' second novel, the tragic story of a doomed affair between a Second Empire courtesan and the son of a respectable family.

ISBN 0 86299 264 8 £2.95

☐ **WAY OF REVELATION**
Wilfrid Ewart

One of the finest novels to come out of the terrible years 1914–19. Highly praised for its authenticity.

ISBN 0 86299 288 5 £3.95

☐ **THE MANCHESTER MARRIAGE**
Mrs Gaskell

Six stories representative of Mrs Gaskell at her best, set in the remote mountain valleys of Wales and Lancashire and in the green seclusion of rural England.

ISBN 0 86299 247 8 £3.95

HIS MASTERPIECE
Émile Zola

Part of the Rougon Macquart series, complete in itself, centring on the art world of Paris in the final years of the Second Empire.

ISBN 0 86299 293 1 £3.95

TRAVEL CLASSICS

ON HORSEBACK THROUGH ASIA MINOR
Colonel Frederick Burnaby

An adventurous ride of 2,000 miles across wild, inhospitable country in the winter of 1876 7 by the author of *A Ride To Khiva*.

ISBN 0 86299 231 1 £3.95

THE BIRDS OF SIBERIA: TO THE PETCHORA VALLEY
Henry Seebohm

In *The Birds of Siberia* Seebohm's narrative skill is put to good use in describing the birds he and Harvie-Brown found, together with vivid descriptions of their exciting experiences in this remote and hostile territory.

ISBN 0 86299 259 1 £2.95

THE BIRDS OF SIBERIA: THE YENESEI
Henry Seebohm

Seebohm was anxious to carry his ornithological and ethnological researches further eastward than those described in *To the Petchora Valley*. In this he was entirely successful but it was a long and adventurous journey. Truly a classic of travel.

ISBN 0 86299 260 5 £2.95

THE WEST INDIES AND THE SPANISH MAIN
Anthony Trollope

Trollope's journey through the West Indies, Central America and British Guiana in 1858 9 is full of personal anecdote told with all the detail and colour of which he was a master.

ISBN 0 86299 220 6 £3.95

PARIS AND THE PARISIANS
Fanny Trollope

The Paris of Chateaubriand, George Sand and Franz Liszt brought vividly to life by the author of *Domestic Manners of the Americans*.

ISBN 0 86299 219 2 £3.95

Prices subject to change

Available from your bookshop. If you wish to be kept up to date with forthcoming titles please write to:

*The Sales Department, Alan Sutton Publishing,
30 Brunswick Road, Gloucester GL1 1JJ
England.*

ALAN SUTTON PUBLISHING, 30 BRUNSWICK ROAD, GLOUCESTER GL1 1JJ